7/02

DATE DUE		11/01
JUN 26 02		
OCT 2 1 2002		
GAYLORD		PRINTED IN U.S.A.

Another America

Native American Maps and the History of Our Land

Mark Warhus

ST. MARTIN'S GRIFFIN ✾ NEW YORK

A THOMAS DUNNE BOOK.
An imprint of St. Martin's Press.

Library of Congress Cataloging-in-Publication Data

Warhus, Mark.
    Another America : Native American maps and the history
of our land / Mark Warhus.
        p.   cm.
    "A Thomas Dunne book."
    ISBN 0-312-18702-5
    I. Indian cartography—North America.   2. Indians of North
America—Maps.   3. Geographical perception—North America.   4.
America—Discovery and exploration—Maps.
    I. Title.
E59.C25W37   1997
970'.00497—dc21   96-44903
                                                                          CIP

First St. Martin's Griffin Edition: August 1998

10 9 8 7 6 5 4 3 2 1

This book is dedicated to the peoples whose world is glimpsed in these maps.

Contents

Illustration List

Acknowledgments

This book began with a grant from the National Endowment for the Humanities, without whose help, and that of the many scholars, Native American consultants, and librarians that participated in the project, the book would never have been started. Equally instrumental were the many archivist and collections keepers who enthusiastically contributed their time and expertise and generously shared the riches of their collections during the course of my research.

I am particularly grateful to the Newberry Library of Chicago, and David Buisseret, whose unfailing support resulted in the first exhibition of these maps. The insights and support of the scholars in the Newberry's D'Arcy McNickle Center for the History of the American Indian and the Hermon Dunlap Smith Center for the History of Cartography continually enhanced and expanded my perspective. Special thanks are due to Margaret Pearce, whose thorough research on several of these maps set a standard that I can only hope to have approached, and to James Akerman, Robert Karrow, Francis Jennings, John Aubrey, Frederick Hoxie, the many employees of the Newberry Library, and the director and staff of the History of Cartography Project, all of whom were helpful and supportive.

This book would not be possible without the scholarly spade work of G. Malcolm Lewis. His years of research into Native American maps literally unearthed many of the maps featured here, and the generosity and selflessness with which he shared his research and expertise have been both a gift for myself and many others, and an example of the highest in scholarly integrity. Finally, I must express my gratitude to the late J. B. Harley. His enthusiasm for the context, sub-text, and meaning of maps, and the good humor and intelligence with which he communicated this information, taught me how to "read" a map, a skill that helped reveal whatever insights there are to be found here.

Another America

Introduction

"The landscape I had grown up in, and felt myself part of, had been wiped clean of this other past. . . . different people living for centuries where we now trod, different people, with their own calendar and reverences and ideas of human association, different houses or huts, different roads or paths, different crops and fields and vegetation, different views, speeds, reasons for journeys, different ideas of the ages of man, different ideas of the enemy and fellowship and sanctity and what men owed themselves."

V. S. NAIPAUL, *A WAY IN THE WORLD.*

I N SEPTEMBER OF 1800 PETER Fidler, a surveyor and explorer for the Hudson's Bay Company, established Chesterfield House at the junction of the Red Deer and South Saskatchewan rivers, just east of present day Alberta. One of the western most outposts of the Hudson's Bay Company, Chesterfield House represented the edge of European knowledge. To the north, west, and south lay a territory whose features and dimensions were unknown to western people. Three centuries of exploration had not yet penetrated this part of the continent. Except for a few sketchy descriptions of the lower Missouri River, the regions west and north of the

Mississippi, the great central plain of the North American continent, were still a native place at the beginning of the nineteenth century.

In contrast, the Native American knowledge of this landscape was deep and detailed. For centuries Native Americans had traversed the Plains, hunting the herds of buffalo and meeting to exchange goods and ideas with other native peoples. Their trading parties crossed the Rocky Mountains and followed routes down to the Pacific coast. Their knowledge and networks extended to east of the Mississippi River, and from the Arctic regions to the Indian societies of Mexico. The Native American traditions contained a map of North America that had been forged through centuries of experience.

Like nearly all the European explorers, Peter Fidler relied upon Native American informants to fill in the features of areas he had not seen. At Chesterfield House he met with the Blackfoot, Kootenay, Snake, and Nez Perce Indians that came there to trade. Throughout the winter of 1800 and 1801 Fidler collected information from these informants. In February of 1801 Ac ko mok ki, a Blackfoot chief, visited the post and met with Fidler.

In response to Fidler's request Ac ko mok ki offered to draw him a map of the region. It is very probable that Ac ko mok ki sketched his map in the snow outside the trading post. Fidler described the surviving copy as "reduced 1/4 from the original." In laying out his picture of the land, Ac ko mok ki would have first related it verbally, for that was how the information was organized and stored—in the oral record of the Blackfeet. He started the map from the place where they were standing, and showed the Red Deer and Saskatchewan rivers coming from the west. He then made two long parallel lines down the length of his map. This represented the Rocky Mountains extending to the south. Ac ko mok ki drew in and named the prominent features of the range, and noted the number of days journey between each one. To the east he drew in the major tributaries of the Missouri River, from the Milk River in Alberta down to the Bighorn River in central Wyoming. On the other side of the Rocky Mountains, Ac ko mok ki sketched in the Columbia and Snake rivers, and the coast of the Pacific Ocean. Fidler's record indicates that Ac ko mok ki provided information about the quality of the land, where there were trees and woods or only grassland. After filling in the major physical features of this vast area, Ac ko mok ki proceeded to draw a picture of the social landscape. He placed circles to indicate the locations of thirty-two different Indian tribes, giving their names and populations to the English surveyor.

In all, Ac ko mok ki sketched out a detailed picture of more than two hundred thousand square miles of North America. His map is one of the great documents of western exploration. Copied and annotated by Fidler, it was sent back to the headquarters of the Hudson's Bay Company in London with a note stating that it showed regions "hitherto unknown to Europeans." Until Ac ko mok ki made this map, the area he represented had been unknown to the west. Ac ko mok ki's map reflects just how thoroughly the landscape was known to North America's native inhabitants. It is a glimpse of North America as it was mapped in Native American history and traditions. Unfortunately, the area Ac ko mok ki pictured would not remain blank to the West for long. The year after Fidler sent his copy of Ac ko mok ki's map to London, the information was added to a western map of the continent. Three years latter Lewis and Clark would be following his directions to open up the Northwest for the rapidly expanding United States.

The map that Ac ko mok ki drew is an illustration of the Native American's oral landscape. Unlike western society, maps were not created as permanent documents in Native American traditions. The features of geography were part of a much larger interconnected mental map that existed in the oral traditions. The world was perceived and experienced through one's history, traditions, and kin, in relationships with the animal and natural resources that one depended upon, and in union with the spirits, ancestors, and religious forces with whom one shared existence. This system of beliefs and perceptions had evolved for many thousands of years in North America; the Native Americans' world had been explored, named, and integrated into their experience long before the first Europeans came to the continent. This indigenous knowledge was passed down in songs, stories, and rituals, and the understanding of the landscape it imparted was as sophisticated as that of any western map.

The primary maps for Native Americans were these oral documents. When a map was needed to show the way or convey a message, it would be drawn out on the ground, in the snow, or in the ashes of a campfire. These drawings were transitory illustrations for the oral documents. Those Native American maps that have survived are like pictures from a story in which the words are missing. Nevertheless, they provide a glimpse of North America as it was conceived by the continent's indigenous peoples.

To read these Native American maps it is necessary to suspend western preconceptions of what makes a map. Unlike western cartography, where the primary document is the physical map and the conventions of scale, longitude, latitude, direction, and relative location are believed to "scientifically" depict a static landscape, Native American maps are pictures of experience. They are formed in the human interaction with the land and are a record of the events that give it meaning. Far from being unsophisticated or "primitive," these Native American maps were as functional and transmissible as the products of Rand McNally or National Geographic. Evidence of extensive Native American geographic knowledge and the efficiency of their methods of orientation and travel can be seen in the continent-wide network of trade and communication that is documented in these maps. The archeological record is rife with examples of goods, ideas, and peoples moving over great distances on the continent. And, the detailed knowledge of geography, political allegiances, and economic relations that is recorded in some of these Native American maps reveals an added depth of indigenous understanding and insight. Combined with their missing oral components these maps easily fulfill all the functions and attributes associated with conventional western maps.

But to look only for parallels to western cartography is to miss the wealth of information these maps contain. As graphic documents from oral cultures these maps provide a rare glimpse into the Native American's perception of the world. They open a window on a rich multidimensional landscape shaped by history, geography, human belief and experience, and an ever-present spiritual world. The maps are important documents for the understanding of Native American cultures. They reveal not only the sites of past habitations but also the social and historical relationships in which their societies functioned. At one time the human history of the North American continent was preserved in the Native American's oral traditions. Today only fragments of their history, like the pieces of their landscape that can be glimpsed in these maps, remains.

The loss of this Native American history is the result of the European invasion. Beginning in the fifteenth century North America was named, claimed, and taken over by the forces of western civilization. In this process the continent itself was remade in the image of western society. Western concepts of ownership, possession, and land use transformed the way the land was perceived. The European powers defined a new landscape that reflected their imperial ambitions. New England, New France, and New Spain now shaped the continent as if the Native Americans' millennia on the land had never existed. The colonists who followed the European explorers believed that these lands rightfully belonged to them by dint of discovery and the moral superiority of their civilization. Native Americans were forcibly removed to make way for the "higher use" these new immigrants wished to make of the land. As the North American nation states developed, these policies continued until the "savages" that once occupied the continent were confined to reservations.

The path of this western invasion left a trail of destruction for the Native Americans. Native American social tradition, arts, architecture, literature, and intellectual achievements were lost or destroyed. Whole populations of native peoples were wiped out as western society turned the continent into its possession. These maps provide a Native American record of this encounter. They document the fullness with which Native Americans once inhabited the continent and the disastrous effects of the European invasion. They are important both as a Native American perspective on these events and as a record of the effect of western society's advance on other people. Like a double-sided mirror they illuminate the trail of repression, exploitation, violence, and death that transformed the face of North America and they hold up this image as a seldom acknowledged aspect of the western historical record. The window these maps open on this other side of North American history is one of their most important contributions.

The maps are also documents of Native American resilience and survival. In the space of four hundred years, Native American culture was brutally transformed from a way of life that filled North America to an impoverished and repressed remnant confined and controlled on reservations. That Native Americans were able to survive this ordeal is testimony to the strength of their identities and traditions. That they have continued through an additional century of persecution and are experiencing a cultural resurgence is an epic tale of human endurance. The history retained through these maps helps to preserve and maintain a part of these Native American traditions.

These Native American maps survive today because they entered the western record. From the earliest encounters through modern anthropological studies, western persons have asked Native Americans for geographic information. This exchange was often made in the form of maps made or related by Native Americans. In this process Native Americans may have unwittingly contributed to the foreign dominance of the continent, but they also used their knowledge to barter advantages from the Europeans. The majority of known Native American maps were made in the course of such encounters. A few documents were given or obtained in their original form, many more were copied from Native American originals drawn on the ground or sketched on bits of paper, still others were compiled on the basis of Native American oral information. As Native Americans came to understand the power western people attributed to their "writings," various chiefs and tribes adapted the technology and produced their own maps in the hope that the claims they represented would be respected. Originals, copies, and transcribed versions of these Native American maps have made their way into archives, libraries, and museums throughout western Europe and North America. The oldest can be found in the colonial archives of the western powers while contemporary maps, made within the last decade, are often produced and retained by Native American groups that use them to assert their place and their identity.

The maps reproduced here have been chosen for their range of form and content. They are meant to provide an overview of the way Native American societies expressed and recorded their perceptions. They have also been chosen for the insight they provide into Native American cultures and history. The descriptions of the maps are presented in a series of roughly chronological chapters. Each chapter explores a different aspect of Native American maps and how they reflect specific periods of North American history and the history of Indian-white relations. Throughout, the styles and content of the maps, the events recalled and the features of the landscape that are emphasized, are discussed in terms of Native American experience. The maps are used as a starting point for a discussion of the tribal and ethnological history that shaped the perceptions of the landscape. And they are explored as graphic comments on the western record of events that coincides with the maps' creation.

Despite the important historical information and cultural insight that can be gleaned from these maps, it is their human aspects that are most compelling. Each document was at one time the product of a particular human being. Whether recorded in the hand of the maker or compiled from oral testimony, the maps reflect an individual's experience and perception of his or her environment. In the European history of exploration there is a category of inquiry that lionizes the accomplishments of explorers like John Smith, Francis Drake, or William Parry. Affectionately referred to as the "maps and chaps" version of history, the school celebrates the deeds of bravery and nobility that are recorded on the explorer's maps. In the same way the lives and accomplishments of the Native American individuals who made these maps are worth recording. Thrown into difficult circumstances by contact with a culture that they did not invite or understand, these Native Americans responded with the intelligence and tools of their traditions. Among the mapmakers to be encountered here are a "peace chief" desperately trying to explain his people's history on the land to a government bent on taking it away from them; the last known member of a tribe recording the extinction of her people; and an elderly warrior recalling the brave deeds and accomplishments of his youth. Their maps are a record of the human experience of the land. More directly than words they picture one's place in the world and the people and things that give it meaning. As such the maps move beyond descriptions of geography, even beyond their importance as historical documents; they are windows on the lives of people who have gone before us, a means to share in their existence.

1.

Mida oduhkoa atis
Village of woods at confluence

Mandan Town

Mian adomeru ait
Mud dwelling creek

An Overview of
Native American Maps

LIKE ALL PEOPLES, THE INDIGENOUS peoples of North America named and mapped the places of their landscape and the geography of their world. Whether they were hunters and gatherers, agriculturists, or the inhabitants of cities, the land and its resources were a vital part of their identity. Throughout the continent indigenous societies looked upon the earth and the environment as active partners in a web of being; they shared the world with plants, animals, natural forces, and spiritual beings. The native societies that evolved with this view of the world were fully developed cultures. Their technologies enabled them to occupy the diverse environments of North America and they participated in an elaborate trade and communication network. The experience, beliefs, and technologies that enabled these Native American societies to flourish were all held in the oral tradition. These were highly efficient oral cultures. The record of events, the body of beliefs and behaviors, and the materials and methods used in their technologies were all passed down without the use of written language.

As graphic documents from oral cultures, Native American maps are a unique record of these societies and their ways of life. They are striking examples of the sophistication of their oral traditions. Unlike western cartography, where the "map" becomes one's picture of the landscape, Native American maps are always secondary to the oral "picture" or experience of the landscape. Routes, landmarks, sacred sites, and historical events formed a "mental map" that wove together geography, history, and mythology. Lacking the artifice and conventions of western maps, these Native American maps are windows on a multidimensional landscape. Their richness is found in the unwritten text of history, mythology, and spiritual belief. When viewed through the oral tradition, and what has been recorded of the peoples and individuals who are represented, it is possible to glimpse the different ways in which Native Americans perceived their land and how their cultures and technologies enabled them to share the universal human experience of place.

The form and content of the maps are the product of indigenous North American technologies and graphic traditions. Since the geographic information needed for finding one's way was held in the oral tradition, Native cultures seldom produced maps as permanent documents. When a picture was needed it would be sketched in the dirt or sand where it would illustrate the oral map and then disappear. The Native American maps that have survived were either obtained or copied by peoples from western cultures. They have been collected by explorers, commissioned by anthropologists, and requested by surveyors. Some Native American maps were made for presentation to the invading Europeans and others were originally made for indigenous communication. Despite their varied origins and the missing oral component, these maps are a reflection of Native American perceptions and technologies.

The graphic systems used in the maps are often adapted from picture writing traditions used to visually convey information. Far from primitive, these picture-writing systems used an economy of detail to convey their messages and could be easily read by anyone familiar with the oral geography of the region. To read the maps it is necessary to see how picture writing functioned within the oral traditions of these societies.

The materials the maps are made on——the skins, bark, and rocks——are examples of the natural products used in Native American technologies. Native Americans obtained and used these products in an amazing variety of ways. Their technologies ranged from highly specialized hunting and gathering techniques to tanning methods that prepared skins differently depending upon their intended use. Natural products were adapted and used throughout Native American life and the rituals of obtaining these resources were part of Native traditions. When the Europeans arrived with paper, pencils and other drawing implements the Native Americans quickly adapted these western materials to their own ends. Many of the maps document this combination of western media with indigenous graphic techniques.

The subject matter or content of the maps is also uniquely Native American. At one level they are a reflection of the native routes and networks of communication, but the maps can be read more deeply. They reveal the great expanses of land and the generations of time that were held in the oral traditions. They are a record of the people, places, and events that made the landscape meaningful. The maps are also a Native American portrayal of the western presence that was invading their territory. They record the Native American experience of the encounter. They are a unique record of these indigenous cultures and their experience of the land.

The maps presented here provide an overview of Native American forms and content. More significant, however, is the human experience that is expressed in these maps. The stories of the individuals and peoples who made the maps, the traditions that formed their view of the world, and their experience of the transformation of North America are an invaluable record of human experience. The maps document the wars and diseases that reduced native populations, the misunderstood and deceptive treaties that took their lands, and the arbitrary and inhuman policies that white society inflicted on Native Americans in an effort to "civilize" them. They are also a record of Native American resilience, the pleasure they took in their world, and their noble efforts to keep their traditions and maintain their place in the landscape. They chart the demise and the survival of Native American groups and serve as a record of human history.

These examples of Native American maps have survived because of western preservation. Retaining maps as documents was not the Native American practice. The oral traditions passed on their cultural knowledge and records. The few extant maps that were made solely for indigenous use are either religious and mythological representations of space, or maps that were meant to be discarded but somehow fell into western hands. The "Map drawn by Indians on Birch-Bark" is an example of a map left for other Indians to read and discard, but the map was found and kept by a British soldier, and it entered the stream of western history. The majority of Native American maps entered the historical record as part of an exchange of information and goods between Native Americans and representatives of western society. The Indian Miguel's map, made during an interrogation by Spanish colonial authorities in 1602, is a far more common example of a Native American map than those accidentally found by Europeans. Others, like Notchininga's map, were presented to western authorities as part of diplomatic, treaty, and land sale negotiations. Often these maps were copied by western persons and became part of the holdings of western society where history is retained and passed on in documents. Today Native American maps can be found in the national collections of the North American colonial powers and in U.S. and Canadian archives and national libraries. Other maps were collected or acquired by western peoples exploring and surveying the landscape or studying native cultures, and are now held in libraries, archives, and museums.

That these Native American maps were created and retained as part of the western record makes them documents at the intersection of two histories. They are simultaneously a picture of Native American perceptions and experience and documentation of their interactions with western peoples. Together, these maps and the historical and cultural circumstances that surround them tell another side of the North American story. They are part of a record of events seen from the Native American perspective. This new view on the continent's past and the peoples that inhabited it is probably the most significant contribution these maps can make to western history. The equally complex and diverse landscape that they chart for the future, a map in which both the Native American and western presence is represented, is perhaps their most significant implication.

The anonymous Indians who made this map on birch bark (Figure 1) were traveling through the lakes and rivers of the Northeast sometime in the first half of the nineteenth centu-

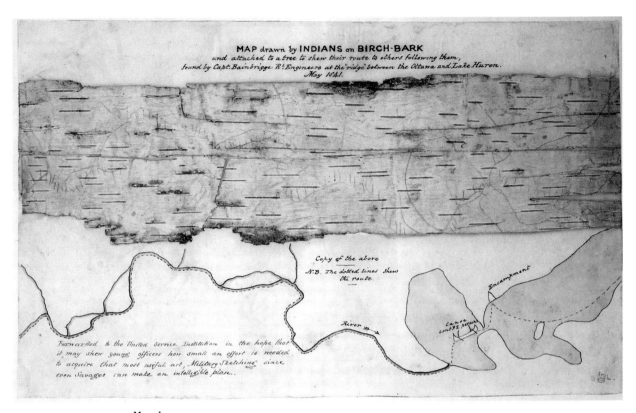

FIGURE 1. **Map drawn** *by Indians on Birch-Bark, c. 1841. Size of the original 3 ½ x 15 inches (8.8 x 38 cm). By permission of the British Library, Map Library, R.U.S.I. (Misc.)*

ry. They left this message to inform those following that they were a day ahead and proceeding along a certain route. It is not known if the party following found the map. All that is recorded is that Captain Bainbrigge, a surveyor with the Royal Engineers, found the map and was intrigued enough to keep it and send it home to England where it ended up in the collections of the British Library. The map is an example of the Native American practice of making and leaving directional messages.

The original map is incised upon the section of birch bark mounted in the upper half of the paper. Captain Bainbrigge had the map mounted and added the descriptive endorsement, "Map drawn by Indians on Birch-Bark and attached to a tree to show their route to others following them, found by Capt. Bainbrigge RI. Engineers at the 'ridge' between the Ottawa and Lake Huron. May 1841." Bainbrigge is also credited with redrawing the map and adding the notes and comments.

Temporarily disregarding the English additions and looking at the birch bark alone, it is a reflection of indigenous North American technologies and of the trade and communications routes used by Indians of the Northeast.

Birch bark, like many of the natural products utilized by American Indians, had been adapt-

Another America

ed for use in a variety of ways. It was used in the manufacture of canoes; as a material for forming containers, bowls and other domestic implements; and as a building material in both permanent and temporary houses. Birch bark was also widely used as a medium for making pictographic messages. One form of these pictographic records is birch-bark scrolls which use a highly stylized picture language to record myths and religious beliefs. They were made as mnemonic devices to aid in the memorization and recitation of sacred information and they continue to have religious significance for many Indians today. The more common form of pictographic records are temporary messages etched in birch bark or other materials. These messages were posted at campsites or houses, or left in prominent places along the trail. They were used throughout the Northeast to inform someone of where the message maker had gone, or to give directions on the route to follow.

In writing or inscribing their messages, northeastern Indians used a form of picture writing that employed both symbolic and representational elements. Their pictographic language appears to be quite ancient and to have developed along with the oral traditions. People, places, routes, and events were recorded in the form of line drawings. These drawings can be faintly seen on the birch-bark map. They represent a lake, a camp, and the route which the mapmakers wished to convey. The map notes that the two Indians, shown in the canoe, had camped for one night and then continued their journey up the river that flows into the lake. Like many American Indian maps, the drawing is not to scale; the size relationship of the canoe to the lakes and rivers was not relevant to the information conveyed. Another common characteristic of Native American maps is the lack of differentiation between rivers, portages, and trails; the map simply represents the route taken as a continuous line.

Without the oral record, the length and events of the mapmaker's journey cannot be known and the route they were taking can only be speculated. But given that the map was found on the "ridge" between the Ottawa River and Lake Huron, it is possible to extrapolate. The "ridge" on which Bainbrigge claims he found the map may refer to the divide between rivers draining to the east and those flowing south and west into Lake Huron. The Ottawa River, which flows towards the St. Lawrence, lies on the other side of the watershed from rivers and lakes that form part of the drainage into Georgian Bay on Lake Huron. The route described on the birch bark map may have followed the Ottawa River from Montreal to the Mattawa River across the short portage to Lake Nipissing, and down the French River to Georgian Bay and Lake Huron. This route was of considerable interest to the Royal Engineers who surveyed the area in the 1830s, and may have brought Bainbrigge to the "ridge" were the map was found. These rivers and lakes were part of a major thoroughfare for the Algonquin and Ojibwa Indians bringing furs and other goods to trade in Montreal. The route avoided the much longer southern course through Detroit and the lower Great Lakes, and reduced the threat of having to deal with the Iroquois Federation that controlled the upper St. Lawrence River.

The birch bark map was not meant to be a permanent document. Since the routes through the area were well known to Native Americans, there was no need for a map except to indicate which route or paths had been taken. It is very likely that the map would not have survived had Captain Bainbrigge not taken such an interest. Like many Native American maps, more is known about the European who obtained the map than the two Indians who made the original artifact. Captain Philip John Bainbrigge of the Royal Engineers had been educated at the Royal United Service Institute (R.U.S.I.) in London. There he was taught the skills of drafting and topographical sketching before being posted to the Canadian provinces. When Bainbrigge arrived in Canada, the area between Lake Huron and the Ottawa River was still Indian country, inhabited mainly by Ojibwa and Algonquin Indians. The military undertook a survey of the area to plan the roads and settlements needed for the growing numbers of settlers. They even contemplated the construction of a canal to route commerce from Lake Huron down to Montreal and help speed the development of the area.

Part of Bainbrigge's North American service was performed in the Royal Engineers Office in Ottawa where he "certified" maps, evidently receiving maps and survey reports from engineers throughout the provinces. Some time during this period he obtained the map on birch bark. In preparing to send the map back to London, he mounted it on a stiff paper, gave it a title, redrew the map in the lower half of the paper, and added his comments on the map's value.

Bainbrigge's redrawing of the map accurately represents the Northeast Indian pictographic messages, and his interpretation of the map content is probably correct. Before sending the map to the United Services Institute in London, Captain Bainbrigge felt compelled to add a comment on the map for his friends and superiors back at the school where he had been taught the skills of mapmaking. Perhaps the craftsmanship of the maps he had been certifying at the Royal Engineers survey office was below par, or maybe his comments were meant as a jolly good joke for the boys back home; either way, retrospect makes Bainbrigge's gibe seem more a comment on his own lack of understanding than on the quality of the map. In the note he added below the map he states that he was forwarding the map, "in the hope that it may shew young officers how small an effort is needed to acquire that most useful art, Military Sketching since even Savages can make an intelligible plan."

(Figure 2) a message map incised on birch bark, is an example of the efficiency with which Northeast Indians could communicate using picture writing. The message, or wikhegan, was made by Sapiel Selmo, a chief of the Passamaquoddy Indians, a tribe living in northern Maine. Although made as an illustration of Passamaquoddy picture writing, it is much like the map on birch bark in that it is the type of message that would be left for another Indian to find and read. Sapiel Selmo reads the message as the story of two Indians who go hunting, traveling together until the river forks and then each following a separate way. They both build their winter wigwams, shown at the numbers "4" and "5" etched into the bark, and carry on with their hunt. The Indian who followed the river to the left kills a moose, which is shown in the upper left. The other finds a bear's den under a tree, pictured in the right of the message. He attempts to stab the bear but misses his vital part. The bear then grabs and bites the hunter, inflicting a mortal wound.

The wounded hunter returns to his wigwam and, worried that he is going to die, makes this message on a piece of birch bark. When his friend comes he finds the hunter dead in his wigwam. He also finds these marks made on a piece of birch bark which he reads, and immediately knows that his friend has been killed by the bear. Following the hunter's tracks he also finds the bear which has died from its wound.

(Figure 3) is an example of picture writing used to illustrate history. The oral history of the event, as it was told by the Ojibwa who made the drawing, states that ninety-one winters ago (1797), twenty-five Ojibwa were encamped on a small lake (labeled "o" in the middle of the map)

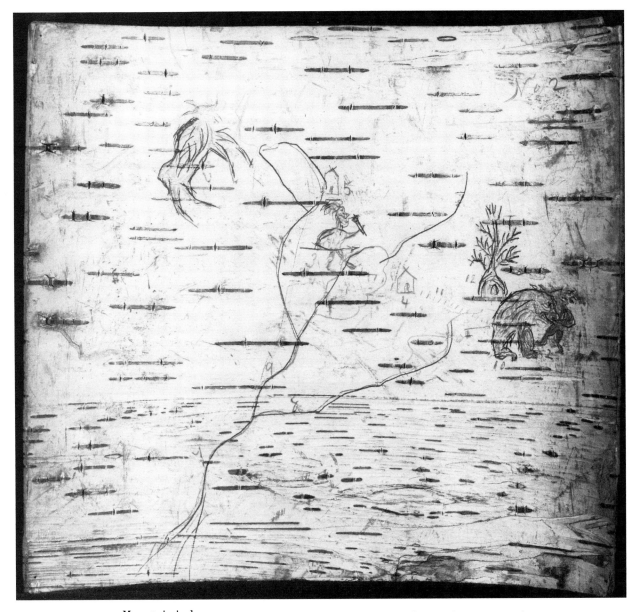

FIGURE 2. **Message incised** *in birch bark, c. 1877. National Museum of Natural History, Smithsonian Institution, 77-8466.*

just west of Mille Lacs, Minnesota. The chief's lodge (a) was erected a short distance from the lake. Because of recent Sioux hostilities, a party was sent out to reconnoiter the area around a nearby lake (labeled "m" towards the bottom of the map). They discovered a force of three hundred enemies and quickly sent back word for the women and children to be taken to a place of safety. Three older women refused to flee. Their lodges are shown (c, d, and e). The Sioux surrounded

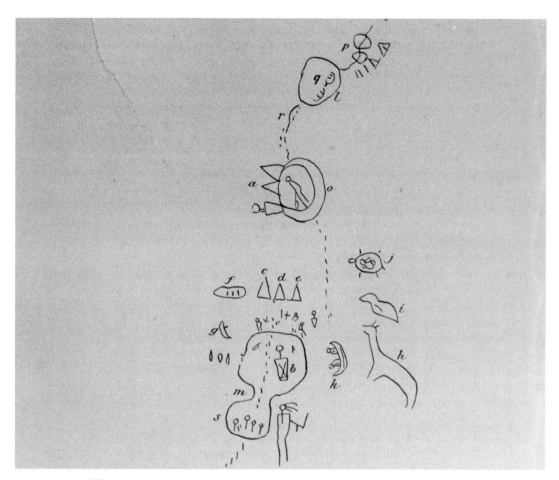

FIGURE 3. **Ojibwa map** *of a battle in 1797. In 1888 an Ojibwa Indian told the anthropologist Garrick Mallery the history of a battle between the Ojibwas and the Dakotas that had taken place ninety-one years earlier. While doing so he drew this map to illustrate the oral record. The map demonstrates how the history and characteristics of a place, those things that gave it meaning for the Ojibwa, were held in the oral record. The picture-writing record was not retained; the oral history, the story, was the record that stayed with the Ojibwa. When illustrating his story the Ojibwa Indian used several pictographic elements such as lakes, canoes, lodges, and the depiction of a route, that are similar to those used in the map on birch bark. His drawing was copied and redrawn in Mallery's published report on "Picture-writing of the American Indians." Mallery also annotated the map with the alphabetical key to locate the events.*

the lake and the fight took place on the ice (warriors, paths, and methods of escape are pictured on and around the lower lake). All the remaining Ojibwa were killed, the chief being the last to die.

Pictured alongside the lake are the deer (h), grouse (i), and turtle (j), which represent the game hunted there during various seasons, and the canoe (k) indicating that they hunted along the lake shore and in the streams that connected the three lakes shown. The map demonstrates

Another America

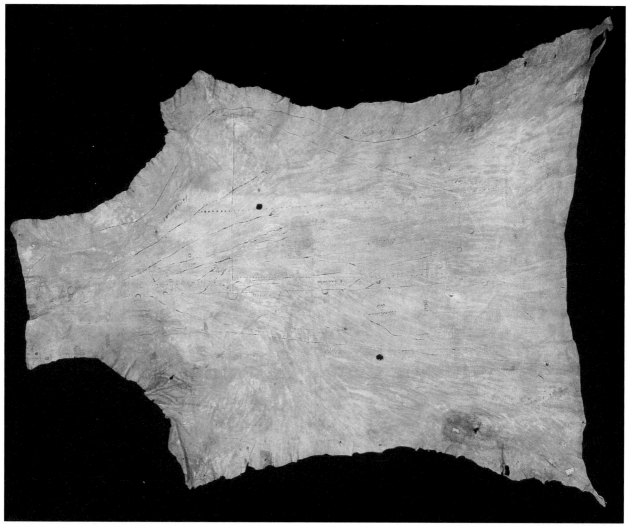

FIGURE 4. **Map on** *skin. Size of the original 54 x 36 inches (137.2 x 91.4 cm). By permission of the British Museum, Department of Ethnography.*

the interaction between the oral traditions where history and cultural information were held, and the use of graphic images, including maps, to illustrate the oral record.

Just as bark and other plant products were adapted for use by Native Americans, animals provided another important resource. Throughout the continent animals were a primary source of food. Their bones were used to make tools, sinews were used for thread, organs for containers and carriers, and their skins for everything from cloths to coverings for homes. The relationships between Native Americans and the animals they depended upon often included a spiritual kinship between man and animal. Interwoven throughout many indigenous cultures were rituals, practices, and stories that tied human groups to animals and their spirits. These relationships helped to teach the skills of hunting and managing game animals and reinforced the roles and responsibilities of hunters, warriors, and others within the community.

In addition to their use in clothing and domestic items, skins were used as a medium for painting and record-keeping. Painted skins have been found throughout the continent, from the pages of the codices or picture-writing books of the Aztecs and Mayans to the illustrated winter counts of Plains Indian tribes and the decorated clothing and implements of the Arctic peoples. The use of skins as a medium for graphic expression began before the historical record. Examples from both before and after the encounter demonstrate a fully developed tradition of making visual messages on skins.

The "Map on Skin" (Figure 4) is an interesting example of a painted skin showing geographic features, tribal territories, and land cessions. The lines and graphic information on the map are probably original Indian, while the English language words for features and Indian groups may have been added later. Nothing is known about the history of the map before 1825, when it is reported to have been given to England's Stonyhurst College by the son of a wealthy citizen of St. Louis, Missouri. He, in turn, may have obtained the map as a curio item or memento——the area around St. Louis is represented on the map. It is also possible that the map was commissioned to record a land sale made during this period of confusion in the sale and cession of Indian lands. Given the date of the map's appearance, the area it represents, and the Indian tribes and places that are painted on the map, it is possible to read the image as a reflection of Indian and white relations at the beginning of the nineteenth century.

Although the lines on the map are very faint, the representation that it gives of the region between the Mississippi and Ohio rivers is a timely picture of the Native Americans' meeting with western society. The rivers represented on the map are named in English. The Mississippi is drawn on the top (west), with the Illinois, Embarras, Wabash, and Ohio rivers arranged across the skin and turned to meet at the neck. The area covered on the map includes what are now central and southern Illinois, Indiana, and Ohio. It is characteristic of Native American maps to bend or alter the shape of geographic features or the courses of rivers to fit the size and shape of the object on which the map is being made. In this case it demonstrates the efficiency with which the oral tradition could represent spatial information. A western map confined to the same space would not be able to represent the extent of the area shown.

Rather than the spatial relationships, it is the people, places, and things in this landscape that are the focus of the map. Three Indian tribes are named: The Kaskaskia Indians are noted in the left near the river which bears their name, the Wea and Piankashaw Indians are named along tributaries of the Wabash river in the middle of the skin. Circles, an indigenous symbol for human settlements used throughout North America, note Indian villages and the site of forts and trading posts. Paths are pictured by dotted lines.

At the time the map was made this was an area in transition. Over the previous two centuries American Indian groups had been steadily migrating west. Native populations were displaced when European diseases entered the continent with the first explorers. Small pox, influenza, and other diseases ravaged various Indian groups and caused others to move. In the seventeenth and eighteenth centuries the trading and military alliances introduced by the British and

French fur trade resulted in further inter-tribal conflicts and displacement. And in the nineteenth century the United States was rapidly expanded its territory and simultaneously displacing Indians from the east. By the 1840s displacement became the official policy of the United States, with the forced removal of Native Americans to areas west of the Mississippi River.

The Kaskaskia, Wea, and Piankashaw Indians who occupied parts of the territory represented on this map had been effected by these events. The Kaskaskia, an Algonquian-speaking tribe and part of the group of tribes known collectively as Illinois Indians, once occupied the area around the Illinois and middle Mississippi rivers. By the time of this map, pressures from hostile Indians and growing white settlements confined them to the strip of land between the Kaskaskia and Big Muddy rivers.

The Wea and Piankashaw Indians on the other side of the map were closely associated with the Miami Indians who lived along the upper Wabash. The three had established themselves in the region by the middle 1600s and for the next century and a half had contacts with French, English, and finally American traders and colonial representatives. They maintained a traditional way of life with their summer camps spread out along the rivers and their winter hunting expeditions. By the nineteenth century the United States started to pressure these tribes to move west, while other displaced Indian tribes began to enter their territories and deplete the game. In response the Miami, Wea, and Piankashaw began to sell their lands in Illinois territory and move across the Mississippi.

The map documents the loss of Indian territory. In the lower right between the representations of the Ohio and Wabash Rivers is the notation "Piankashaws sold," recording a previous land cession. And the straight line painted across the left half of the map has been interpreted as a treaty or boundary line indicating lands that the Indians could no longer claim.

Because of the unknown provenance of the map and the confused history of the region in the early nineteenth century, it is impossible to say which treaties or land cessions may be recorded here. At the time the Weas, Piankasaws, and Kaskaskias were in the process of ceding their territories and moving to allotted sites west of the Mississippi River. By 1840 all three tribes no longer lived in the area represented on this map. They had been removed to territories they were forced to share with larger and stronger tribes. By the end of the century all three tribes had either been incorporated into other Indian groups or become so thinly dispersed that they could no longer maintain their identity. Within sixty years of their removal, the Kaskaskia, Wea, and Piankashaw Indians no longer existed as peoples.

Lone Dog, a Yanktonai Dakota or Sioux Indian, painted this skin (Figure 5) from his own experience and the tribal memory as it was passed on by the elders of his tribe. The winter count, as such paintings are called, uses a distinguishing event or circumstances to represent each year as it passes. Several winter counts have been recorded covering different and overlapping periods of tribal history. Lone Dog's count begins at the center with the thirty lines representing the thirty Dakotas killed by Crow Indians in the winter of 1800–01. The pictures representing subsequent years continue in a counterclockwise spiral to record seventy-one winters for the Dakotas with images representing the events that marked each year in Dakota memory. The second image, a figure with spots, records the arrival of smallpox among the Dakotas in the year of 1801–02. The spotted horse pictured two images later records the winter of 1803–04 and the Dakotas' success-

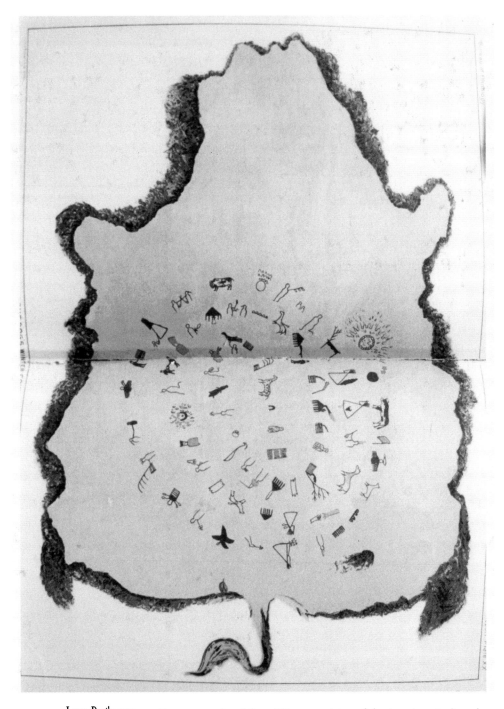

FIGURE 5. **Lone Dog's** *Winter Count, reproduced from "Picture-writing of the American Indians by Garrick Mallery,"* Tenth Annual Report of the Bureau of Ethnology, Smithsonian Institution. *Washington: Government Printing Office, 1893.*

Another America

FIGURE 6. **Map Rock,** *Native American petroglyph located by the Snake River near Givens Hot Springs, Idaho. Rock, approximately 10 feet x 9 feet x 5 feet. Courtesy of Idaho State Historical Society, photograph by Thomas J. Green.*

ful horse raid against the Crows. In that raid the Dakotas stole some "curly horses," a breed in which the hair grows in curled tuffs as indicated by the black spots on the figure.

Like other picture-writing techniques, painted winter counts supplemented the oral history of the tribe. They also give insight into the events that stood out in Dakota memory to organize time, history, and geography. Among the symbols on the map are representations of ceremonies that marked the beginnings of wars, of diseases that struck the tribe, of coups counted against their enemies, and the establishment of western trading houses in the Dakotas' territory. The outer circle records events from the 1840s through 1871. Near the top (neck) of the buffalo hide on which the count was originally painted there is a circle representing a Brule (Sioux) camp and semi-circles moving away from it to indicate the hoof-prints of the horses that the Crows stole from the Brules in 1849–50. This image is followed by a picture of a buffalo with a human figure drawn inside it, which has been interpreted as a Dakota religious symbol noting a reaffirming event that occurred in 1850–51. The next picture with two figures distinguished by different hair styles facing each other with arms extended and holding pipes, represents a peace treaty made with the Crows in 1851–52.

The winter count ends with two pictures painted on the right at the middle of the skin. The first, a dark circle with two lighter stars, records an eclipse of the sun that took place in the summer of 1869 and was total within the territory of the Dakotas. The image represents the sun as colored dark with the stars coming out bright. The final figure on the count records a battle between the Hunkpapas (Uncpapas) band of Dakotas and the Crows. The circle at the center represents the Crows' village or fort, while the surrounding figures are the Hunkpapas whose bullets fly towards the fort. It is the first image on this winter count in which the Indians are shown using guns.

Map Rock (Figure 6). Over ten thousand years ago, Native American hunters and gatherers pursued mammoths along the Snake River valley. The area forms a natural corridor linking the high plains of what is now Montana, where the beginnings of the Missouri River flows east, to the Snake and Salmon river systems that drain west towards the Pacific Ocean. The region offered a wealth of resources to these ancestors of modern Indians. Salmon migrated up the Snake each spring; cammas roots could be harvested in the lowlands; elk, deer, and antelope could be hunted in the mountain valleys; and, before grazing transformed the landscape to a sagebrush scrubland, the upper part of the Snake River plain was a grassland where buffalo could be taken. This was the Native American landscape and for thousands of years groups of American Indians traveled through the region on their seasonal rounds of hunting, fishing, and following the buffalo out onto the plains.

The Indians who traveled through this region left a record on the rocks of their comings and goings. Hundreds of etched and painted rocks can be found along the Snake River and on the Columbia Plateau. Most are prehistoric, from long before the European invasion, and are no longer part of living traditions. The meaning of these images can only be speculated. They are mute testimony to the centuries of Native American inhabitation, and graphic expressions of the unique concepts and beliefs with which the inhabitants organized their world.

Petroglyphs are rocks that have designs scratched, pecked, and otherwise cut into them. Pictographs are rocks on which the design has been painted. "Map Rock" is a petroglyph with the design deeply etched or scratched into a basalt boulder. The geometric and animal designs of "Map Rock" have much in common with other petroglyphs found throughout the region, although the long curvilinear line that dominates the front of the rock is less common. The petroglyph has been known as "Map Rock" ever since white men entered the region, and the design has been interpreted as a map of the upper Snake River and the surrounding environment for just as long.

One interpretation is that the rock is a map or representation of the territory of the Shoshone Indians. They first entered the area in the fifteenth century using the region as a seasonal hunting and fishing ground. When the region's cycle of seasonal travel was interrupted by the introduction of horses and European weapons in the eighteenth century, the newly armed and mounted Blackfoot Indians pushed the Shoshone out of Montana and on to the Snake River Plain and Salmon River area. The Shoshone shared their new territory with the Bannock Indians and maintained good relations with their Paiute and Nez Perce neighbors. They adapted to the seasonal cycle of the region, fishing, gathering, and hunting as they moved back and forth between the plains and the mountains. "Map Rock," on which an outline of the Snake and Salmon Rivers can be interpreted, and where etchings of the animals that the Shoshone hunted can be seen, may be a symbolic representation of the Shoshone's territory. Without a tradition to verify this theory, however, it is impossible to make an interpretation with certainty.

Rather than try to solve the riddle of who made the petroglyph and what geography it represents, it is more fruitful to read the rock in the context of Native American life. As stationary art, petroglyphs were located in places that individuals or people had to come to. Some were purposely isolated, others were placed along game trails or at sites that were visited during the seasonal round. Some petroglyphs may simply have been made to note the boundaries of one's territory. Many of these rocks have been interpreted as shamanistic and ritual expressions made to guarantee the success of the hunt or to mark spiritual and social locations of cultural importance. The animal designs, images of people, spiritual entities, and abstract patterns painted or etched on the rocks mirror the multidimensional world of Native America. Human, animal, and spiritual elements existed together in a universe where actions in one realm effected outcomes in the other.

Like other examples of Native American graphic art these images undoubtedly included an oral component that gave context to the image. The message of these petroglyphs was wrapped up in the ritual retelling of the oral history and spiritual significance of the place. At the same time the graphic systems used in rock art provide early examples of Native American artistic traditions——traditions that would reach their full expression in bead work, pottery design, painted hides, and other media.

"Map Rock" is located in a field of petroglyphs about three hundred yards from the Snake River, south and east of present-day Boise, Idaho. It is in a spot that could easily be seen as one traveled along the river. The remains of winter lodges from four thousand years ago have been found in the vicinity, and the rock may mark an ancient crossing point. The line running across the rock connects a series of geometric designs and anthropomorphic figures. The rock includes representations of buffalo, deer, mountain sheep, elk, antelope, and human figures. As a representation of the rivers and the locations of animal resources the rock would have been redundant in the oral cultures of Native Americans. But as an expression of the spiritual relationship between the land, its resources, and the people who depended upon them, "Map Rock" would be in a similar category with the speculated meaning of much of the region's rock art. The petroglyph may have been made as part of a ritual meant to keep all these elements in balance and to secure the continued health of the people. Interpreted in this manner the petroglyph represents both the corporal and the spiritual elements that coexisted in the Native American world.

(Figure 7) Note the similarity between the line that meanders across the front of the rock and a map of the Snake River crossing south central Idaho from its source in the lakes around Yellowstone National Park. This similarity has led to the interpretation of the petroglyph as a map of the Snake and Salmon rivers, describing the territory of the Shoshone and Bannock Indians. The redrawing also shows several of the animals represented on the rock. According to the geographic interpretation of the petroglyph, the animals are represented in their approximate locations from the river, for example the buffalo to the east on the Great Plains. It is also possible that the animals and the river were represented along with the other designs on the rock as part of a religious message seeking continued success in the hunt and continued spiritual favor for the people who left these marks on the rock.

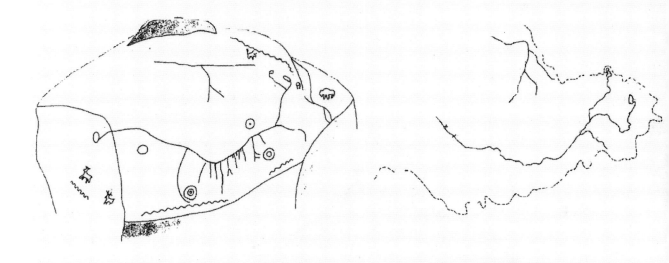

FIGURE 7. **A redrawing** *of the major features of Map Rock compared with a map of the middle and upper Snake and Salmon Rivers. Based on an interpretive drawing by G. Malcolm Lewis.*

(Figure 8) These redrawings of petroglyphs from South Dakota show some of the regional variations of rock art. Made by the ancestors of Plains Indians, the petroglyphs show how geographic information was incorporated into graphic images used in the retelling of mythical or historic events. They are excellent examples of early Plains Indian art, an artistic tradition that continued on in the painted hides and ledger-book drawings of the nineteenth century. For the Indians of the Plains, landscape was formed in the history and experience of individuals and groups. Geography formed the backdrop on which events were depicted. The events represented on these petroglyphs, the exploits of an individual warrior and an unknown journey, foreshadow similar depictions of warrior exploits, travels, and raids in nineteenth-century drawings by Cheyenne, Dakota, Hidatsa, and other Plains Indians.

The drawing on the top depicts two human figures, or possibly the same figure at different points in time, on either side of a vertical line which may represent a stream or pass. The dotted line or track is the route of the figure who has crossed this boundary. The track continues across the face of the panel and up to another heavy line that may represent a river or mountain pass. The petroglyph is the representation of a journey, but the reason for the journey and the events it records are not known.

The drawing on the bottom shows the battle exploits or coups of an individual warrior. The depiction of warrior prowess is a favorite subject of many Plains Indian artists. This theme has been recorded on rocks, skins, and paper. The warrior figure in the petroglyph is depicted with his rounded shield decorated with a horizontal band and a series of dots. He carries a spear or stick from which hang two diamond-shaped objects representing the heads or scalps of his enemies. The dashed line represents the trail of the warrior—the path he took to make his raid. The

Another America

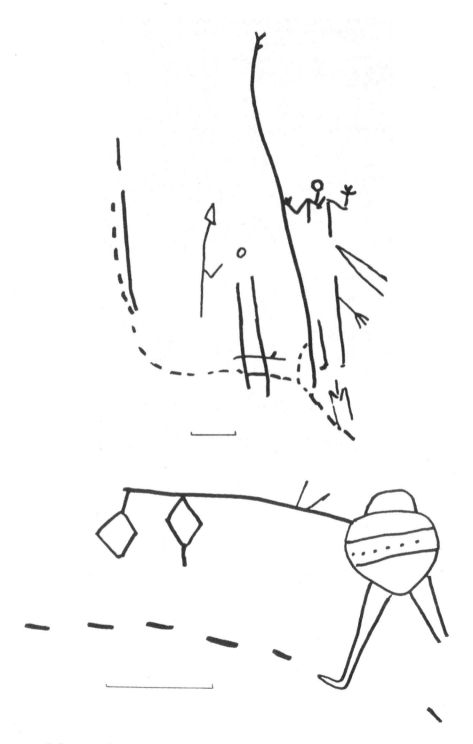

FIGURE 8. **Redrawings of** *Rock Art from Western South Dakota. Courtesy of Linea Sundstrom.*

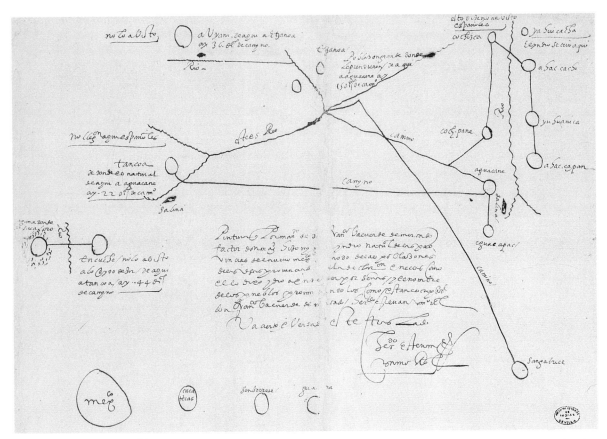

FIGURE 9. **Pintura q** *Por mando de don Franco Valuerde de mercado factor de su magd hizo myguel yndio de las pro vincias del nueuo mexco ...1602 [Sketch which, by order of don Francisco Valverde de Mercado, factor of His Majesty was made by Miguel, an Indian, native of the provinces of New Mexico...] Size of the original 12 x 17 inches (31 x 43 cm). Courtesy of the Archivo General de Indias, Seville.*

drawing might be interpreted as depicting the shield-bearer, whose personal identity is given in the decorations on the shield, having traveled to the enemy camp and killed or counted coup on two enemies.

The oldest recorded Native American map (Figure 9) was made by an Indian named Miguel, who had been captured by the Spanish on the south central Plains of what is now the United States. After his capture Miguel was taken to Mexico City, where he was interrogated as part of an official inquiry into Don Juan de Oñate's expedition to the territories beyond the province of New Mexico. During the inquiry Miguel was instructed to mark with pen and ink on a sheet of paper the pueblos of his land. This is the notarized copy of Miguel's map. Made at the time of the inquiry, the map was sent back to Spain as part of the official record and stored in the colonial archives in Seville.

The area represented on Miguel's map includes those places he had seen or traveled to,

Another America

places that he was aware of, and settlements he had visited while a captive of the Spanish. The map includes a large but unknown area of the south central Plains and demonstrates the extensive networks and geographic knowledge of Native American societies. The map, and the inquiry that accompanied it, is also a reflection of the Spanish interest in the region. Its coming into being as a written document is the result of the encounter that began with the Spanish invasion of the Native Americans' land in the sixteenth century.

In 1598 Don Juan de Oñate, "governor, captain, general, and pacifier of the provinces of New Mexico," crossed the Rio Grande River with four hundred men, one hundred thirty families, eighty-three carts, and seven thousand head of cattle. He was undertaking the conquest and colonization of New Mexico, a right he had been granted by the Spanish crown. A wealthy citizen of Mexico, Oñate's wife was the granddaughter of Cortés and the great granddaughter of Montezuma. Related by marriage to the Aztec King and the Spanish Conquistador, Oñate hoped that he too would rule a province as rich as Mexico. His crossing of the Rio Grande marked Spain's first serious effort to extend its empire into the Pueblo country since Coronado's expedition in the 1540s. As colonizer, Oñate could enrich himself with the Indians' tribute, he would profit from the gold he hoped to find, and reap the rewards of developing the new lands and their agricultural riches.

Oñate's expedition was undertaken for the glory of God and Spain. He was accompanied by eleven Franciscan friars who would work to convert the Indians to the holy Catholic faith. International criticism of Spanish cruelty towards the Indians, and the Franciscans' successful argument for saving their eternal souls, had recently resulted in new policy. The "savages" were now to be baptized rather than enslaved, and it was the responsibility of Don Juan de Oñate to see that this policy was carried out. Each baptism brought as much glory to the empire's holy mission as did further conquests or the discovery of more gold.

News of Oñate's arrival must have spread quickly throughout the Southwest and the Great Plains. By the time of the Spanish invasion the Indian societies of the Pueblo country had developed an extensive trading and communications network. Their commerce extended across the plains to the Indians of the Mississippi Valley and south to the Aztecs and other Indian civilizations of Mexico. Apaches coming from the southern plains would bring buffalo hides, meat, fat, and other animal products to trade for corn, blankets, tobacco, and precious rocks from the Pueblos. These indigenous networks had evolved over the twelve thousand years in which Native Americans had lived in this region. First coming as hunters and gatherers, about five thousand years ago they began to adapt maize cultivation. With the beginnings of agriculture these Southwestern societies slowly changed, evolving into the civilizations with monumental architecture, domesticated animals, irrigation systems, distinctive pottery, and mining that existed around 1300. The entrance of the Spanish into this well-established world was probably looked upon as a curiosity by the indigenous societies of the Southwest.

Don Juan de Oñate's expedition moved north along the Rio Grande into modern-day New Mexico. He established his colonial capital at San Gabriel, represented by the circle labeled "Sangabriel" in the lower right of the map. This was along the Rio Grande River between what are now Albuquerque and Santa Fe. From here, Oñate and his soldiers set about obtaining "Acts of Obedience and Vassalage" from the Indians of the nearby Pueblos. These oaths of allegiance to the Spanish king undoubtedly meant very little to the Indians, as did the ministrations of the friars who set about trying to convert them. Most of the Pueblos peacefully accepted the temporary inconveniences of Spain's claim to their territory, but in 1599 the Pueblo of Acoma, a "sky city" perched atop a mesa, rebelled. They refused to give the tribute demanded by the Spanish, and Oñate sent his nephew Juan de Zaldívar to deal with the situation. When Zaldívar intervened, he and several other members of the expedition were killed by the residents of Acoma.

The Spanish revenge upon the Pueblo was merciless. Oñate appointed Zaldívar's brother, Vincente, to lead the avenging force. They laid siege to the pueblo, burning it to the ground and causing the death of many of the people. Gaspar Perez de Villagra, an officer who accompanied Oñate's expedition, described the burning of Acoma and the capture of the survivors in his historical ballad, *Historia del la Nueva Mexico :*

"Note, most worthy lord, those high walls, roofs, and lofts, tottering and crumbling in a thousand parts, then crashing in an inferno of flames, engulfing the unhappy inhabitants. Note those wretched beings who in their last despair seek death by hurling themselves from those awful heights. See the savages, men and women, who with their little ones rush amid the raging flames, lamenting their misery and their fate.

"The sergeant was moved to compassion by the terrible slaughter. . . . so Zaldívar urged (the) savages who had surrendered to plead with their people to yield and cease this terrible self-destruction. He assured them on his word of honor that he would spare them all if only they would end this awful sacrifice."

Villagra's interpretation was meant to flatter the Spanish. His poem goes on to tell of the peaceful surrender of the survivors, but the reality came out in later inquiries. Others at the battle noted that after surrendering, the Indians gave the corn, blankets, and turkeys as had been demanded, but Zaldívar refused their offerings and confined the natives as prisoners. Under Zaldívar's direction they were taken out of the prison one by one, murdered, and thrown over the mesa's cliff.

The Spanish revenge was completed in February 1599, when Oñate himself officiated at the sentencing of the Acoma survivors. For having killed eleven Spaniards and two servants, and for failing to submit peacefully when Vicente de Zaldívar came to punish them, Oñate sentenced all males over the age of twenty-five to have one foot cut off and to give twenty-five years of service. Males between twelve and twenty-five and all females over the age of twelve were given twenty years of service. In other words the entire population over the age of twelve was forced into slavery. The children were given over to be raised in convents or by the friars. Two Hopi Indians, captured at Acoma, had their right hands cut off and were sent home as a warning to others.

Such cruelty may have earned Oñate the continued submission of the Pueblos, but it did nothing to further the colonial goals of the conquistador. Villagra was more accurate in his "Historia" when he recorded the story of two Indians who had escaped the destruction of Acoma only to be captured by the Spanish and imprisoned. First, they barricaded themselves in the prison for three days. When further resistance was futile they are reported to have cried out:

"Castilians, if you are not yet satisfied with the blood you have shed, and if you must still wreak your vengeance upon us, we will grant you this satisfaction. Send us two sharp daggers, and we will cut our throats and die here. We would prefer this rather than have it said that we died at the hands of such infamous dogs as you."

Despite Oñate's conquest of the Pueblos, his enterprise was not going well. Winters in New Mexico were hard and many of the settlers abandoned the colony. And the friars were not successful in converting the Indians. In 1602 it was reported that only about sixty souls had been baptized and these were mostly children or women who were slaves in service to the Spanish. Oñate's investment was in danger and his expeditions outside the province had yielded no gold or other riches to reward the venture.

Between the "official" expeditions of Coronado in 1541 and Oñate's colonial enterprise in 1598, several Spanish adventurers had entered the regions north of Mexico in hopes of enriching themselves. Although these explorations established no permanent Spanish presence in New Mexico, the Indians who had accompanied these forays brought back stories of rich tribes and fertile lands to the east. To Oñate this represented a way to save his colony. The Indians' descriptions could only be of Quivira, the land visited by Coronado and described as "the best I have ever seen. . . the land itself being very fat and black and being very well watered by the rivulets and springs and rivers, I find everything they have in Spain. . ." Here was the possibility of fertile lands with agricultural bounty and an Indian civilization with potential wealth for the colonizer.

In 1601 Oñate set out for Quivira. Taking approximately eighty men and guided by a Mexican Indian, he headed east on to the buffalo ranges. The line labeled "camino" (road) that extends from San Gabriel towards the center of the map may represent the route of Oñate's exploration. The expedition followed the Canadian River through Texas and Oklahoma. They met with nomadic Apache Indians and saw the Plains so filled with buffalo that it was difficult to believe their eyes. After several days the expedition entered the territory of the "Escanxaques." These Indians, believed to be another group of Apaches, were camped for their summer hunt in a temporary village of five thousand people. Miguel represented the village of the Escanxaques at "aguacane," the circle in the right center of the map connected by roads and paths to the network of Native American settlements. The Escanxaques told Oñate that the village he sought was two days' journey from there, and they warned the Spanish not to trust these Indians, the Quiviras. Oñate took several Escanxaques as guides and continued on to the great Indian village between the rivers. Others of the tribe followed the Spanish at a distance.

The Native American societies that Oñate encountered had begun to migrate on to the Great Plains in the eleventh and twelfth centuries. Linked together by trade and traditions, they relied upon a combination of hunting, trade, and agriculture for their subsistence. The buffalo was their major source of food and material goods, and the warrior ethic and tribal animosities that shaped these societies were well established before the encounter with Europeans.

The settlement at which Oñate eventually arrived is referred to, but not clearly represented, near the center top of the map. It is believed to have been along the Arkansas River in modern-day Kansas. The inhabitants, called Quiviras by the Apaches, were Wichita Indians, and their settlement extended for three days' travel between the banks of the Arkansas and its tributaries; parts of this fertile land still carry the name Quivira. The Wichitas were an agricultural people, taking advantage of the land to grow corn, beans, and squash. They lived in permanent circular grass houses formed around poles stuck into the ground. Oñate's soldiers counted over two thousand of these houses in the Wichita village. They were scattered throughout the settlement and erected in groups of thirty of forty with fields of corn and other crops planted between them.

Initially, the Wichitas came out to meet Oñate, bringing tribute and promising friendly relations. But the Escanxaques were enemies of the Wichitas. They told the Spanish that these were the Indians who had killed the earlier Spanish explorers, and still held one captive. To investigate these charges, Oñate decided to take some of the Wichitas hostage and hold them in exchange for the Spanish captive. The next day, when a delegation from the settlement came out to meet with the Spanish, this was done. When the Wichitas saw the Spanish working with their enemies, and seizing five or six of their delegates, they left, temporarily abandoning their settlement and having nothing more to do with the Spanish.

With the Wichitas away from their settlement, the Escanxaques who had followed the Spanish proceeded to sack and burn the Wichita village. According to the Spanish, they attempted to stop this, telling the Escanxaques to take food but leave the Wichita's settlement alone. The Spanish then proceeded to explore the village, going at least half way between the two rivers that bordered the settlement before returning to their original camp and finding that they were now in a vulnerable position.

The Spanish, a relatively small force of less then eighty armed men, received reports that the inhabitants of the village were assembling to attack. The soldiers petitioned Don Juan de Oñate to return to San Gabriel rather than continue the expedition. The governor reluctantly granted their petition. As the Spanish returned through the Wichita settlement they found a force of Escanxaques camped with their women and children. These Escanxaques opened fire on the Spanish. The resulting skirmish lasted four hours, in the course of which the Spanish captured a few of the Indian women, several boys, and the Indian Miguel. The Escanxaques mounted a fierce attack and several of the Spanish soldiers received wounds. In order to halt the hostilities Juan de Oñate ordered the release of the women prisoners. At the request of the friars they kept the Indian children to instruct them in the holy faith, and the Indian Miguel, so that "he might furnish information about all this land." The Spanish returned to San Gabriel with Miguel as a captive.

Six months later Miguel had been taken to Mexico City to participate in the inquiry "concerning the New Discovery Undertaken by Governor Don Juan de Oñate Toward the North beyond the Provinces of New Mexico." The Viceroy of New Spain had called the inquiry to find out what had taken place on Oñate's expedition and to gather information on whether the area Oñate had entered contained resources that would make it worth the effort of colonization——"In order to establish the truth," as the royal commission said, "and to permit the most appropriate measure to be taken for the service of God and the king, our lord."

The inquiry was recorded by Hernando Esteban, a royal notary. His account of the proceedings is quoted below, and his signature appears with a flourish at the bottom of the endorsement in the center of the map. Questioned during the inquiry were five of the soldiers who had accompanied Oñate on the expedition, and the "Indian prisoner seized in a skirmish in the newly discovered settlements of the Indians who roam the buffalo plains and follow the multitudes of these animals, and this Indian, though he did not speak or understand any language in which he could express his thoughts, gave important details about the land by signs." The testimonies of the Spanish soldiers form the basis for much of what is known about the expedition. Miguel's testimony, on the other hand, records a different view of the Plains and Pueblo area and of the Native American experience of the Spanish invasion.

The questioning of Miguel took place on the last day of the inquiry. Hernando Esteban described Miguel as being well built with good features, and somewhat darker than the Mexican Indians. Miguel was first asked to make the map. Esteban's account notes that:

> Miguel proceeded to mark on the paper some circles resembling the letter 'O,' some larger than others; in a way easily understood he explained what each circle represented, and I, by order of the factor, wrote in each one of the circles what the Indian said they represented, to make it clear. Then he drew lines, some snakelike and others straight, and indicated by signs that they were rivers and roads; they were also given names, according to his explanation.

Except for San Gabriel, located along the Rio Grande in central New Mexico, the only other places noted on the maps whose location is known are the four Mexican cities represented by circles in the lower left of the map. In the middle, guadiana (Durango), a city in north central Mexico is represented; next is Sonbzerese (Sombrerete) a city where it was recorded that Indians captured in New Mexico were taken to be sold as slaves. The next circle represents çacatedac (Zacatcas), a mining city somewhat north of Mexico City. The final circle labeled "mex^{co}" represents Mexico City, where Miguel was being interrogated. He may have passed through these places on the way to his interrogation, or the Spanish may have placed them on the map in the hopes of giving a western orientation to the document. The locations of the places represented above these cities cannot be confidently related to a western map, but Miguel's explanation provides insights into the Native American geography.

Esteban records that, "After making this picture map the Indian explained by signs the place where he was born, how he was taken prisoner and carried away by the enemy to other lands where he grew up, how he came to fight the Spaniards and was taken prisoner."

Miguel claimed that he was being held captive by the Escanxaques that attacked Oñate. He explained that he was originally from "Tancoa," which he represents as a village between two rivers in the left center of the map. The notes explain that Miguel described this as a twenty-two-day journey from "Aguacane," connected on the right by the "camino" that crosses the map. Miguel claimed that he had been taken to the Escanxaques' village, Aguacane, when he was still a young boy. If Miguel's statement is true, he could have been a member of any number of tribes on the south central Plains. But the stories of Spanish cruelty had undoubtedly proceeded Oñate's expedition onto the Plains. After the fight with the Spanish at Quivira, Miguel suddenly found himself held captive by the destroyers of Acoma, the Spaniards who had burned the Pueblo and condemned the survivors to slavery. It is easy to see the motivation Miguel might have had for establishing himself as different from those who had fought against Oñate. Later inconsistencies in Miguel's testimony add further weight to this possibility. Still, Miguel's map presents a picture of the knowledge he possessed of important sites outside of his immediate territory.

In laying out the map, Miguel used a common Indian measure of distance by indicating the number of days' journey between places. In addition to the twenty-two-day journey between Tancoa and Aguacane, Miguel notes that from Aguacane to the great village where the Spanish

FIGURE 10. A Wichita *village from the mid-nineteenth century. The thatched-grass houses are much like those described by the members of Don Juan de Oñate's expedition to the great Indian settlement on the Arkansas River in 1601. The cluster of houses are arranged at the center of the radiating cornfields. From* Exploration of the Red River of Louisiana, *U. S. War Department, [c. 1850]. Courtesy of the Everett D. Graff Collection, The Newberry Library, Chicago.*

took him prisoner was fifteen days' travel. Other locations near the top of the map are described as *"no lo a visto,"* meaning they were locations that the Spanish had not seen. The area described is considerable, showing Miguel's knowledge of places and peoples as much as forty-four-days' journey apart.

After Miguel made his map the questioning continued. The Spanish officials showed him plants, animals, and other Indians in an effort to obtain information about the new area and the people and resources it contained. The officials then ordered everyone to leave except Miguel and the notary Esteban, and the most important part of the inquiry began. The Spanish produced samples of gold, silver, copper, and brass and asked Miguel if any of these metals were found in his land or the places he had marked on the map. Miguel then demonstrated, by placing objects on the map, part of the trading network used by the Indians of the Southwest and Plains. He said that gold was brought to his native pueblo of Tancoa from Encuche (represented in the middle left and described as a forty-four-day journey from Tancoa); there the gold was traded for meat and hides. When asked if the gold was mined at Encuche, Miguel answered that it was "obtained from a lake beyond Encuche which is about the depth of a man." He then added on to his map,

Another America

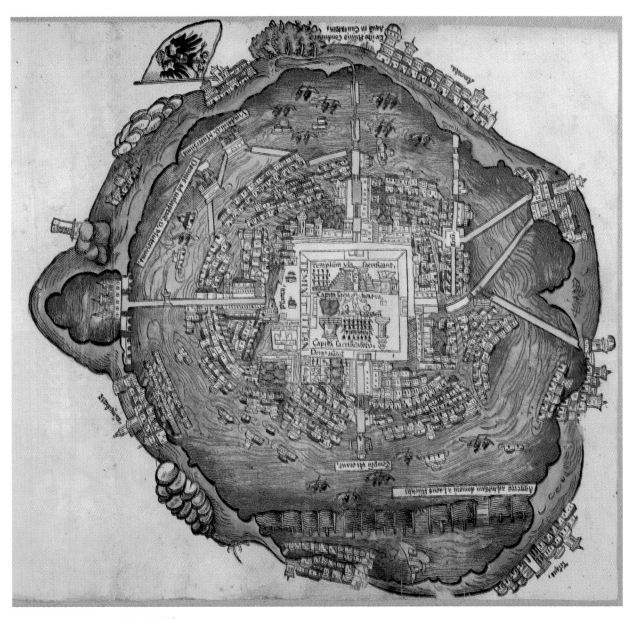

FIGURE 11. **Tenochtitlán,** *the Aztec capital as it was pictured in the second letter of Hernán Cortez published in Nuremberg in 1524. The map, while European in design and execution, does show some of the pre-Columbian features of the city of Tenochtitlán. The temple square, where the market may have been held, is featured in the center. The city is shown sitting in the middle of Lake Texcoco, on which it was originally built. The shallow lake offered protection for the imperial city and it may be the same lagoon Miguel was referring to when he added it to his map as the place where gold can be found. Miguel said he had only heard of this place; ironically, he may have been in the same city as a Spanish captive. Courtesy of the Edward E. Ayer Collection, Newberry Library, Chicago.*

with the path from Encuche crossing the river to a large settlement, represented by the circle on the extreme left with the hatch marks around it. This place is titled "the lagoon where gold can be gotten" (*laguna donde se saca oro*). It is speculated that this might represent the Aztec Capital of Tenochtitlán (Mexico City), located in the middle of a shallow lake and the scene of a large native market where gold and many other goods were traded with people from throughout the continent.

Trade between the Pueblos of the Southwest and Mexico City has been documented, and it is possible that Miguel was aware of the availability of gold in Tenochtitlán. However, Miguel claimed to have been an adult when he witnessed gold being processed in his native village of Tancoa. He also said that he had never returned to this village since his childhood capture by the Escanxaques. This contradiction was noted by the Spanish, but went unaddressed as the interrogators had no way of explaining the contradiction to Miguel.

Misunderstandings across the gulf of language and culture that separated Miguel from his Spanish interlocutors were probably quite common. And Miguel's experience with the Spanish could easily have influenced his testimony. Nevertheless, Miguel's map gives an intriguing if unknown view of the Native American landscape and the intricate networks American Indians had developed.

After giving his testimony, Miguel was returned to the house of the chief *alguacil* or bailiff, "where he is kept by order of his lordship," and no mention is made of him again. Hernando Esteban copied and signed the map, which was sent with the record of the inquiry back to Spain and the Archivo General de Indias. Oñate's colony continued to experience difficulties; a lack of riches, few souls for the church, and growing discontent among the settlers and Indians. In 1608 Oñate resigned as governor. Later he was stripped of his glory and charged in the Spanish court for his cruelty at Acoma. The Spanish maintained their colony, sending missionaries to look after the few converts the Franciscans had made. In 1610 a new capital was established at Santa Fe. In 1680 the Pueblos united in a revolt against Spanish rule, successfully pushing the invaders out for the next twelve years.

Matonabbee's Map (Figure 12). Matonabbee was a Chipewyan or Northern Indian from the Barren Grounds west of Hudson's Bay. He was a well-known trade leader who periodically brought furs to the Hudson's Bay Company's post at the mouth of the Churchill River on western Hudson Bay. In 1762, the factor of the trading post asked Matonabbee and Idolyazee, another Chipewyan Indian, to make a map to the largest rivers to the north. Five years later Matonabbee returned with the original of this map. Made at the request of a non-Indian, the map uses Chipewyan cartography to represent the extensive area of western Canada that Matonabbee was familiar with. The map indicates rivers, lakes, coasts, and resources located throughout the area of northwestern Canada from Hudson's Bay to Great Slave Lake and north to the Arctic Ocean.

Matonabbee's map is a picture of a landscape formed in the oral traditions. Ties of kinship and the rituals of the hunt sustained Matonabbee and his people along with the other Indians who inhabited this region. Their mythology, traditions, and sense of the world were all adapted to a life of hunting and gathering on the tundra. The land and its resources shaped their lives, and their technologies enabled them to produce a good living from this harsh environment. Like the wolves, whom the Chipewyans looked upon as their spiritual brothers, the Chipewyans depended upon the Barren Grounds caribou, preferring this animal to fish, furbearing creatures, and all other ani-

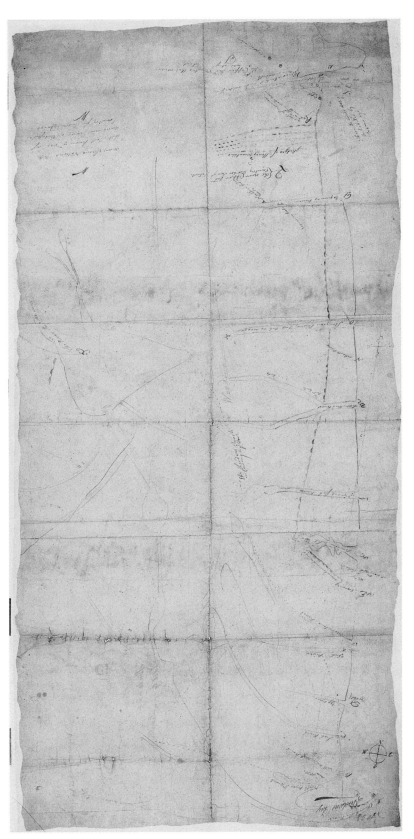

FIGURE 12.
Matonabbee's Map *(copy by Moses Norton), 1767. Size of the original 27 x 56 inches (68.5 x 142 cm). Courtesy of the Hudson's Bay Company Archives, Provincial Archives of Manitoba.*

mals. The rhythms of Chipewyan life followed that of the caribou. In the spring and fall when the caribou gathered in great numbers for their annual migrations, the extended families of the Chipewyans would gather as well. Hunting parties would place themselves along the migration routes for the great killing. In good years enough caribou could be taken to sustain the band until the next season. The Chipewyans' ties to the caribou extended into almost every part of their life. Their oral traditions and religious beliefs centered on the caribou, and the animal spirits that came in dreams imparted power over the herd. The Chipewyans used the animal's bones, hides, and visceral parts so skillfully that they had little need for outside trade goods. And their preference for the animal's meat earned them the epithet "Caribou eaters" well into the twentieth century.

The communal hunts during the caribou migrations were also a time of celebration. The Chipewyans would gather at their seasonal campgrounds where they feasted, exchanged goods, arranged marriages, and held the rituals and ceremonies that helped to maintain their traditions. With the end of the hunt the large regional band would disperse into smaller bands of forty or fifty people. These groups would spend the winter in the forest hunting caribou and other game. In spring, when the caribou migrated back out on to the tundra, the extended clan would gather again, only to disperse until the next migration.

This cycle of gathering and then dispersing was adapted to the environment of this subarctic region. Except for the caribou migrations, the land could not support a large group of people and the regional band would break up into small groups that could successfully exploit their hunting territories. Chipewyan identity reflected this situation. The Chipewyans and their neighbors did not maintain an overall tribal structure; instead they were "dene," the people. Each band had its leaders, members, and traditions and there was no need to label themselves as anything different. Social cohesion for the Native peoples of this region was maintained through a network of kinship. Family members moved back and forth between bands and through marriage and other exchanges spread themselves throughout the region so that one always had relations that could be depended upon in time of need. In 1771, when Matonabbee led the explorer Samuel Hearne across much of the territory depicted on this map, Hearne remarked how Matonabbee had friends or relatives in almost every band they encountered.

In a good year after the fall migration when the winter's supply of caribou had been secured, Matonabbee would take the furs he had traded from Indians to the west and north, and set off for the trading post on Hudson's Bay. With his many wives carrying the loads of furs, Matonabbee would follow the forested edge of the tundra or the courses of rivers, crossing the watersheds of the Canadian Shield until he reached the rivers draining into Hudson's Bay. Matonabbee's knowledge of this area was extensive. The map that he and Idolyazee returned with in 1767 was one of the earliest maps to give Europeans a glimpse of the vast interior of northwestern Canada. On it Matonabbee included the major water routes, the size and central location of Great Slave Lake, the existence of rivers draining from the Barren Grounds into the Arctic Ocean, and the Mackenzie River forming a link from Great Slave Lake to the Beaufort Sea. This area comprises nearly half of western Canada, much of which had not yet been seen or understood by the white man.

Matonabbee made his map at the request of the Europeans. It was a tool for the Hudson's Bay Company to use in its pursuit of Canada's environmental riches. The company built its trading post on the Churchill River in hopes of opening fur trade with the Chipewyan Indians and others to the north and west of the Bay. The Chipewyans proved to be a disappointing source for

Another America

the highly prized pelts. Most of what the Chipewyans needed they obtained from the caribou. Instead of trapping furs themselves, the Chipewyans developed an intermediary role. They gathered furs and pieces of copper from their northern relatives, the Yellowknife and the Dogrib Indians. They would bring these to Fort Churchill where they could be traded for manufactured goods. In turn the Chipewyans would mark up these goods when trading again for furs with their subarctic neighbors. Chipewyan trade leaders became well known and respected. Like skillful hunters they could support a large family.

The Hudson's Bay Company post where Matonabbee came to trade was a formidable structure. In 1731 the company replaced its original fort with a large stone structure called the Prince of Wales Fort. When traders arrived, only the Indians' leaders, often dubbed "Captain" by the English, were allowed inside. Matonabbee and his fellow captains would bargain with the factor, or company representative, on behalf of their people.

In 1762 Moses Norton became the factor of the Prince of Wales Fort. For years pieces of copper and rumors of rich ore deposits to the north had come to the fort with the traders. Norton made it his mission to find and exploit these copper mines. It was he who commissioned Matonabbee and Idolyazee, "to go & trace to ye mouth of ye Largest River to ye Northward." When they returned five years later, it was Moses Norton who copied and annotated their map.

Because of its non-western geometry the map is difficult to read even in an annotated redrawing (figure 12). Matonabbee's drawing is a picture of the Native American landscape rather than a western map of the region. Distance, direction, and orientation were part of traditional knowledge. They were part of one's "mental map," and a graphic system was not needed to express them. At the same time, the Chipewyans' knowledge of the region enabled them to regularly undertake considerable feats of travel with the certainty of meeting extended relations at the appointed time and location.

Matonabbee's map covers the western coast of Hudson's Bay from the Churchill River—represented at the bottom of the map with a symbol for the Prince of Wales Fort —north to Chesterfield Inlet—"M" on the map labeled "Little Head River." The geography represented on the map then jumps across the lower part of the Melville and Boothia Peninsulas to Chantry Inlet on Canada's Arctic coast— "N" on the map—and across the top of Canada to Coronation Gulf and the Coppermine River (called "copper mine river") pictured at the top of the map. The interior of the map centers upon Great Slave Lake which is shown in a remarkably accurate profile. It is worth noting that the Chipewyan mapmakers were able to grasp the proportions of a body of water some three hundred miles long and encompassing over ten thousand square miles. They placed an enlarged picture of this lake at the center of their map, like a hub from which the region's travel routes extended. Included is the river "Kiscachewan" flowing northwest and soon to be renamed the Mackenzie.

To the Hudson's Bay Company the coasts and the rivers offering access to and from the interior were most important. But to Matonabbee and the "dene" of the region, the map is perhaps best read starting at Great Slave Lake. This would be a central location for the communal hunts of spring and fall, and the source of fish and other game animals in the other seasons. The routes which extend from here were the well-known routes of rivers, lakes, paths, and watersheds crossed in the Chipewyans' annual round of hunting and gathering.

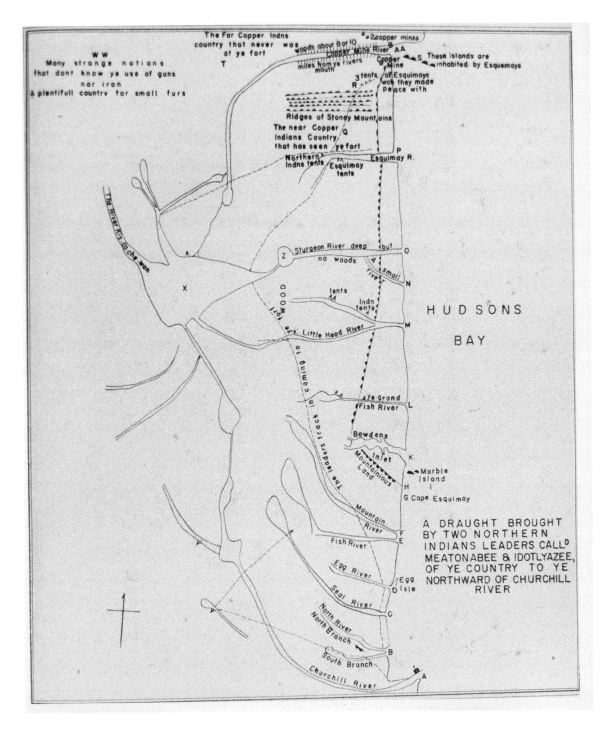

The Far Copper Indns
country that never was
at ye fort

woods about Bar IQ
miles from ye rivers mouth
Copper Mine River

2 copper mines
AA
Copper Mine
S These islands are inhabited by Esquemoys

WW
Many strange nations
that dont know ye use of guns
nor iron
A plentifull country for small furs
T

3 tents of Esquimays
R wch they made peace with

Ridges of Stoney Mountains

The near Copper
Indians Country
that has seen ye fort
Q

Northern
Indns tents
XX
Esquimay
tents
Esquimay R.
P

The River Kis fa che wen

Sturgeon River deep but no woods
Z
a small river
O
N

tents
Indn tents
M

WOOD coming to nothing

X

HUDSONS
BAY

Little Head River

Ye Grand Fish River
L

Bowdens
Inlet
K
Marble Island
Mountainous Land
H
I
G Cape Esquimay

The leadest track

Mountain River
F
E

Fish River

A DRAUGHT BROUGHT
BY TWO NORTHERN
INDIANS LEADERS CALL D
MEATONABEE & IDOTLYAZEE,
OF YE COUNTRY TO YE
NORTHWARD OF CHURCHILL
RIVER

Egg River

Egg D Isle

Seal River

C

North River
North Branch

B

South Branch

Churchill River
A

FIGURE 13. **Matonabbee's Map**, *as redrawn by R. I. Ruggles in* Historic Atlas of Manitoba. *Courtesy of Dr. Richard Ruggles, British Columbia.*

Another America

A NORTH WEST VIEW of PRINCE of WALES'S FORT in HUDSON'S BAY, NORTH AMERICA, by SAM.¹ HEARNE, 1777.

London Published Jan¹ 1ˢᵗ 1796, by Cadell & Davies, Strand.

FIGURE 14. **The Hudson's** *Bay Company's Prince of Wales Fort, built at the mouth of the Churchill River, where Matonabbe and other Indians of the Northwest came to trade. Illustration from Samuel Hearne's* A journey from Prince of Wale's Fort in Hudson's Bay to the Northern ocean in the years 1769, 1770, 1771, and 1772. *1795. Courtesy of the Courtesy of the Edward E. Ayer Collection, The Newberry Library, Chicago.*

Notchiningas' map (Figure 15). Notchininga, a chief of the Iowa Indians, presented this map at a Peace council held in Washington D.C. in the fall of 1837. The map is a both a picture of the Iowas' tribal memory and a reflection of the different conceptions of land-ownership and land use that existed between Indian and white societies.

The council that Notchininga and the Iowas attended had been called by the secretary of war. He was concerned that the hostilities among the Indian tribes crowded into the region between the Mississippi and Missouri Rivers might spill over into the white settlements. In addition to the Iowas, the secretary invited delegations of Sac, Fox, Sioux, and other Indians of the Missouri and Mississippi river valleys.

Notchininga, whose name translates as "No Heart of Fear," was the second chief of the Iowa Indians at the time of the council. He was there to present the Iowas' claim to lands that they

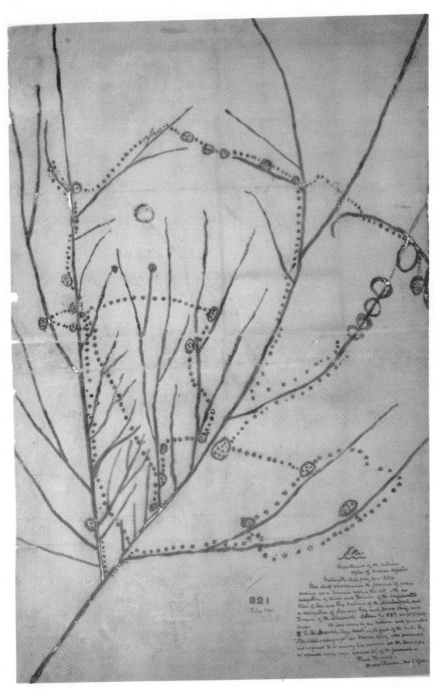

FIGURE 15. **Notchininga's Map**, *1837. Size of the original 41 x 27 inches (104 x 68.5 cm). Courtesy of the National Archives and Records Administration, Cartographic and Architectural Branch, Washington, DC. RG 75, Map 821, Tube 520.*

Another America

believed had been wrongly taken by the U.S. Government and other Indians during the previous decade.

The Iowas' grievances reflect those of many of the upper Mississippi Valley Indians during the first part of the nineteenth century. In past treaty negotiations it had been the U.S. policy to push the Indians to outline their tribal territories on a western map, a process that went against the land-use and land-tenure traditions of many of the Indian groups. The American Indians looked upon their hunting grounds as lands held in common, and when asked to outline their territories, a Winnebago chief spoke for many when he explained that, "it would be difficult to divide it [the land] up—it belongs as much to one as the other."

The government's insistence on its policy contributed to the transformation of the American landscape, imposing on it a system of ownership that resembled that of European societies. The government's policy also made it easier to obtain land cessions. By recognizing the claims of one tribe over those of another, the government could negotiate cessions from one rather than many tribes. This practice took advantage of the Indians' warrior traditions and played into the hands of larger and stronger tribes. The latter would claim large territories, usurping the claims of the smaller and weaker tribes, and then cede that land to the government. In this fashion, the Iowas felt they had been robbed of their right to part of their ancestral homelands. The claims of other tribes had been recognized, and the land ceded without the Iowas receiving proper recognition or compensation.

The Iowas believed they had been cheated in this fashion following the Treaty of Prairie du Chien in 1825. At that time the Iowas had given up their lands east of the Mississippi River and moved to a strip of land between the Mississippi and Missouri rivers. In this new territory the Iowas suffered from both U.S. government policies and their Indian neighbors. As more tribes were pushed west of the Mississippi, hostilities developed over conflicting land claims and scarce resources. The weakened Iowas were raided by Sacs, Sioux, and other powerful Indian tribes, their horses and livestock were taken, and their stocks of game depleted. For nearly ten years the proud Iowa had suffered these indignities. It was with the hope of redressing these grievances that Notchininga and the Iowa delegation prepared for the council in Washington D.C.

The Indians' arrival in the nation's capital created a minor sensation. The *Washington National Intelligencer* described delegations of Sioux, Sac, Fox, Missouris, and Iowas walking around in their finery, "Carrying about with them in the streets their bows and arrows, tomahawks, and pikes...." During the council several of the delegates visited the race track and the National Theater, and quite a few, including Notchininga, had their portraits painted for the War Department's collection.

The actual council meetings were held in a rented Presbyterian church. Joel Poinsett, the secretary of war, and Carey A. Harris, the commissioner of Indian affairs, presided over the sessions. On the morning of October 7, 1837, Notchininga presented the Iowas' case:

"My Father," he began, "you have sent for me. I have come. I am now in the house of the Great Spirit of the Earth and the Sun witnesseth what I say..."

Notchininga then brought out his map. He pointed to the rivers, villages, and paths pictured upon it. "This," Notchininga said, "is the route of my forefathers it is the land that we have always claimed from old times we have the history we have always owned this land it is ours it bears our name."

The area depicted on the map extends from Green Bay on Lake Michigan to west of Omaha on the Missouri River, and down the Mississippi River from north of Minneapolis to south of St.

Louis. The diagonal from the lower left to the upper right represents the Mississippi River, and the vertical line on the left side of the map represents the Missouri. The network of lines flowing into these two represents the tributaries that flow into the Mississippi and Missouri river valleys. Along this network the Iowas placed circles to represent village sites, and the dotted line represents the meandering path of their migrations. Like most Native American maps, it is in the light of the Iowas' oral traditions and cultural history that the map is best seen.

Notchininga's map goes back to the very beginnings of his people; the point, both geographically and historically, at which the Iowas became a separate tribe. The ancestors of the Iowas were part of the Oneota culture that evolved in the area of the upper Mississippi valley and west-

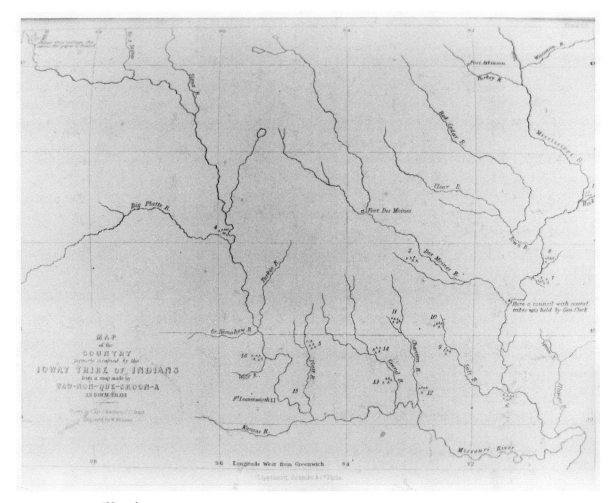

FIGURE 17. "Map of *the Country formerly occupied by the Ioway Tribe of Indians from a map made by Waw-Non-Que-Skoon-A, an Ioway Brave." The map traces back sixteen migrations of the Iowas from their reservation on the west side of the Missouri (number 16) to their pre-contact settlement along the Rock River on the east side of the Mississippi. The map covers much of the same area and settlements as those represented on Notchininga's map. From Henry R. Schoolcraft,* Historical and Statistical Information Respecting the History, Condition, and Prospects of the Indian Tribes of the United States . . . *part III, 1853. Courtesy of the American Geographical Society Collection, University of Wisconsin–Milwaukee Library.*

ern Great Lakes between the fourteenth and seventeenth centuries. This tradition is the cultural ancestor of several groups of Siouan speaking peoples including the Oto, Missouri, Winnebago, and Kansa Indians. The Iowas trace their particular origins to the Winnebago. Iowa oral history recalls that "...we came down around the Great Lakes and were one tribe with the Winnebagos. The time came when the Winnebagos, our Fathers, wished to stay by the great water to fish, but we went towards the southwest until we came to a river, the Mississippi."

FIGURE 18. Notchininga at *around the age of sixty. Photograph courtesy of the National Anthropological Archives, Smithsonian Institution.*

Another America

The Iowas' earliest settlements, the place at which their tradition started, are in the area around Green Bay. When Notchininga pointed to the map he indicated the circle in the upper right, saying it was "the residence of our forefathers. ...they built our village on the banks of Lake Pepin the Sacs call it Green Bay."

The dotted line that begins at this ancestral village represents the Iowas' movements over time. It connects the ancient settlements where the Iowa began, and ends with the sites they inhabited in the nineteenth century. The map is not simply a picture of territory; it is a map of the tribal memory; noting the places and events that made this land part of the Iowas. To Notchininga and his people, this was the land of their ancestors, the land that "bears our name."

History records that the area on either side of the Missouri River and along the upper Mississippi to the east and west was once part of Iowa territory. In 1836 the Iowa had petitioned President Jackson with their claim to this territory, stating that no one could deny the remains of their earth lodges and towns that were scattered across this landscape. The map Notchininga presented at the treaty council was another attempt to get recognition for what the Iowas saw as their ancestral territories. Perhaps the Iowas hoped that by using a map, a powerful image used by white societies to define territory, their claim would be recognized over that of the others.

There is no record of how Notchininga's map affected the council. But the Iowas were not successful in getting recognition for their claim. Several days after Notchininga presented this map, the Iowas removed themselves from the council, and refused to sign the resulting treaty. But by 1838 William Clark, the superintendent of Indian affairs, persuaded the demoralized Iowas to sign the treaty and accept the government's offer for their lands. The Iowa ceded the last of their traditional territory, and removed themselves west of the Missouri River into an area that was not a part of their ancestral lands.

In the years that followed Notchininga went on to become the principal chief of the tribe. He helped his people through the beginnings of reservation life in this new territory, a strip on the Kansas–Nebraska border that remains the Iowas' homeland today.

Like Notchininga's map (Figure 15), Sitting Rabbit's map of the Missouri (Figure 19A–G) is as much about the history and beliefs of his Mandan people as it is about geography. Sitting Rabbit was a Mandan Indian living on the Fort Berthold reservation in North Dakota. In 1905 the secretary of the State Historical Society of North Dakota commissioned Sitting Rabbit to make a map showing "all the old villages of the Mandan and Gros Ventre [Hidatsa] . . . and the banks and islands of the [Missouri] river just as they used to be." Sitting Rabbit was to paint the history of Mandan settlements in North Dakota. His map is a picture of the Mandans' "tribal memory," documenting the power of the oral tradition to preserve history. Painted on an oblong piece of canvas, Sitting Rabbit's map divides the meandering course of the Missouri River into several sections. The map uses elements of traditional Plains pictography in its representation of features and locations, and includes transliterated Mandan words and English annotations. The map was completed in 1907, before the building of the Garrison Dam changed the river and its surrounding areas and formed Lake Sakakawea.

The ancestors of the Mandan Indians migrated to the area around the Missouri River about eight hundred years ago. While they and their neighbors practiced agriculture, their survival, like that of all Plains peoples, was made possible by the abundance of the buffalo. This combination

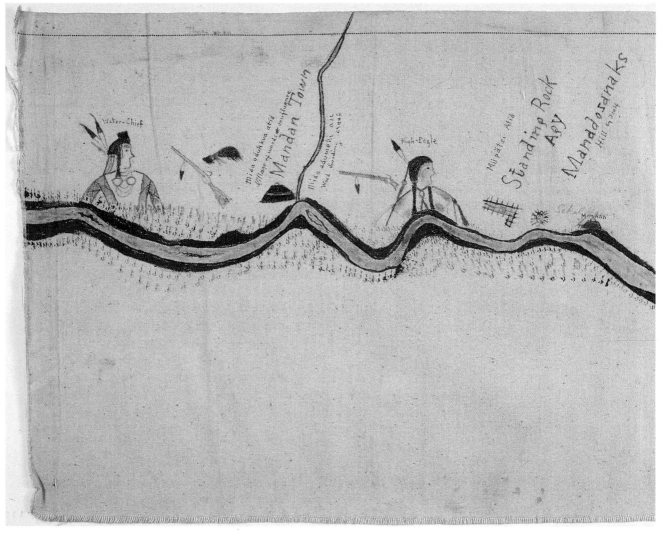

Sitting Rabbit's *Map of the Missouri River in North Dakota, 1907. Size of the original 17.8 inches x 23.2 feet (45.2 x 701 cm). Courtesy of the State Historical Society of North Dakota.*

FIGURE 19A. *The first section of Sitting Rabbit's map.*

enabled the Mandans to evolve a unique way of life and a rich cultural heritage. Over time their oral traditions filled the landscape with mythical and historic events that gave names and meaning to the geography of their world, only to have it nearly obliterated in the epidemics and tribal wars that accompanied the arrival of the white man. Sitting Rabbit's map, made after the Mandans had reached their nadir and, many thought, no longer existed as a people, records part of their history and language. It is a visual testimony to the strength and endurance of Mandan culture, an image of their ties to the land.

Another America

Following the course of the Missouri River on the map is like following the history of the Mandan people. The earliest Mandan sites on the river date from around 1250 and the remains of settlements as they moved up the river show the evolution of Mandan life through the centuries. The map begins near the border of North and South Dakota and continues north and west, following the course of the Missouri to its confluence with the Yellowstone River at the border of Montana. Reading the map from left to right is going up the Missouri River with locations on the west side of the river pictured toward the top of the map.

The Mandans were accomplished farmers. They grew corn, beans and squash, rationing the crops during the growing season and preserving part from one year to the next. This largess enabled the Mandans to get through bad years and to trade their corn for hides and trade goods from other Plains Indian tribes. Agriculture required at least a partially sedentary life and the bluffs along the Missouri enabled the Mandans to establish their villages on high ground overlooking their fields. Early in their life along the river the Mandans lived in small villages where they built defensible earth lodges. Sitting Rabbit uses the symbol of the earth lodge throughout his map to mark the locations of Mandan, Hidatsa, and Arikara villages. An example of one can be seen below the words "Mandan Town" on the first section of the map (Figure 19A). These half-subterranean structures could accommodate an extended family group within a space that was warm in winter and cool in summer.

From their villages the Mandans would go out to hunt the buffalo on foot. A successful hunt required ritual preparation and highly organized techniques. The Okeepa, the Mandans' major annual ceremony, helped to focus the people on the traditions and the spiritual relationships needed to ensure their survival with good crops and successful hunts. The ceremony began with "Lone Man," the mythic maker of the earth, opening the ceremonial lodge for the Okeepa. The elders would then ritually retell the great stories of the Mandans, repeating their history from the beginning of the world down to the present. These stories reaffirmed the Mandan beliefs and traditions, and reinforced the rituals and behaviors that put the community first. On the second section of Sitting Rabbit's map (Figure 19B) he pictures "Turtle Fall Creek," a name and location associated with Lone Man. A Hidatsa woman explained that "in his work as creator Lone Man made four turtles, but one got away and slipped back into the water. This turtle now supports the dry land and prevents it from sinking." The mythical location recognizes the importance of arable land to the Mandans and their spiritual relationship with the landscape.

A little further north on the Missouri, Sitting Rabbit pictured a buffalo hunt with Indians pursuing the buffalo into a pound. The Mandans' relationship to the buffalo, like their relationship to other animals, was partly spiritual. During the Okeepa this relationship was ritualized in the buffalo dance when men dressed in buffalo skins mimicked the action of the buffalo and others acted the parts of animal or spiritual beings. This and other hunting rituals helped to bring the buffalo to the Mandans. Hunting required that groups work together just as Sitting Rabbit pictured them, driving the animals off a jump or into a corral where they could be killed. The buffalo were an important resource for the Mandans; almost the entire animal was used, from the meat which was eaten or preserved, to the bones and sinews which were used to make tools and household items. The hides were used for blankets or covers, and they were stretched over wooden frames to make the bull boats that the Mandans and their neighbors used to cross the Missouri River and its tributaries.

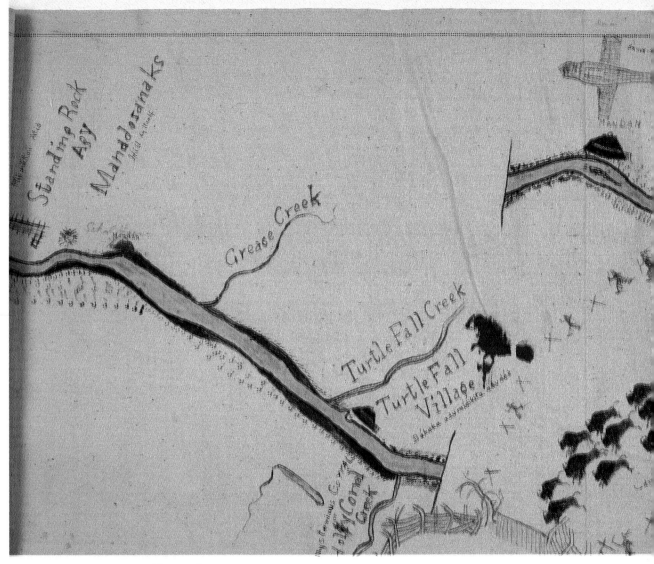

The history of the Mandans is intertwined with the migrations of the Sioux and other Indians of the Plains. Indians repeatedly raided the Mandans' crops and homes, leaving their small villages vulnerable and forcing the Mandans to move up the river and gather into larger fortified villages. Sitting Rabbit's map includes many different sites that had been occupied during different periods of Mandan history. Villages recorded by Lewis and Clark in their 1804 journey up the Missouri are shown on the map (Figure 19C), as are the sites of villages abandoned by the Mandans in the centuries before Sitting Rabbit made his map. The location and names of these villages were

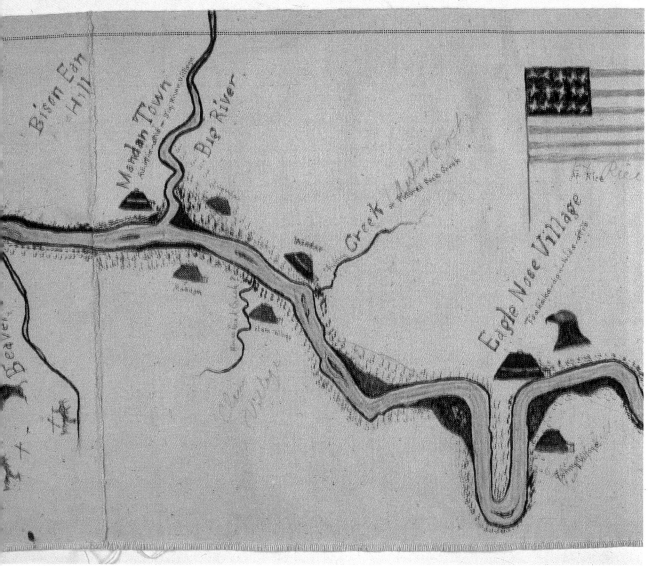

FIGURE 19C. **The third** *section of Sitting Rabbit's map.*

part of the Mandan tribal memory. Past the picture of the buffalo hunt, Sitting Rabbit includes two villages, one labeled "Mandan Town," on either side of the "Big River" [the Cannon Ball River] at its confluence with the Missouri. The two villages shown alongside the river corresponded to pre-historic archeological sites of early or "proto"- Mandan settlements, one dating back to about 1500. Sitting Rabbit's map documents Mandan history going back four hundred years.

Further up the river Sitting Rabbit pictures the town of Bismark (Bismarck) North Dakota, with its grid of streets and the railroad line running through it (Figure 19D). Above Bismarck is

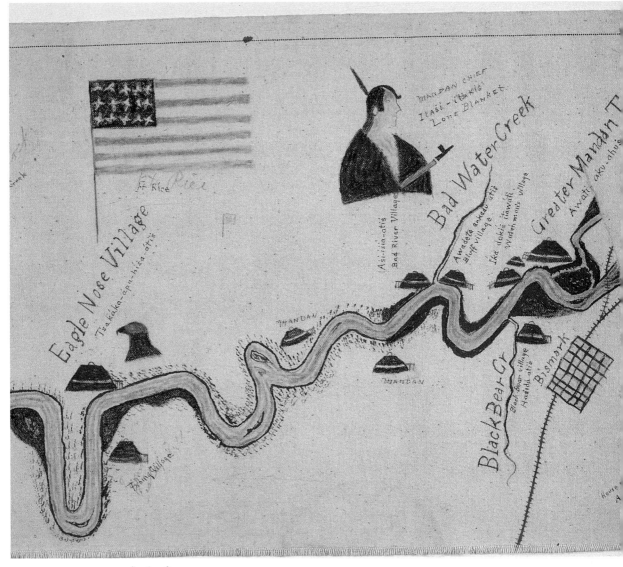

FIGURE 19D. **Section four** *of Sitting Rabbit's map.*

pictured the mouth of the Heart River and several earth lodge symbols labeled "Greater Mandan Town." The Heart River, which continues on the next section of the map (Figure 19E), is considered the "heart" of the Mandans' universe. As the Mandans concentrated in larger settlements, they eventually established seven large villages here around the confluence of the Heart and Missouri rivers. Sitting Rabbit pictures several of them on his map. In these villages they constructed the large rounded earth lodges that have come to be associated with the Mandans. These lodges were built to accommodate the increased numbers of people who lived in the villages and

Another America

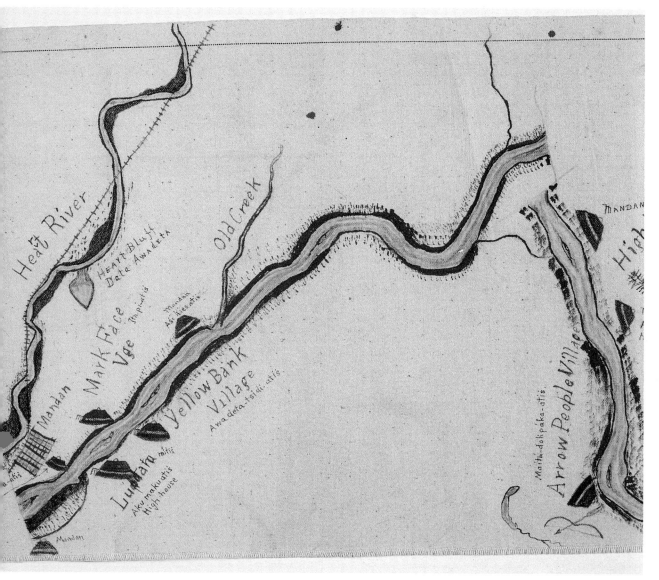

Text visible within the map image: Heart River, Heart Bluff Data Awadeta, Old Creek, Mark Face Vge Itapiatis, Mandan Asi-kisa-atis, Yellow Bank Village, Awadeta-tsidi-atis, Mandan, Lui data mitig, Aku mokua-atis High house, Mandan, Marta-dohpaka-atis, Arrow People Village, MANDAN, High

offered protection from raiding enemies. The skills the Mandans developed in farming, hunting, and trading enabled them to maintain these large sedentary villages and develop a culture that was different from those of many of the other Indians living on the Plains. Around 1700 the villages pictured around the Heart River were home to approximately seven thousand Mandans. It was one of the largest concentrations of Native Americans on the northern plains.

North along the Missouri, Sitting Rabbit pictures the trading post at Fort Clark and the "Five Villages" located below the Knife River (Figure 19F). These are the five Mandan and

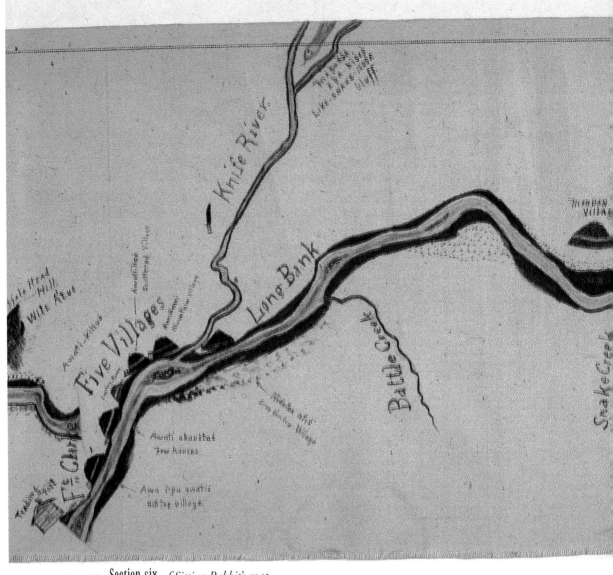

The map shows labels including: "Knife River", "Like-Snake Nose Bluff", "MANDAN VILLAGE", "Long Bank", "Five Villages", "Buffalo Head Hill", "White Atus", "Awati Kihus", "Awati Hise Scattered Village", "Mountain Village", "Battle Creek", "Hidatsa atis Gros Ventre Village", "Snake Creek", "Awati akavitas Few Houses", "Awa tipu awatis Hilltop Village", "Trading Post", "Ft Clarke".

FIGURE 19F. **Section six** *of Sitting Rabbit's map.*

Hidatsa villages visited by Lewis and Clark during their expedition to the Northwest. Located on the bluffs of the Missouri, these villages offered the Mandans protection from raiding enemies and access to the river and their fields. They were recorded by the artists Karl Bodmer and George Catlin whose pictures helped to form the popular image of the Mandans and their ceremonies. On the other side of the Knife River is pictured the "Gros Ventre Village," the Hidatsa settlement painted by Catlin in 1832.

   These villages were also the site of the terrible small pox epidemic that ravaged the Mandan

Another America

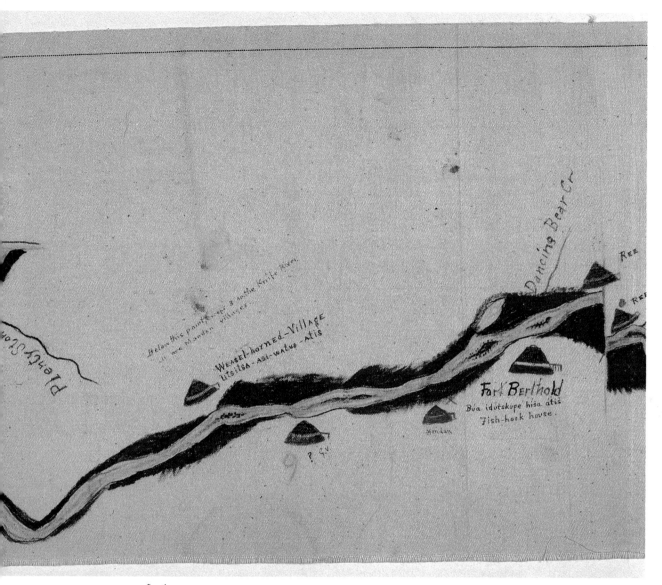

FIGURE 19G. **Section seven** *of Sitting Rabbit's map.*

people in 1837. In July of that year smallpox invaded the Mandan villages. Some believe it arrived with crew members on a steamboat that had sailed the upper Missouri. Regardless of its immediate source, smallpox was originally brought by the white man. It was unknown to Native Americans before the encounter, and the Mandans' lack of immunity left them to the mercy of the imported disease. The smallpox spread through the Mandan villages with speed and violence, killing its victims in a few hours and leaving the survivors devastated. The Mandans were the first to experience the disease. Their neighbors, the Arikaras and Hidatsas, fled up the Missouri and escaped the full force of the epidemic. The hapless Mandans were forced to remain in their villages. Sioux war parties had surrounded the villages and prevented the Mandans from fleeing. As a consequence the smallpox nearly destroyed the Mandans. It is estimated that the Mandan population fell from approximately eighteen hundred in June of 1837 to less than one hundred by the end of the year.

The epidemic's destruction led to the popular misconception that the Mandans are no longer a living people. The surviving Mandans eventually left their villages along the Knife River and joined up with groups of Arikaras and Hidatsas. With so few people, the Mandans' tribal organization broke down and the continuity of their traditions was strained and broken. By 1839 the Mandans had joined the Hidatsa. Together they migrated further up the Missouri River trying to rebuild their tribal life. In 1844 they selected a site for their winter camp at a bend in the Missouri River. The village was called "Like-a-fish-hook." Sitting Rabbit pictures it as "Fish-hook house" near Fort Berthold (Figure 19G).

This settlement became the permanent home of the Mandans and the Hidatsa. "Like-a-fish-hook" village was the beginning of the modern Mandan homeland, the Fort Berthold Reservation. Today the Mandans share this reservation with the Hidatsas and Arikaras, tribes with whom they are affiliated. The population of the affiliated tribes is now over six thousand with more than thirty-five hundred living on the reservation.

Sitting Rabbit's map, made near the beginnings of this remarkable resurgence, demonstrates the power and strength of Mandan cultural and oral traditions. The Mandans have survived epidemics and wars to keep the history of their land for over five hundred years.

In 1832 the artist George Catlin journeyed up the Missouri River. Among the many pictures he made of North American Indian life were his studies of the Mandans and this image (Figure 20) of the Hidatsa or Gros Ventre village along the Knife River. It is pictured as the "Gros Ventre Village" on Sitting Rabbit's map (Figure 19F). Catlin's picture shows the relative size of the earth lodges and their placement on the bluffs above the river. In describing the scene Catlin noted the "wild and garrulous groups of men, women, and children . . . wending their way along the [river's] shores, or dashing and plunging through its blue waves, enjoying the luxury of swimming, of which both sexes seem to be passionately fond."

Pawnee Sky Chart (Figure 21). The mingling of religious belief, mythology, and cultural traditions that shaped the Native American environment is epitomized in this celestial chart made by Pawnee Indians. The chart was collected by James Murie, a half-Pawnee field worker for Chicago's Field Museum of Natural History, in 1906. The map is of the stars in the night sky and is believed to be quite old. The spiritual relationship with the stars that the chart expresses was part of what it meant to be Pawnee.

Different theories exist on the origin of the Pawnee, but as Caddoan-language speakers, the cultural tradition from which they came had its origins in the Southwest over one thousand years ago. Their cultural ancestors developed the agricultural skills and the semi-sedentary way of life that characterized these Plains Indians. When the Pawnees and their relatives, the Arikaras and Wichitas, moved out onto the plains they brought the cultivation of corn, beans, and squash with them. They lived in semi-permanent settlements where they would tend their fields and leave and

FIGURE 20. George Catlin, *"Hidatsa Village" from* Illustration of the Manners, Custom's, and Conditions of the North American Indians, with Letters and Notes, *9th ed. vol.1. Courtesy of the Edward E. Ayer Collection, the Newberry Library.*

return on the annual buffalo hunts. Agriculture gave the Pawnees an advantage over the more nomadic Indians with whom they shared the plains. They participated in an elaborate trading network in which skins and animal products were exchanged for corn and other products from as far away as the northwest and Mexico.

The tradition of wars and raids that developed among Plains Indian cultures had their effect on Caddoan culture as well. The large grass lodges arranged in widely dispersed villages such as those built by the Wichitas along the Arkansas River in the 1600s gave way to the more compact village pattern of earth lodges placed close together and situated in an easily defended position on the high ground. By 1700 the Skidi band of Pawnee, who made the Sky Chart, were established in eight villages along the Platte and Loup rivers in eastern Nebraska. It is said that their villages were arranged along stellar patterns; certainly the construction of houses was planned to correctly place the smoke hole—the opening in the center of the roof—so that the night sky could be easily observed. Through this hole Pawnee priests would watch for the arrival of the constellations that signaled the time for the ceremonies that regulated Pawnee life.

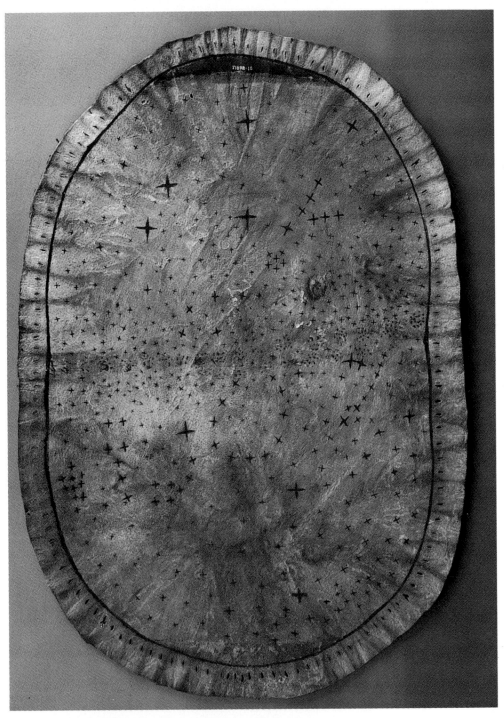

FIGURE 21. **Pawnee Sky** *Chart. Size of the original 26 x 18 inches (6.5 x 46.1 cm). By Permission of the Pawnee Indian Tribe of Oklahoma, and the Field Museum of Natural History, Chicago. Negative 16231c.*

Another America

The Pawnee trace the beginnings of all people and things to the nighttime sky. Above all was Tirawahat who made the heaven and the stars. But it was the Morning Star who started the creation of the world and set mankind in motion. He was the most powerful world-making being. The Pawnees' star mythology reflects the universal constructs of myths; opposing forces of light and dark and death and renewal that must be overcome in order for the people to continue. The Morning Star, the male hero, must overcome the tests and resistance of Evening Star, the female spirit. During his trials Morning Star appointed the four stars that define the universe and bring the seasons. He provided the earth with water in the form of rain, and created the sun to give the earth heat and light. Finally he lay with Evening Star, and from their union came a girl who descended to earth. There she joined with a boy, the child of the sun and the moon, and together they peopled the earth.

As creator, the Morning Star was a powerful figure and could demand the sacrifice of a human being. When the need to satisfy the Morning Star became strong enough, he would appear to a warrior as a vision and the seer would raid an enemy's camp to capture a young girl. The captive was put through several months of preparation and rituals. For the sacrifice the young girl was dressed in ceremonial garments representing the resources and spiritual relationships of the Pawnee. Her body was painted, red on the right to symbolize day and the Morning Star and black on the left for night and the Evening Star. The victim was forced to climb a scaffolding where a priest shot an arrow through her heart and her blood was spilled on sacred objects to be burned in a ceremonial fire.

The origins of this ritual began about nine hundred years ago. It may have come from the native cultures of Mesoamerica over one thousand miles to the south. The Pawnee were linked to the Southwest and the home of Native American groups that regularly traded with the Indians of Mexico. Along with trade goods, the concept of ritual sacrifice and celestial relationships could have traveled to the Pawnee. Regardless of its origin, the successful sacrifice meant that the Morning Star had been satisfied and he would continue to look after the Pawnees' well-being.

Not only were the stars the source of creation and renewal for the Pawnee; they dictated the cycle of nature and the Pawnees' place within it. At the end of winter Pawnee priests would mark the arrival of the Swimming Ducks, two stars that signaled the beginning of the spring ceremonies. Twelve sacred bundles were used in these ceremonies. The first bundle, that of the Evening Star, was ceremoniously opened. It contained symbols for the buffalo, for corn, for the wisdom of the chiefs, and for the bravery of the warriors. The opening of the sacred bundles was accompanied by the ritualized retelling of the creation story, methodically recalling how things came to be and symbolically bringing the world back to life for the Pawnee. Other star-guided ceremonies were tied to the spring planting, the summer buffalo hunt, and the harvesting of their crops in the fall.

The relationship to the stars permeated Pawnee life. Each Pawnee village had been given a sacred bundle by one of the stars. The Big Black Star, a star that stood in the northeast, was the harbinger of autumn. He brought the Pawnee the gifts of healing, the buffalo, and skill in capturing their enemies' ponies. Big Black Star also gave the Pawnees their knowledge of the stars, and this star chart is believed to have been part of the sacred bundle given to the Pawnee by the star. The skin was once supposed to have wrapped a piece of a meteorite; such an object, part of a star itself, would have been considered very powerful by the Pawnee. The chart may have been used in a Pawnee ritual, or it may have been a device to learn and remember the names and locations of the stars. As part of a sacred bundle it is to be viewed with the same respect as a western religious object.

The chart does not include the entire sky as it would have been seen by the Pawnee, and the constellations which they recognized are different than those of western astronomy. Still, the names of the stars and constellations that can be read on the chart give a glimpse of how the heavens and the earth were organized by the Pawnee. Ray A. Williamson, in his book *Living the Sky,* identifies several of the stars on the chart and gives their names and symbolism for the Pawnee. The chart is divided across the middle by a series of dots and crosses that represents the Milky Way. To the Pawnee this was the parting of the heavens and the pathway of departed spirits. The North Star is shown as a large star in the lower left quadrant of the chart. Called "The Star That Does Not Walk Around" it was compared to the Pawnees' supreme being "Tirawahat." Near the North Star and towards the center of the chart is a circle of eleven stars that the Pawnee called the Council of the Chiefs. It reminded the Pawnee of the council of stars set up at creation by Tirawahat. Across the Milky Way from the Council of the Chiefs is a compact group of six small stars that represents the Pleiades. The Pawnee marked the arrival of the Pleiades, or the Seven Brothers, as the time for planting ceremonies. Among the many other stars and constellations pictured by the Pawnee is the Bow, a series of five stars arching across the sky near the top of the Milky Way. This was said to represent the first bow given to first man by Morning Star, making it possible for the Pawnee to kill buffalo and other animals.

This stellar mythology served the Pawnee for many generations. Their agriculture and hunting skills helped to provide them with a prosperous life, while the bravery and skill of their warriors helped to defend their villages from the raids of Sioux, Cheyenne, and other Plains Indians. In the second half of the nineteenth century the balance of fortune and power tipped against the Pawnee. With the beginnings of reservation life in Nebraska, the Pawnees' ability to hunt and raid for horses was restricted. At the same time the Sioux continued to raid the Pawnee, stealing their horses, damaging their crops and villages, and preventing them from conducting the hunts needed to get the tribe through the winter. For protection the Pawnee allied themselves with the growing power of the United States. They enlisted as scouts for the U.S. Army in the wars against their traditional enemy, the Sioux. The Pawnee suffered for this during the Civil War, when they were literally abandoned by the United States. Following the war they suffered from government policies that rewarded hostile Indians with treaty and peace gifts while leaving the friendlier tribes to fend for themselves.

On the reservation the Pawnees were continually raided and their horses stolen. But the Indian agents would not let them go out and replenish their supply by raiding others. The toll of reservation life demoralized and destroyed many of the Pawnee. Their population fell from an estimated 12,500 in 1844 to a little over 2,000 in the 1870s. In the 1870s the Pawnee were removed from their homeland in Nebraska and assigned to a reservation in the Indian Territory of Oklahoma. Here the difficulties and decline of the Pawnee continued until less then seven hundred tribal members remained at the end of the century. Despite these trials the Pawnees retained their language and their identity. In the 1940s the birth rate of the Pawnee began to exceed the tribe's mortality, and the Pawnee once again began to grow.

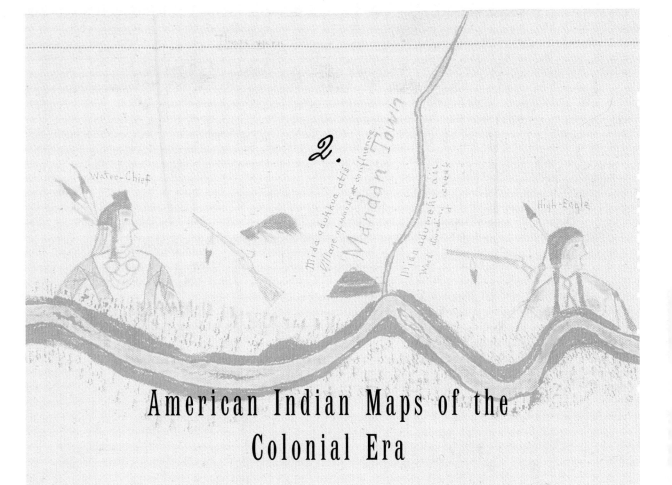

American Indian Maps of the Colonial Era

WITHIN ONE HUNDRED AND FIFTY years of the European encounter, the North American continent was the site of an international scramble. Spain, France, England, the Netherlands, and Sweden all established colonies on the continent, each one dubbing its enterprise "New" in the ethnocentric belief that the continent, as a discovered land, could be claimed. Native Americans were largely ignored in this conception of the Americas. Their centuries of inhabitation were scarcely recognized and their land use patterns deemed insufficient to constitute a claim to the territory. The official policies towards Native Americans seldom recognized their rights or dealt with them as sovereign peoples, and the colonial traders, administrators, and farmers usually looked upon Native Americans as a resource to be exploited or as competitors for colonial land.

European societies were in the midst of building great empires; spreading their beliefs, technologies, and ways of life to distant lands they believed themselves justified in exploiting. In their western ideology kings, rulers, and explorers had exclusive rights to lands they could claim to have discovered. European technologies transformed these foreign landscapes, dividing them into individually owned parcels that could be mapped and recorded. The western social and legal systems, with their dependence upon written records, used these maps and deeds to organize and control the land and its resources. And the Europeans' military weapons and armed traditions enabled the imperial powers to take the land and enforce their claims. In these societies the deed, the map, and the official record were the means of determining ownership. Paper was the medium through which one's perception of the landscape was organized and expressed.

The western system stands in marked contrast to the oral traditions of Native American societies. Indigenous traditions did not perceive land as a commodity to be owned. Hunting and fishing grounds, fields for planting, and areas where food could be gathered were often held in common. The oral traditions assigned certain areas to one group or band, who could in turn invite others to plant or take game. This concept of land fit the indigenous settlement patterns. Unlike European villages most Native settlements were mobile, moving between semi-permanent sites to plant, hunt, fish, and gather as the seasons or tradition required. Tribal animosities and the native traditions of warfare also changed the landscape. One tribe would take over the hunting grounds of another or usurp their fields and resources. Use of the land changed according to season, tradition, and military fortunes; the idea that a paper gave one exclusive ownership of the land was a foreign concept.

The Native American maps made in exchanges with the European colonists were, therefore, usually made in response to some need or request by the invaders. The circumstances of these maps and the history of the peoples and events they reflect, are a microcosm of the experience of colonization. They tell the story of invasions; first by foreign diseases and trade goods; and then by foreign peoples bent on taking all the land they could acquire. They reflect the European's ethnocentric belief in their own superiority, justifying the displacement of native societies for the higher civilization of self-righteous Christians. And they record the human costs of enslavement, land thefts, indiscriminate murder, outright genocide, and extinction that was exacted in the name of establishing this civilization.

The maps are also a record of the Native American response to this invasion. They give insights into the strategies Native Americans used to stave off the colonists' thirst for land, and record their attempts to resist the colonists or to accommodate and survive in the face of western society's overwhelming power.

The maps reveal the Native Americans' lack of preparedness when faced with an encounter they did not invite. The social and cultural systems that had evolved in North America provided no means of making the united effort needed to stop the monolithic advance of the Europeans. The structure of Native American societies, in which traditional enemies would raid one another's territories, where the warrior ethic resulted in a cycle of vengeance raids and counter raids, worked to the disadvantage of Native Americans in their conflicts with the Europeans. Early on the colonial powers took advantage of traditional Native enmities, forming alliances with one

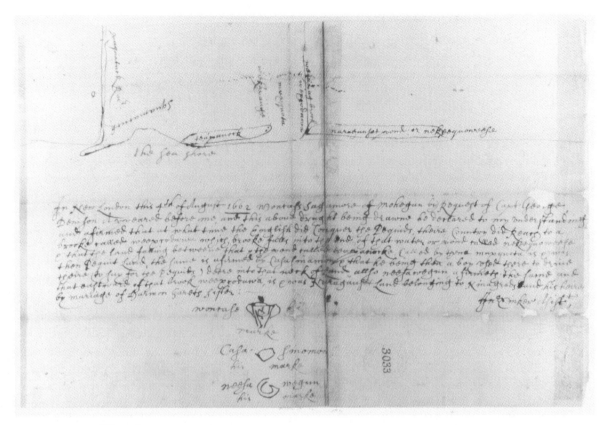

FIGURE 22. **"Plan of** *the Pequot Country,"* *1662. Massachusetts Archives, Vol. 30, p. 113 (Maps and Plans #3033), Archives of the Commonwealth, Boston.*

group against the other and favoring them with weapons and access to trade goods that upset the existing balances of power. Those Indian groups who had a tradition of confederation, like the League of the Iroquois in the Northeast or the Cherokees and Creeks in the Southeast, profited in this system and strengthened their positions. The smaller, less centralized tribes found themselves stuck between well-armed land-hungry colonists on the one hand and well-armed Indian Nations demanding tribute and subservience on the other. The consequences of the Native American inability to unite against a common enemy are reflected in maps that record the colonists' reliance upon their Indian allies. They would enlist the Native Americans to capture slaves or defeat hostile Indians, only to later turn upon these same allies when the need for land or the pressures of coexistence became too much.

The establishment of European colonies in North America set in motion a conflict over land and resources that continues to characterize the relationships between Native Americans and the western cultures. Regardless of the ideological beliefs, misguided policies, or simple ignorance that can be explained as products of the times, the process of colonization established the pattern of persecuting Native Americans. They were driven from their lands, and their traditions were systematically destroyed to make way for the expansion of western society.

"Plan of the Pequot Country" (Figure 22). When European society began its colonization of North America the Pequot Indians were one of the major powers in southern New England. They occupied the land between the Connecticut and Pawcatuck rivers in what is now the state of Connecticut, and held dominion over Indians living throughout the Connecticut valley and across the Sound on Long Island.

There is evidence that Pequot culture had developed along the northeast Atlantic coast for many generations. About eight thousand years ago the ancestors of the Pequots adapted to a life of hunting and gathering. Approximately one thousand years ago the warming of the climate led to their widespread adaptation of maize agriculture. In the area around Narragansett Bay, in what is now Rhode Island, Pequot, Narragansett, Niantic, and Mohegan Indians practiced the cultivation of corn, beans, squash, artichokes and tobacco. They supplemented their crops with hunting, fishing, and gathering foodstuffs from the environment. Around 1615, at the same time that English explorers were planning the establishment of colonies in New England, the Pequots numbered approximately thirteen thousand individuals.

Less than fifty years later this map was made to help determine the extent of land formerly occupied by the Pequots. In the Pequot War of 1637 the English and their Indian allies had nearly wiped out the Pequot Indians and condemned the survivors to live as wards of the state. The New England colonies were now the dominant force in this part of North America, and the Indians' lands were the objective of colonial machinations. The Pequot's western boundary was to serve as the boundary between the new colonial entities of Connecticut and Rhode Island. The map is focused on the area that begins just west of the modern border of Connecticut, the Pawcatuck River——"paquatuck Riur" on the map——and extends east along the seashore to "naraganset pond," now known as Quonochontaug pond on the Rhode Island coast. Three Indian informants were called in to help make the map; their "marks" can be seen below the drawing. According to their statement, prior to the war the Pequot territory extended to the brook called "wekapag," represented as emptying into the Narragansett pond. While colonial politics eventually moved the Connecticut/Rhode Island border west to the Pawcatuck River, the map documents the transformation that European colonization brought to the region and the lives of the Indians.

The history of the Pequots' encounter with the European invaders parallels the experience of many Native Americans. Prior to the arrival of the colonists, diseases brought by early explorers swept through the region. Between 1617 and 1619 epidemics of smallpox and bubonic plague devastated the Indians living along the Atlantic coast. A further epidemic struck in 1633. Without natural immunities to these imported diseases, the mortality rate among Indian societies was extremely high. By the time the English began the colonization of Connecticut in 1635, the Pequot had been reduced to about three thousand people, a 77 percent drop in the tribe's population.

Conflicts over land began as soon as the colonists arrived. Early European traders had participated in the established Native American trade networks. They required only a minimal amount of space in which to conduct the exchange of goods. Colonists, on the other hand, wanted land to farm and build villages. In their view the continent was an object to be owned and used for their benefit. The colonial policy was based in the belief of ownership by right of discovery. The king or his appointees possessed the land and they could grant, charter, or sell it as they saw

Another America

fit. In this system Indians were viewed as non-persons, as temporary occupants who held no title to the land. In the opinion of the Puritans, the godless, lazy, unproductive, and unworthy savages could be rightfully dispossessed for the "higher use" of the colonists' farms and towns.

Obtaining the Indians' land involved the creation of documents that satisfied the needs of the English legal system; treaties, deeds, or records of land sales could be used to displace the Indians and bar them from occupying or using their land in the future. This entire process was contrary to most Native American traditions. In the Native American view a piece of paper or a "writing" did not establish title to land for which there was an oral tradition that told of the Indians' historic relationship with the land. As the colonial appetite for land increased, friction with the Indians grew. Treaties and land cessions were sometimes successfully used to obtain Indian lands, but the really big acquisitions of Native American land were made in wars against the Indians. In New England the Pequot War was the first major conflict of this type, and it set the tone for much of what was to come.

The Pequots lived between the colonies of Connecticut and Massachusetts, and the English immediately perceived them as a threat. In 1635 the English established Fort Saybrooke at the mouth of the Connecticut River. The following year colonists from Massachusetts Bay founded several settlements in the Connecticut valley and established the outpost of Springfield on the Connecticut River. As these settlements grew, the need for land and the desire to secure the settlements from Indian attack increased tension with the Pequots. At the same time inter-tribal hostilities contributed to the level of tension. The Pequots struggled with the Narragansett Indians for control of the fur trade with the English. When the Pequots triumphed, the Narragansetts allied themselves with the colonists. The Mohegans, who had been the subjects of the Pequots, broke out of their subservient role. Under the leadership of Uncas, whose "mark" appears on this map, the Mohegans joined the Narragansett–English alliance.

When the Pequots attacked the settlement of Wethersfield, killing several settlers and taking others prisoner, it provided the excuse for a war of extermination. Connecticut and Massachusetts colonists joined forces with the Narragansetts and Mohegans to plan an attack upon the Pequots' fort on the Mystic River.

In preparing the attack Roger Williams, the future founder of Rhode Island, met with the Narragansett Indians to seek their support and council. The Indians advised him in preparing the campaign:

> "That the assault would be at night, when they (the Pequot) are commonly secure and at home, by which advantage the English, being armed, may enter the houses and do what execution they please."
> "That before the assault be given, an ambush be laid behind them, between them and the swamp, to prevent their flight, etc."
> "That it would be pleasing to all natives, that women and children be spared, "

The Pequot fort on the Mystic River was much as it is pictured in John Underhill's 1638 description of the battle (Figure 23). A palisade stockade with two narrow entrances, there were as many as seventy dwellings lined up along the settlement's streets. It is estimated that seven hun-

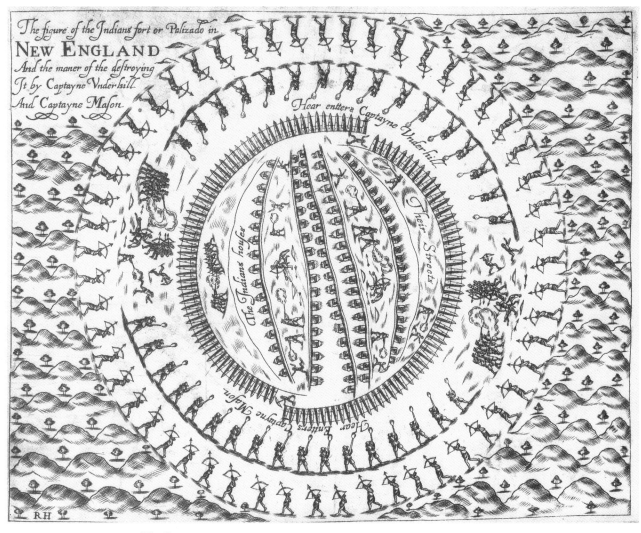

FIGURE 23. "The figure *of the Indians' fort . . .*" *from* Newes From America, *by John Underhill, 1638. Courtesy of the Edward E. Ayer Collection, The Newberry Library, Chicago.*

dred Pequots, including women and children, occupied the fort. Just before dawn on the morning of May 26, 1637, an army of English soldiers led by captains Mason and Underhill, together with their Mohegan and Narragansett allies, attacked the fort. The two English captains entered the fort from either side while the Indians waited outside to catch those trying to flee. The element of surprise worked in favor of the English and they were able to attack several houses before the general alarm was sounded and the Pequot began to respond. At this point Captain Mason ordered that the dwellings in the fort be set ablaze. The reeds, grass mats, and wood of the Pequot structures quickly ignited into a fire that consumed the fort and incinerated several hundred

Another America

Pequots. Those who escaped the blaze were cut down by the English soldiers and their Indian allies. It is reported that no more than seven of the Pequot Indians in the fort survived.

Hearing of the massacre, those Pequot who were not in the Mystic Fort either rushed to attack the English or fled into the countryside. In the three months following the attack, the English carried out a systematic campaign to exterminate the Pequot. Hundreds were hunted down and killed, or captured and enslaved. The vindictive view of the English and their desire to eliminate the Pequots is reflected in the letter from Israel Stoughton, the leader of an English military expedition, to the Connecticut governor. In his letter Stoughton describes how he had given many of the captured Pequot slaves to the Narragansett, and that he was sending forty-eight or fifty women and children to the governor. But, the letter continues:

> "there is one, that is the fairest and the largest that I saw amongst them, to whom I have given a coat to cloathe her. It is my desire to have her for a servant, if it may stand to your liking.... There is a little squaw that Stewart Calacot desires, to whom hea has given a coat. Lieutenant Davenport desires one, to wit, a small one that hath stroaks upon her stomach, thus !!!"

The war ended when the leader of the Pequots made his way to Mohawk territory, where he hoped to enlist the Iroquois in an alliance that would drive out the English. But the Mohawks were already deeply involved in their own trading alliances with the European nations. To elevate their position and prove their worth as preferred trading partners, the Mohawks executed the Pequot leader and his followers, sending their scalps back to Boston.

To the English, their triumph in the Pequot War marked the true beginnings of their hegemony on the continent. The Pequots' destruction was proof of the colonists' righteousness, and the savagery with which the genocide was accomplished became abstracted as the will of god. The few remaining Pequots were legally terminated—no longer recognized as a people in 1638, stripping them of the status needed to make any future land claims. A 1643 Puritan account of the war credited the victory to divine intervention rather than the colonists' savagery:

> "God's hand from heaven was so manifested that a very few of our men in a short time pursued through the wilderness, slew, and took prisoner about 1,400 of them, . . . so that the name of the Pequots (as of Amalech) is blotted out from the under heaven, there being not one that is, or (at least) dare call himself a Pequot."

The Pequots' extinction became so fixed in colonial history that it was to serve as the metaphorical name for the ill-fated vessel in Herman Melville's *Moby Dick*. In 1851, he described the "Pequot" as "a celebrated tribe of Massachusetts Indians, now extinct as the ancient Medes."

But the Pequots did survive. Though legislated out of existence, the Pequots continued as wards of the colonists. Some lived with the Mohegans, who, under the leadership of Uncas, had continued their alliance with the English. In 1667 a Pequot reservation was set up at Mashantucket with Casasinomon, whose signature is also on this map, as the leader. For the next three hundred years the Pequots lived under state supervision suffering population loss and the

FIGURE 24. **Untitled map** *by King Philip and John Sassamon, 1666. Records of the Plymouth Colony [MPLms I(1): 21]. Size of the original 1 1/2 x 4 inches (3 x 10 cm). By permission of the Plymouth County Commissioners*

division of their territory. By 1983 the Mashantucket Pequots had reorganized themselves. They were awarded Federal recognition and a trust fund was created to allow them to purchase land. The Pequots' near extinction remains a central event in the tribe's history, both a source of pain and a mark of pride in their continuance and survival. Today the Mashantucket Pequots are a thriving community, with a growing population and land base.

King Philip's map (Figure 24) is a record of a land sale made by the Wampanoag sachem, King Philip, to the Plymouth Colony in 1666. Following the sale, the map was copied into the Plymouth Colony's *Book of Indian Records For Their Land.* This is the book of deeds that the colonists made to document their purchases of Indian land. Over time the ink has bled through the page, obscuring some of the map, but the double-lined diagonal labeled "this is a River" can be clearly seen.

The map is best read by turning it over with the "River" flowing down towards the right between the two semicircular necks of land that embrace it. This represents the area known as

Another America

Sippican Neck in Buzzards Bay south of Cape Cod. The area behind it includes the land on which modern day Rochester, Massachusetts is located. Philip, whose mark appears above the map, is quoted in the endorsement as saying he was "willing to sell the Land within this draught; . . . [and] I have set downe all the principall names of the land wee are not willing should be sold." Philip's desire not to sell all the land and retain a home for the Wampanoags reflects the growing tensions between the Native Americans and the land-hungry English. Forty-six years earlier, in 1620, Philip's father, Massasoit, had welcomed the Pilgrims to Plymouth. Now the English farms and villages were swiftly displacing the Wampanoags. In a little over a decade, these frustrations would erupt into the largest Indian war in New England colonial history, King Philip's War.

At the beginning of the seventeenth century the Wampanoag Indians, also known as the Pokanokets, occupied the area of southeastern Massachusetts east of Narragansett Bay including Cape Cod, Martha's Vineyard, and Nantucket Island. With an estimated population of over six thousand they lived in small villages, practiced slash-and-burn agriculture, and hunted and gathered in the surrounding countryside. Like most of the Algonquian Indian groups in the region they lived in small semi-permanent settlements with each village having a sachem or leader. They would sometimes work together with the other Wampanoag villages to farm, hunt, make war, and provide for the common defense.

Prior to the arrival of the Pilgrims, epidemics of European disease had diminished the power and security of the Wampanoags. Some of their villages had suffered considerable population loss and became prey to their traditional enemies, the Narragansett Indians. Massasoit, the chief Wampanoag sachem at the time of the English arrival, is believed to have embraced the newcomers and forged an alliance with them partially out of the desire to protect his people. Whatever his reasoning, Massasoit entered into a formal treaty of friendship with the Plymouth colonists, establishing a peace that was maintained until his death in 1662.

During that time a considerable amount of the Wampanoags' land was sold or taken by the English. English trade goods and tools were of particular interest to the Wampanoags, and they "sold" parts of their land to obtain the goods they wanted. But the Wampanoags' concept of land ownership and sale differed dramatically from that of the English, and this difference helped to set up the conflicts that would result in King Philip's War. To the Wampanoags, "selling" their land meant giving a neighbor or potential kinsman the right to participate in the use of the available land. This practice of shared use is reflected in the words Philip used to describe this map, saying that although he was willing to sell the land, "the Indians that are upon it may live upon it still. . ."

The English, on the other hand, firmly believed in private property and sole possession. When land was purchased, the Indians were to vacate to make room for the sedentary English farmers and the use to which they would put the land. In this way, the "sales" the Wampanoags made whittled away their territories at the same time that Wampanoag culture demanded that they retain a large number of acres to accommodate their slash-and-burn agriculture and their hunting and gathering traditions.

Massasoit's friendship with the colonists may have brought the Wampanoags peace and trade goods, but the practice of accommodating the English eventually resulted in a period of decline. By the time Philip became chief sachem the mutual respect and benefits that had marked the Wampanoags' earlier relations with the English had deteriorated to the point of forced agreements and exploitation. At the same time, Philip and his fellow sachems were well aware of the price of resistance. They had seen how the English dealt with the Pequot when they stood in their way. The colonists' powerful weapons and their military might had been used to slaughter women and children. It was a lesson not lost on Philip and the Wampanoags.

Upon his ascendancy, Philip, who was also known as Metacomet, was given the title of king by the English. He continued his father's policy of selling land while recognizing the need to maintain a homeland for his people. Samuel Drake, in his history of the American Indians, lists over twenty deeds of sale on which Philip's signature and that of other Wampanoag sachems are found. Many of these deeds were witnessed by John Sassamon, a christianized Indian who served as Philip's interpreter and scribe.

Sassamon, the first American Indian to attend Harvard, personifies the difficulties faced by the Wampanoags and other Indians when dealing with the English invaders. While Sassamon benefited from the education and religion of the English, he was still an Indian and often intimately tied to the fate of his people. As a christianized Indian, Sassamon had accepted English domination as the best alternative, a view that made him an anathema to his own people. On the other hand, Sassamon's familiarity with the English made his services essential in many cross-cultural dealings. Philip evidently relied upon Sassamon to negotiate several of the Wampanoags' land deals, a position Sassamon is believed to have taken advantage of by claiming some of the land for himself. Philip eventually dismissed Sassamon from the Wampanoag court, and Sassamon went to the English with accusations that Philip was preparing to make war on one of their settlements. The colonists were not able to verify these charges, but not long afterwards Sassamon was found murdered. The deed was commonly attributed to Philip, and Sassamon's murder became one of the excuses for the coming war.

The English either found or fabricated a witness to Sassamon's murder, and they quickly tried and hung three of the Wampanoags. This English justice was just one more injustice to the Wampanoags. Their oral testimony was not considered legitimate by the courts, just as the Indians' oral records were not regarded as legal documents in disputes over land. The English practice left the Wampanoags with no access to justice and no recourse to a higher authority.

As tension between the Wampanoags and the colonists grew, John Easton of the Rhode Island Colony asked Philip and the Wampanoags to Providence to see if he could work out the difficulties. There, Philip listed some the Wampanoags' grievances. He complained how "if 20 Indians testified that an Englishman had done them wrong, it was nothing, but if one of the worst Indians [serving his own interests] testified against any Indian or their king [Philip], when it pleased the English, that was sufficient." Another grievance noted that when the Wampanoag sachems sold land, the English would take more than they had agreed to, and a "writing [a map or document]" would be used as proof against the Wampanoags. This English duplicity resulted in the Wampanoags having "no hopes left to keep any land." In his complaint Philip summarized the Wampanoags' history with the English:

> The English who came first to this country were but an handful of people, forlorn, poor and distressed. My father was then sachem, he relieved their distresses in the most kind and hospitable manner. He gave them land to plant and build upon. . . they flourished and increased. By various means they got possession of a great part of his

Another America

territory. But he still remained their friend till he died. . . . Soon after I became sachem they disarmed all my people . . . their land was taken. But a small part of the dominion of my ancestors remains. I am determined not to live until I have no country.

Philip's desire to keep a homeland was shared by other Indians in the region. In June of 1675, Philip's frustration with the English erupted in raids upon colonial settlements. This marked the beginning of King Philip's War, and the Wampanoags were soon joined by the Nipmucks, Norwottocks, and Narragansett Indians. In time Philip's insurrection even spread to the Algonquian tribes of Maine.

This rising up of Indians throughout the region is indicative of the growing Native American anger with the English colonists. But it was not a united effort. Others, like the Mohegans who had gained from their alliance with the English, or the Pequot, who had suffered the consequences of an English military campaign, stayed out of the conflict.

The battles of King Philip's War started as a series of raids upon English settlements and skirmishes between Indian groups and colonial militias. The Indians' attacks on frontier settlements in the Connecticut River Valley created an atmosphere of alarm among the colonists. It is not known if Philip and his allies dreamed of driving the invaders out of New England. But once the conflict began it became, for the colonists, a holy war. Puritan preachers denounced Philip as the seed of the devil himself, and the violence that accompanied the war only confirmed the growing Puritan conviction that sharing their soil with the savages was not what god intended. With the human and military resources of the United Colonies, the English gathered a superior force, and before the winter of 1675 they began burning Indian villages and crops, cutting Philip and his allies off from the supplies they needed to continue the war.

Philip planned to spend the winter of 1675–76 in the relative safety of the western frontier above New York. But the governor of New York had no desire to let the trouble-making Wampanoags find succor in his colony. He enlisted the help of the Mohawks who, in their zeal to maintain their prominent position in the fur trade, had no qualms about attacking their Algonquian brethren. They surprised Philip and dealt his warriors a mortal blow. The demoralizing effects of this battle may have prevented Philip from widening the alliance he hoped to form against the English. By the summer of 1676 Philip and his allies were weakened by hunger and the losses in battle. In August, as Philip was making his way towards his home at Mount Hope on the Pokanoket peninsula, his camp was surrounded by the English and Philip was shot.

As the mortal enemy of the Puritans, Philip was not to be given a proper burial. His death was to serve as an example for others. Philip's wife and child were sent into slavery, and Philip's body was beheaded and quartered. His quarters were hung in separate trees and a hand was cut off as a reward for the man who had betrayed him. Philip's head was given to the Plymouth colonists, who placed it upon a spike and exhibited it to passersby for decades. The Wampanoags suffered in defeat as well. The war had greatly reduced their numbers. Like the Pequot, the surviving Wampanoags were handed over into servitude or became the wards of the state. Under the care of the colonists they suffered several generations of neglect, only to reemerge as a presence in New England in the twentieth century.

Following King Philip's War the remaining Wampanoag lands were confiscated by the victorious colonists. Among the lands taken was the Sippican Neck pictured on Philip's map of 1666. Only ten years earlier this had been part of the "land wee are not willing should be sold."

This map (Figure 27) endorsed as a "Discription . . . given from an Indian called Jacka-napes . . ." is an example of a map solicited from an Indian informant but actually made for use by the European colonists. In this case the map provides information on the number of Susquehannock Indians living with the members of the Iroquois League. It was solicited by Rando Brandt, an official of the Maryland Colony. Brandt either redrew the map from the Indian origi-nal or composed it from the information provided by Jackanapes before sending it to the council. Brandt's explanation of the map is written above his signature in the lower right. The Indian infor-mant, identified only as "Jackanapes"——a derogatory name that is in itself a comment upon the English view of the Indians——described as a Mattawoma ("Mattawoman") Indian who recently escaped from a period of captivity among the Cayugas ("Quiaquos" on the map). Brandt evident-ly interrogated Jackanapes shortly after his escape, obtaining the information that is represented on the map.

The area represented on the map includes the upper portion of the Susquehanna River and its tributaries, encompassing central New York State and part of Pennsylvania. The diagonal from upper left to lower right labeled "A great River that comes into the Bay" represents the Susquehanna River from right below the present Pennsylvania–New York border, and the Chemung and Cohoctan rivers continuing northwest into the territory of the Seneca Indians in western New York. The intersecting diagonal to the upper right labeled "Branch of said River" is the north branch of the Susquehanna continuing into northeastern New York State. Across the top of this area the five nations of the Iroquois League are pictured as circles and named with sev-enteenth-century synonyms——From left to right: the Senecas ("Sinniquos"), the Cayugas ("Quiaquos"), the Onondagas ("Annodoguns"), the Oneidas ("Wittassons"), and the Mohawks ("Cannagains"). Further to the east the trading center of Albany is noted as the "Scituation of English and French." From the three tribes represented in the middle, routes pictured as dotted lines lead to a circle labeled "A place of genrall Rendesvous from the Nations . . . ."

By 1681 this geographic information was readily available to the governor and council of the Maryland Colony. The information of most interest is that which Brandt obtained from Jackanapes concerning the number and locations of Susquehannock Indians living with the Iroquois. Among the Wittassons (Oneidas) he notes, "not good with them 17 Susquahs." It is the same with the Annodoguns (Onondagas) where there are "14 Susquehannahs," and the Quiaquos (Cayugas), "our supposed friends 8 Susquehannohs with them. . ." The colonists' concern stems from the history of their treatment of the Susquehannock Indians.

In 1675, the colonists and their Indian allies had ruthlessly attacked the Susquehannocks, driving them from Maryland territory and on to the frontier. When the Susquehannocks retaliat-ed with raids on the outlying settlements, the peace of the region was threatened. To quell the vio-lence the governor of New York offered sanctuary to the Susquehannocks and protection from their enemies. Most of the Susquehannocks moved up into the area represented on this map where they lived among and received the protection of the Iroquois.

Shortly after this the Susquehannocks lost their tribal identity in the series of treaties that came to be known as the Covenant Chain. These treaties brought peace to the colonies by putting

PHILLIP alias METACOMET of Pokanoket.
Engraved from the original as Published by Church.

FIGURE 25. **Portrait of** *Philip alias Metacomet of Pokanoket, from Samuel G. Drake,* Biography and History of the Indians of North America. *Boston: C. L. Perkins. 1834.*

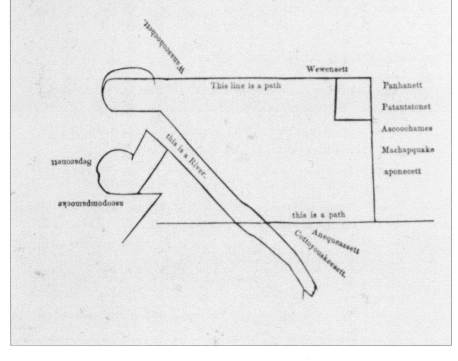

BOOK OF INDIAN RECORDS FOR THEIR LANDS.

THIS may informe the honor⁴ Court that I Phillip ame willing to sell the Land within this draught; but the Indians that are vpon it may liue vpon it still but the land that is [waste] may be sold and Wattachpoo is of the same mind; I haue set downe all the principall names of the land wee are not willing should be sold.

ffrom Pacanaukett
the 24ᵗʰ of the 12ᵗʰ month 1668.   PHILLIP: P⸱ his mark.

FIGURE 26. **Printed version** *of King Philip's map, from* Records of the Colony of New Plymouth in New England, *vol 12,* Deeds & c, *vol.. 5, 1620-1651,* Book of Indian Records For Their Land, *1861. Courtesy of the Newberry Library, Chicago.*

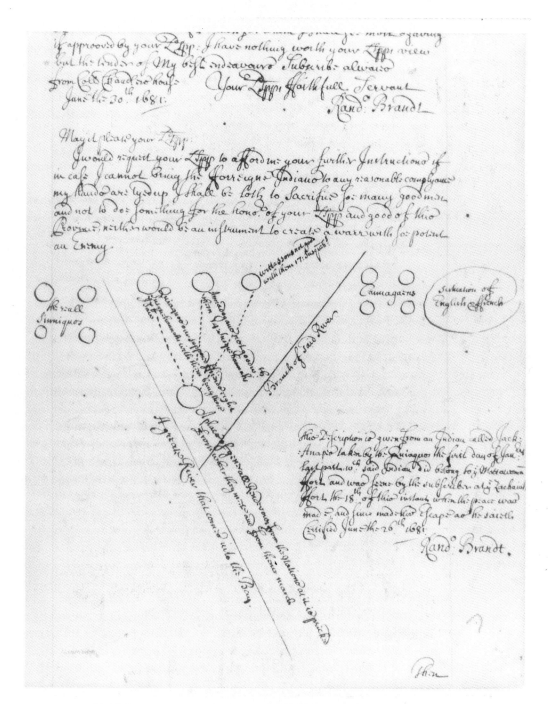

FIGURE 27. **Untitled map** *of the Susquehanna River and the League of the Iroquois, 1681. Maryland State Archives/GOVERNOR AND COUNCIL (Proceedings) R. p. 204 Drawing of Indian Routes [MSA S 1071-8].*

the League of the Iroquois in the preeminent position and granting them authority over the other Indians of the region. Consequently, smaller tribes like the Susquehannocks were no longer recognized as nations. Far from actually disappearing, the Susquehannocks found advantage in their protected status among the Iroquois. They would accompany their protectors on raids into Maryland territory whenever uncooperative Indians——the same Indians who had joined the colonial militias in attacking the Susquehannocks——needed to be taught a lesson about the workings of the Covenant Chain. This resurgence of the Susquehannocks, and the colonists' fears that they might take revenge for the way they had been treated by Maryland, were the reason Rando Brandt and others wanted to know exactly how many Susquehannock warriors were living among their supposed friends, the Iroquois.

The Susquehannocks' resurgence was not sufficient to prevent their ultimate dispersal and loss of cultural identity. Their experience is like that of many Native American groups caught in the shifting balance of political ties and military alliances that accompanied the expansion of the English colonies. Prior to the arrival of the English, the Susquehannocks had played an important part in the native societies of the Northeast. Of Iroquoian background, the Susquehannocks were first evident in the middle of the sixteenth century along the river that bears their name. By 1580 they had established a settlement along the Susquehanna River near present-day Lancaster, Pennsylvania. Like their Iroquoian and Algonquian neighbors the Susquehannocks practiced maize agriculture and hunted and gathered throughout the region. But their strength and their prominent position came from the role they played in regulating trade on the Susquehanna River.

The Susquehanna River was a major conduit of trade for Native American civilizations. People, goods, and ideas traveled in all directions on the river; from the Chesapeake Bay to the Finger Lakes and east to the Mohawk and Hudson rivers valleys, from the Delaware valley to the Great Lakes, and over the Appalachians to the Ohio River. For more than two thousand years the Susquehanna had been a major artery in the networks that tied the peoples of North America together. When John Smith arrived in 1608, he sailed up the Susquehanna as far as the falls. There he met the Susquehannocks or "the people of the falls." At that time the Susquehannocks claimed possession of the entire Susquehanna River Valley and territories on both sides of Chesapeake Bay. Smith noted that they could raise six hundred warriors and lived in palisade towns. An estimate from the 1640s puts the Susquehannock population at approximately six thousand.

The Susquehannocks' control of trade on the river must have enriched them and enabled them to support such a large population. European trade goods, introduced early on in the encounter, proved highly desirable to Native Americans, and the Susquehannocks profited from their strategic position in the indigenous trade network. In 1630 an Englishman, William Claiborne, established a trading post on the Chesapeake Bay from which he dealt extensively with the Susquehannocks. When Lord Baltimore attempted to exercise his rights under the Maryland Charter and seized Claiborne's enterprise, Claiborne incited his trading partners, the Susquehannocks, to hostilities. The Maryland Colony declared war on the Susquehannocks in 1642, and hostilities continued off and on until 1652 when the Susquehannocks made peace with the colony and ceded a considerable amount of their territory.

In the years that followed, the rulers of Maryland made alliances with whomever could most benefit the economic and territorial ambitions of the colony. In the 1660s this was the Iroquois, and in order to make peace with them the colony had to remove the Susquehannocks. To get the

Another America

Susquehannocks out of the way, Governor Calvert "invited" or put pressure on the Susquehannocks to leave their territory and move south to an abandoned Piscataway Indian fort on the Potomac River. This move proved disastrous for the Susquehannocks. Living on the border with Virginia, the Susquehannocks were blamed for any Indian troubles that occurred in that colony. In 1675 the Virginia militia mounted a campaign against the Susquehannocks and requested the assistance of Maryland. The Maryland colonists mobilized 250 troops to join in the attack. With their Indian allies the combined Virginia and Maryland militias laid siege to the same fort that the Maryland governor had recently invited the Susquehannocks to take as their new home. In one instance five Susquehannock chiefs were given safe conduct to meet with their attackers, only to be seized and put to death on orders of the Maryland captain. Following a prolonged siege the Susquehannocks escaped and launched a series of retaliatory raids on remote settlements of the colony.

That is how things stood in 1676 when the governor of New York invited the Susquehannocks into the protection of his colony. The governor issued a similar invitation to several other hostile tribes, including those who had been defeated in King Philip's War. The invitations were part of a move to consolidate power over the Indians in the hands of the Iroquois, with whom Governor Andros of New York was on good terms. The treaties that formalized this agreement, the Covenant Chain, recognized the five members of the Iroquois League and the Delaware Indians as the only legal entities with whom the colonists could deal. This regulated the Susquehannocks to the status of non-persons. Without an official presence the colonies could not make treaties with the Susquehannocks. But, as JackAnapes's map shows, the non-existent Susquehannocks continued to haunt the Maryland Colony. The archives record an Indian informant telling Lord Baltimore in 1679 that "the Susquehannocks laugh and jeare at the English saying they cann doe what mischief they please for that the English cannot see them."

With the blessing and sometimes assistance of their Iroquois guardians, the Susquehannocks continued to make vengeance raids upon those Maryland Indians who had assisted the colonists. Around 1690 some of the Susquehannocks left these wars to resettle along the Susquehanna River. They settled at the confluence of the Conestoga Creek and Susquehanna River, taking on the name of Conestogas. There they intermixed with Shawnees, Delawares, and other Indians that had migrated to the region as a result of the displacements taking place throughout the colonies. The Susquehannock-Conestogas attempted to sell the Susquehanna valley to William Penn in 1700, but the sale was disputed by the Iroquois. Gradually the Conestogas became dependent upon the protection and economic help of the Pennsylvania Colony.

Like New York, the Pennsylvania Colony eventually allied itself with the League of the Iroquois and gave them power over the Indians along the Susquehanna. Some of the remaining Susquehannocks migrated west, losing their identity among the various Indian groups that were moving into the Ohio River valley to escape the growing presence of the colonies. The rest remained at Conestoga until the French and Indian War (1754–1763). When some of the Pennsylvania colonists suspected the Susquehannock-Conestogas of helping the French and their allies, a vengeful mob known as the Paxton Boys attacked their settlement and massacred what remained of the once proud and powerful Susquehannocks.

Wampum, strings of beads that were sometimes woven into belts, became an important commodity among the Iroquois and the customary gift to be presented at any formal occasion. Wampum belts were often exchanged during treaties between the Iroquois and other Indians and with the English. The exchange of wampum symbolized the importance of the occasion and the truth of the words and promises that were spoken. Figure 28 is a painted reproduction of a belt that is said to represent the League of the Iroquois and has a geographic correlation to the area represented on Jackanapes's map. At the bottom the figure of the Mohawks guards the "east door" of the League near Albany. The white line of beads that extends through the belt is the "peace path" that unites the members of the League. It extends west through the homelands of the five tribes to the cross that represents the Senecas at the "western door" in the area east of modern-day Buffalo, New York.

Figure 29 is a copy of the original map made by the Indian Lamhatty. It is the visual account of his captive journey and eventual escape. In 1707 Lamhatty had been captured in a slave raid that destroyed his people's villages. He was taken by his Indian captors and made to work for them. Lamhatty was then traded to Indians who may have been taking him to sell at the English slave markets. After six months in captivity Lamhatty escaped, making his way to the English settlements of Virginia where he made the original of this map and worked for a time as a servant.

Lamhatty is identified as a Towasa Indian of northwestern Florida. His experience and that of his people is intimately tied to the struggle between the colonial powers for control of the southeastern United States, and to their policies of tolerating or openly embracing the use of Native American slaves. Slavery had been practiced among American Indians for many centuries. The practice ranged from forcing captives to work as slaves and trading them to other tribes, to "adopting" members of a fallen enemy's family into one's tribe. But it was not until the arrival of the Europeans and the need for slave labor in their colonial economies, that the wholesale capture and sale of human beings became a widespread practice in North America. Slaves and indentured servants were used in the Spanish and French colonies, but the English practiced slave-holding on a much larger scale. Many of the American Indian survivors of the Pequot War and King Philip's War were sold into slavery.

FIGURE 28. **Painting of** *an Iroquois Wampum Belt, detail from Rufus Alexander Grider,* A Collection of Pictures of Wampum and Impliments Made & Used by the Iroquois Indians, *Manuscript Scrapbook, 1883-97. Courtesy of the Edward E. Ayer Collection of the Newberry Library, Chicago.*

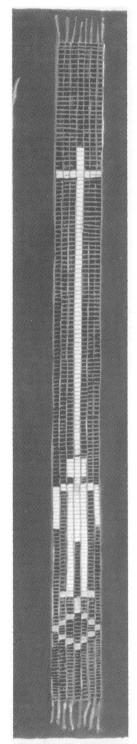

Another America

In the New England colonies the use of kidnapped Indians as slaves was condoned, as was the practice of trading Indian captives for Black slaves from the West Indies. But it was the Carolina colonies that became the center of the Native American slave trade. In the late-seventeenth and early-eighteenth centuries a ready supply of American Indian slaves could be found among the Indians in the Spanish colony of Florida. These "mission" Indians, so-called because their villages were located around the Spanish missions, were easy prey for the parties of Creek, Yamasee, and other Carolina Indians who would raid these towns at the urging of their English allies. Sometimes the Carolina colonists themselves led these raids, gathering captives for the rich trade in human chattel that was carried on in the colonies.

Lamhatty and his Towasa relatives had the misfortune of living around one of the Spanish missions. Towasa Indians were first recorded in 1540 during De Soto's exploration of Florida. Later they were reported living in part of what is now Alabama. By 1700 the Towasa had migrated down to the Florida coast in the area around the Apalachicola and Chipola rivers, which are represented in the lower left of Lamhatty's map draining into the "Saltwater Lake or Sea" which is also called the "Bay of Florida." The named circles in the lower left are the ten towns of the Towasa federation where Lamhatty lived. The Towasa were one of the Timucuan-speaking peoples who populated northwestern Florida. They practiced slash-and-burn agriculture, and relied upon the game and marine life of the area for their sustenance. Estimates of the Indian population of northwestern Florida in the early part of the seventeenth century are between six and ten thousand. The epidemics that followed the arrival of Europeans weakened and reduced the population so that by the time the intensive slave raids from Carolina began, it is impossible to make an estimate of the number of Indians living in this part of the Spanish colony.

In the late 1600s Spain faced a growing threat from French and English encroachment on its Florida colony. To assert their presence the Spanish built a series of missions in the region. These missions provided facilities for Spanish military and political operations, and served as a base for missionaries who attempted to convert the local Indians. These latter efforts were only marginally successful, but because the missions were built near Indian settlements they did serve as a focus for local activities. These mission towns quickly became the target of the English attempts to gain control of the region. Raids led by Carolinians and their Indian allies are reported to have destroyed over thirty-two Indian settlements by 1706, when they began their attacks on the Towasa towns.

Lamhatty's account of his capture and journey was recorded twice: once by the Virginian, Colonel John Walker, to whom Lamhatty was brought when he was first found by the colonists; and again by Robert Beverley, the Virginia aristocrat and historian. Beverley's copy is the surviving copy of the map. Robert Beverley's account ("Acct.") of Lamhatty is written on the back of the map. In both Walker's and Beverley's accounts, Lamhatty's captors are identified as "Tusckaroras" Indians. Modern scholars believe it is much more likely that the Indians who raided and destroyed the Towasa villages were Creek Indians. The Creeks had a history of working with the Carolinians in this manner, and the towns to which they took Lamhatty are in the area inhabited by the Upper and Lower Creek Indians at that time.

According to Beverley's account, in 1706 the Creeks destroyed three of the ten Towasa towns. The next year four more were "swept away" and Lamhatty was captured. The route of Lamhatty's captive journey is shown on his map as the dotted line beginning at the village west of the Apalachicola River (lower left), and continuing up and out of the area Lamhatty was familiar with. The path crosses the "East–West" line that bisects the map. Lamhatty was first taken to a number of Creek towns represented by the circles above the "East–West" line. His captors then took him across the Apalachicola and Flint rivers into the foothills of the Appalachians which Lamhatty represented with a mountainous profile. There Lamhatty's Indian captors forced him to "worke in ye Ground," possibly in a mine, for three to four months. From there he was taken

Another America

across the mountains, shown in an extremely foreshortened line on the map, to the headwaters of the Savannah River along the border of what are now Georgia and South Carolina. This is represented on the map by a circle labeled "Sowanoúka" in the center right. The Sowanoúka are the band of Shawnee Indians that Lamhatty was traded to. The Shawnees took him on several weeks' journey north along the mountains to the headwaters of the Rappahannock River in Virginia. Here Lamhatty escaped his Indian captors and made his way to the English settlements along the Mattaponi River, shown in the upper right of the map. At these settlements Lamhatty is said to have come "naked and unarmed" to the English, who took him to the home of Colonel Walker where Lamhatty was interrogated and the map of his journey was made.

Having escaped his Indian captors, Lamhatty's difficulties were not over. An unidentified Indian coming to the English settlement was not trusted. The settlers first tied him up and Colonel Walker intended to put him in irons. Only after several days, when Walker found him to be "of a seeming good humour," was Lamhatty allowed at liberty about the house. It might be assumed that this means Lamhatty was found to be a useful servant, for Walker ends his letter with a statement that "he [Lamhatty] seems very desirous to stay," and he requests "if I might have yor; Honrs; leave to keep him." Being kept by the English may not have been to Lamhatty's liking. Robert Beverley adds a postscript to his account, noting that Lamhatty was "Sometimes ill used by Walker," and when some of his fellow Indians "were found servants," a possible euphemism for fellow Towasa being taken as slaves, Lamhatty "became verry melancholly often fasting & crying (for) Several days . . . when Warme weather came he went away & was never more heard of."

The Towasa, from whom Lamhatty had been taken, were soon to be "never more heard of" as well. Their villages had been nearly destroyed by the Creek raids, and the surviving inhabitants fled west to Mobile and the relatively benign protection of the French. Over time they emigrated to several settlements in Alabama, losing their identity among the tribes with whom they settled and disappearing altogether in the Creek removal to Oklahoma. The other Indians of northwest Florida did not fare much better. The Carolinians' dependence on the trade in Native American slaves continued to inspire raids upon the Indians of Florida. By the time the Spanish ceded the colony to Britain in 1763 the aboriginal inhabitants of northern Florida had been entirely dispersed or wiped out. Like many of the Native Americans who had the misfortune of being on the wrong side of the colonial struggle, the Indians of northwest Florida were never able to reorganize themselves or gain tribal status in their homeland.

Shortly after Francis Nicholson was appointed governor of South Carolina, representatives of the Indians living on the Carolina piedmont came down to Charleston to have a formal meeting with him. The tradition of formally greeting visitors had evolved among the Southeast Indians long before the European arrival. In the past, visiting headmen or the chiefs of other nations would be met outside the village and ceremoniously escorted in. Similar greetings had been extended to the Spanish explorers when they first attempted to colonize the region in the 1500s. It was only appropriate to inform the new English headman of the Indians' presence and of their desire to maintain good relations. The meeting with Governor Nicholson included the exchange of gifts. Nicholson, an old hand who had already served in several of the colonies, may have prepared packages of trades goods for the visiting dignitaries. It is speculated that the original of the map (Figure 30) was among the gifts the Indians gave him in return. The map would have been

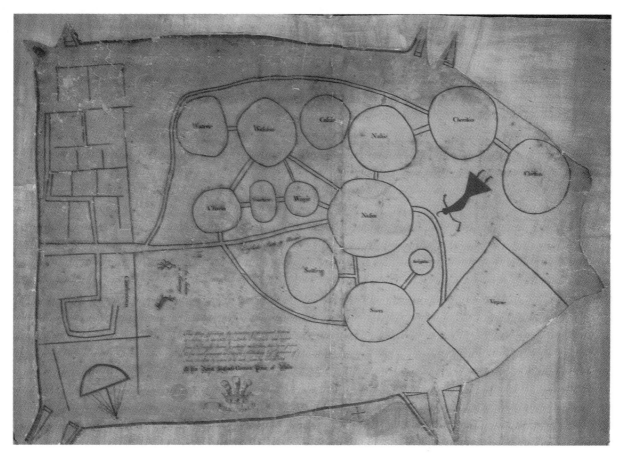

FIGURE 30. *This Map describing the Scituation of the Several Nations of Indians to the N.W. of South Carolina . . . , c. 1721. Size of the original 32 x 44 inches (81 x 122 cm). By permission of the British Library, Additional MS 4723.*

appropriate for a meeting of leaders. Painted on a deerskin the map was a picture of the social and political geography of the region, made to inform the English governor of the lay of the land and exactly who lived where.

Represented on the map are many of the Siouan-speaking tribes that lived above the fall line on the Wateree and Catawba rivers in the Piedmont region of what is now North and South Carolina. In 1721 these diverse peoples were still in the process of becoming the Catawba Nation as it is known today, and they had not yet coalesced into a single entity. The map is a snapshot of an area in transition, one step in the series of changes that transformed the region and its people. As the colonies expanded, many of the Indian groups pictured on the map attempted to both maintain themselves and accommodate the society that threatened their way of life. For the Catawbas this proved a successful strategy for survival.

The endorsement in the lower part of the map explains that it is a copy of the original which was "drawn & painted on a Deerskin by an Indian Cacique and presented to Francis Nicholson

Another America

Esqr. Governour of South Carolina. . ." Nicholson dedicated the copy to "His Royal Highness George Prince of Wales," and sent it to England. There it eventually became part of the manuscript collection of the British Library; a similar copy is deposited among the documents of the North American Colonies in the Public Record Office in London.

Like the original, the paper on which the map was copied is cut in the shape of a deerskin. The area represented on the map is the southeastern quarter of the United States. Charleston ("Charlestown"), South Carolina is represented on the left side of the map with a grid of streets and a boat pictured in the harbor. The Virginia colony ("Virginie") is represented in the lower right of the map. The center of the map is a sophisticated representation of the Indians living to the northwest of Charleston. Eleven circles form an inner network that centers on the Nasaw. The Nasaw were part of the diverse Indian groups that the English referred to collectively as the Catawbas. Their central position has led to speculation that it was one of the Nasaw headman who made the map, and the map is commonly referred to as the Catawba Map.

Radiating from the Nasaws' central circle are a series of double-lined paths or connections to the other circles and to the English settlements of Charleston and Virginia. The mapmaker was not content to merely inform the governor of the presence of this loose confederation of Indian groups; he also wished to portray their central position in the networks of trade and politics that occupied the colonists. Coming from Charlestown is "The English Path to Nasaw" and extending from the Nasaw is a large path to Virginia. By 1720 the Catawbas had developed a dependence upon European trade goods and they carried on an active commerce with traders from both these colonies. Another double line extends from Charleston over the top of the map to the Cherokees ("Cherrikies"). This has been interpreted as the Savannah River leading up to the Appalachian Mountains and access to the Cherokee Indians. Beyond the Cherokees, the map continues down the Tennessee River to the territory of the Chickasaw Indians ("Chickisa") in Alabama and Mississippi.

While the map is unlike a western map, it is far from a primitive representation. The Native American mapmaker used a system of symbols that some speculate is rooted in the great mound-building cultures that inhabited the Southeast about two hundred years before the European encounter. This succinct visual language enabled the mapmaker to picture the intricacies of the local network with the Nasaw at its center and, at a smaller scale, the regional connections from Virginia to Mississippi. The pictorial tools also allowed the mapmaker to differentiate the Native American societies, shown as circles, from the angular settlements of the Europeans.

The network of tribes pictured around the center of the map reflects the Indians' view of each one as a separate entity. The "Catawba," as the English called them, did not exist for the mapmaker; instead it was the Nasaw, Nustie, Succa, and Suttirie that he knew. While linguistically and culturally related, each of these groups represents a separate tradition with its own leaders, kinship network, and territory. For nearly two centuries these people had survived difficulties and upheavals as they struggled to adapt to the changes introduced by the coming of the Europeans. The highly prized trade goods that arrived with the encounter were accompanied by imported diseases and increasingly violent wars. These three factors combined to upset the balance and traditions of the region. Pushed together for protection in an increasingly dangerous world these peoples were finding advantage in mutual defense, in agreeing upon a common spokesperson, and in making a unified response to the growing power of the English colony. At the time the map was made they had begun the difficult process of transforming the many circles shown on the map to the single "nation" they would become by the middle of the century.

The ancestors of the Catawbas had migrated over the Appalachian Mountains many centuries before the arrival of Columbus. They built their towns along the piedmont rivers and creeks and practiced agriculture, growing corn and other crops that they supplemented with hunting, fishing, and gathering. Throughout their tenure the Southeast had been a region of transition.

About eight hundred years ago the cultural and social tradition known as Mississippian had dominated the region and its people. This was a highly complex culture that built large towns with ceremonial mounds and maintained a stratified social structure that extracted tribute from the peoples and villages under its dominion. In the South Carolina piedmont, Mississippian people built the city of Cofitachequi which de Soto visited on his expedition of 1540. While Mississippian culture and its achievements were on the wane at the time of de Soto's visit, they still maintained an extensive trade and information network in the region. De Soto's chronicles note the presence of European trade goods in Cofitachequi prior to his arrival, probably the relics of earlier attempts to colonize the area. The de Soto narratives also record the presence of another product of the European invasion: disease. The army saw "large vacant towns, grown up in grass" and were informed that there had been a "pest" in the land. By the time the Prado expedition visited the town twenty-five years later, the society had declined to the point that the earlier social hierarchies were no longer visible. The exact role imported diseases played in the decline of Mississippian cultural is not known, but by the time the English colonists arrived, Cofitachequi and its people were no longer a major presence on the piedmont .

The diseases that devastated Cofitachequi also affected the Catawbas. It is estimated that about five thousand of these people lived along the rivers and creeks of the Carolina piedmont in 1600. In 1700, the English traveler John Lawson visited several of the piedmont Indian settlements, noting that "many thousand of these Natives" had succumbed to the plagues, leaving less than one sixth of Indians "as there were fifty Years ago." In 1715 the Catawbas are estimated to have comprised only 1,470 people, and a 1720 estimate of all the Indians living between the colonies of Virginia and Carolina——an area that included many more Indian groups than those associated with the Catawbas——listed an entire population of less than five thousand. Epidemics in these proportions were devastating to the social and cultural balance of Native American societies. In these oral societies kinship ties formed the basis of cultural traditions and social learning, designated relatives being responsible for transmitting the oral history and teaching the group's rituals and traditions. The indiscriminate mortality of the epidemics destroyed established relationships, leaving surviving individuals without defined social roles or with duties to perform for relatives that no longer existed. The loss of older members of the population meant the loss of tribal memory and the breaking of traditional continuity. These developments often left the Indians without stable traditions and in need of new forms of social organization.

In addition to diseases, the introduction of trade goods and the colonists' system of Indian alliances put pressure on the Catawbas. The English had disproportionately armed the Indian tribes, favoring those who did their bidding while ignoring other tribes who could only obtain English weapons through trade. This imbalance left the small groups that made up the Catawbas prey to attacks by their traditional enemies. Military pressure also came from the Susquehannock, who began raiding the Virginia frontier in revenge for their ouster from the region in 1676, and from the Iroquois wishing to enforce their dominance over the fur trade. Rifles, shot, and powder gave a considerable advantage in fire-power to these raiders. What had been a tradition of raids with controlled fatalities became massacres that upset whole communities. Where previously a small group could defend itself against a conventionally armed foe, the imbalance in weaponry made it necessary for groups to band together for mutual defense. At the same time, this banding together made it possible for the smaller groups to raise the number of warriors needed to send out their own war parties and gain the honor of revenging their losses upon the enemy.

A third factor influencing the Catawbas' move towards confederation was the desirability of European goods. Manufactured goods, from guns to household utensils, had an immediate appeal for the Catawbas. Like many Indian societies, they happily participated in the fur trade and sought alliances with the colonies and colonial traders that gave them an advantage in the market place. This reliance upon European goods eventually led to dependence and the loss of traditional manufacturing. Early on, the Catawbas opted for coexistence with the European invaders. They contributed braves to the English war against the Tuscarora, and they quickly called a halt to their own hostilities in the Yamasee War when they realized they would be facing the military might of the combined southern colonies. Being uncooperative with the colonists could lead to a trade boycott, a deprivation the Catawbas wished to avoid.

These pressures helped to direct the evolution of the diverse Indian groups pictured on this map. In the early part of the eighteenth century they settled together in the Catawba River Valley. There they were joined by a growing number of refugees, members of coastal tribes who had lost their lands to the colonists, and the remnants of those who had been on the losing side of colonial battles. These linguistically and culturally diverse peoples began to band together, often at the direction or invitation of the Nasaw. Within the federation, groups maintained their separate traditions and authorities, acting together only after council and the identification of a single spokesperson. To become part of the confederation offered one protection and a chance to participate in trade. The alternative was to risk one's own among the competing forces of Indians and colonists, or to become a "Settlement Indian." This latter group included those Indians living on the fringes of the white society. Seldom maintaining their traditions, they picked up odd jobs from the colonists and slowly became part of an obscure underclass that included slaves and freed Africans. This was a dangerous position for a mixed-blood Indian who could no longer trace his heritage, just as it was for an African who could not produce the papers granting him his freedom. The slave-based economy of colonial society was often simply divided between Europeans and others, for whom enslavement was always a possibility.

By providing tribes with a viable solution to the problems of being small and unconnected, the Catawbas grew in influence and attracted new recruits to their confederation. They cemented their political and economic relationships with the English, and offered the safety of numbers in a region that included the formidable presence of Cherokees, Chickasaws, and raiding Iroquois. The creation of this new entity no doubt strained the various traditions and cultures that had to be accommodated, but the Catawbas retained their Indian identity. Each group that joined the confederation brought its own heritage to the mixture, adding to the fund of traditions and technologies that the entire group could draw upon.

The protection of the group did not solve all of the Catawbas' problems. They continued to suffer from epidemics of imported disease. The overall numbers of the Catawbas declined, and in

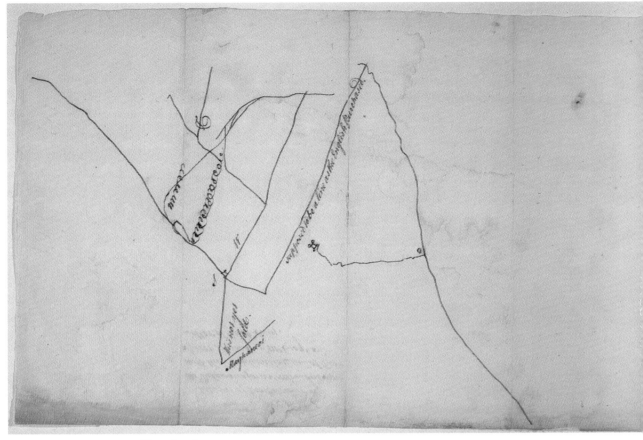

FIGURE 3.1. "Draught of *land desired by the Delawares. . . ," July 30, 1757. Size of the original 12 ½ x 7 ½ inches (31.5 x 19 cm). Record Group 26 Provincial Council Records, Pennsylvania State Archives.*

the second half of the eighteenth century many predicted their coming extinction. At the same time, the relentless colonial pressures for land put the Catawbas at odds with the very power on whom they now depended. The Catawbas had witnessed the decline, dispersal, and disappearance of many of the Indian groups with whom they once shared the region, and it was partly in an effort to protect themselves from this fate that the Catawbas asked to have their lands made into a reservation. This request was in keeping with the Catawbas' practice of accommodating the colonists' demands while working to their own advantage. A reservation would ultimately allow the Catawbas to preserve their culture by creating a boundary between themselves and the encroaching white society, giving them legal recourse to fight colonial incursions. Prior to the reservation, disagreements over the boundaries and sanctity of Catawba lands had become a regular part of the Indians' life. Now, like the English who depended upon maps and deeds to chart and prove possession, the Catawbas had a paper with which to restrain the planters and others pushing into their territory.

In the 1760s the English granted the Catawbas a reservation that encompassed a section of

Another America

their ancestral lands. The English could not honor the guarantees they had promised and the Catawbas suffered corrupt administration, dispossession of their land, and regional dispersal; yet when the time for removal came the Catawbas wished to stay. In the nineteenth century the Catawbas returned to a small remaining slice of the area represented on this map. There they re-established their place in the midst of the society they had learned to live with for over a century. Through accommodation and resistance the Catawbas maintained themselves in a part of their ancestral lands. Today the Catawbas continue to exist as a nation along the river that bears their name.

The "Draught of Land desired by the Delawares" (Figure 31) was presented by the Indian leader, Teedyuscung, at a council between the Delawares and the Pennsylvania Colony held at Easton, Pennsylvania in 1757. The council was called to complete the peace negotiations begun two years earlier when the Delawares ended their short-lived war along the Pennsylvania frontier. Now Teedyuscung was struggling to wend his way through the conflicting political ambitions and pressures of the Quakers, the Pennsylvania Proprietors, and the Iroquois, to secure the title to a home for his people.

Thirty years of manipulation by the colonists and their Indian allies had taught Teedyuscung and the Delawares the importance of obtaining titles, treaties, and documents that the English would respect. Teedyuscung had his secretary draft this map in an effort to show the colonist exactly what the Delawares wanted. With this map and the political skills needed to play one side off against the other, Teedyuscung hoped to be granted the deed to the land west of the Susquehanna River around the settlement known as Wyoming. In exchange for the title, the Delawares would relinquish all grievances and claims against the colony. Teedyuscung proposed that:

> we (the Delawares) intend to settle at Wyoming, and we want to have certain Boundaries fixed between you and us, and a certain Tract of Land fixed, which it shall not be lawful for us or our Children ever to sell, nor for you or any of your Children ever to buy. We would have the Boundaries fixed all round, agreeable to the Draught we gave you, that we may not be pressed on any side, but have a Certain Country fixed for our use and the use of our Children for ever.

For the last hundred years the Delawares had been exploited and abused by the politics and conflicts of colonial North America. They had been cheated of their lands and used as pawns by colonial and Indian powers alike. Now, the "grandfathers" of the Eastern Algonquian Indians hoped to retain a place for themselves in the region they had known for many generations.

The map is centered on the Susquehanna River in central Pennsylvania. The area Teedyuscung was asking for, Wyoming, is marked with a "W" in script along the Susquehanna near the present site of Wilkes-Barre, Pennsylvania. Below Wyoming, at the junction of the Susquehanna and its west branch (which goes off towards the upper left of the map), the English trading post of Fort Augusta is represented by the four-sided symbol for a European fort. To the left (west) of Wyoming the curlicue lines represent the foothills of the Allegheny Mountains, and the line looping over this may mark the western boundary of the land Teedyuscung was seeking. Below Fort Augusta the scripted "S" marks the other Indian settlement in the region, Shamokin, and the Susquehanna River is pictured continuing south to a river labeled "Maghaneoi," marking off an area that is described as "This not yet Sold."

The issue of which lands had been sold was crucial to the Delawares' plan. The diagonal running across the map and labeled "supposed to be a line as the English Purchased," notes the extent of land they had already lost. East of this line was the traditional territory of the Delawares, including the land they lost in the infamous Walking Purchase of 1737. By 1750 very little of it remained in their hands. Instead, the English presence is pictured east of the line. Fort Allen is shown on the Lehigh River, near present day Allentown. The Lehigh flows to the east (right) where it meets the curved line that represents the Delaware River. The circle at the junction of the Lehigh and the Delaware rivers is Easton, where the council was taking place.

The area Teedyuscung hoped to gain for his people was the focus of competing colonial and Indian pressures. The Iroquois wanted to maintain their control over the Susquehanna Valley, while colonists from Pennsylvania and Connecticut were eager to move in and start farming. The Delawares provided a balance for these competing interests, and while they were not given title to the land, they were allowed to move in and act as both a deterrent and a buffer.

The Delaware Indians call themselves the Lenape or Leni Lenape meaning the "real people." The English gave them the name Delaware because they lived along the river and bay of that name. At the time of European contact the Delawares occupied the Delaware River Valley, parts of New Jersey, southeastern Pennsylvania, and southeastern New York west of the Hudson. Delaware tradition maintains that they have occupied the region for several thousands of years, and one record, the Wallam Olum, traces their migration from Asia across the continent to the Northeast, where they became the first or the "grandfathers" of the Algonquian-speaking peoples of the region.

Traditionally the Delawares lived in small, nearly autonomous villages. Tied together by a network of kin relationships and cultural traditions, they did not have a centralized tribal structure. There was no leader or "Chief" of the Delawares. Each village had its own chief, who could act with other village chiefs to organize raids or communal hunting parties. Delaware hunting and fishing grounds were held in common with family and kin group areas defined by tradition. These practices, which had served the Delawares well, came into conflict with the colonists' need for exclusive title to land and with their desire for a recognized "king" or leader with whom they could execute their land transfers.

By the middle of the seventeenth century the Delawares had been in contact with Dutch, Swedish, and English traders and the resulting series of epidemics, trade wars, and colonial hostilities took its toll on the Lenape. Their participation in trade with the Europeans also weakened them by engendering a dependence upon trade goods, particularly alcohol which the Delawares incorporated into their life as a form of recreation and entertainment.

Without a central authority to exert their interests, the Delawares were unable to defend themselves against the growing power of the colonies and the Iroquois League. After a period of hostilities, they petitioned for peace with the Iroquois. Like many of the tribes in the region the Delawares came under the protection and direction of the Iroquois League as part of the Covenant Chain. But, unlike the Susqeuhannock and others, the Delawares were recognized in the treaties. In this process the Iroquois changed the status of the Delawares, making them "women." The Delawares were required to pay tribute to the Iroquois council and forbidden to make war or conduct other business in their own name. The status of "women" has been interpreted as giving the Delawares a special role as peacemakers and council keepers, and its unmanly implications, though later used to taunt the Delawares, were not immediately apparent in the designation.

The Pennsylvania Colony, founded in 1682, proved to be the power that would eventually remove the Delawares from their ancestral lands. At first, William Penn's "holy experiment" treated the Indians with respect and recognized their rights to the land. It was Pennsylvania policy that the Indians' title must be extinguished before land could be divided and distributed to colonists. This led to fair and even-handed treatment of the Delaware under William Penn. Unfortunately, the principles Penn established were not continued after his death in 1728. The new proprietors developed an Indian policy that worked to the Delawares' disadvantage.

Hoping to gain influence with the League of the Iroquois, the Pennsylvania Proprietors embraced the concept of the Covenant Chain. They recognized the Iroquois' ascendancy over the other tribes in the region, and the Iroquois' claim by right of conquest to the Susquehanna River Valley. As the colony grew, the Delawares and other Indians migrated west towards the Susquehanna. New settlements made up of displaced Delawares, Shawnees, Conestogas, and other Indians pushed out by inter-tribal wars or fleeing the dangers of enslavement grew up along the river. These gatherings of dispossessed Indians, open to French influence emanating from the Ohio Valley, troubled the Pennsylvania Colony, who empowered the League of the Iroquois to restrain and direct these smaller tribes on the colony's frontier.

The policy of Pennsylvania still required that the colonial proprietors, William Penn's children, must obtain a clear title to the lands of the Delawares. The representatives of Pennsylvania continued to look for a leader or "king" with whom they could negotiate the deeds extinguishing Indian title. Delaware traditions provided no mechanism for creating such a paramount chief. Instead, leaders of Delaware bands or subgroups were bribed or cajoled into serving as king and signing the deeds the colonists needed. Taking advantage of the Delawares' fondness for alcohol, the Pennsylvania administrators concluded a treaty with the elderly chief of the Schuylkill Delawares. In exchange for their rights and title to lands from the lower Delaware River west to the Susquehanna, Pennsylvania provided a quantity of trade goods and twenty gallons of rum. This represented the last land in southeastern Pennsylvania that the Delawares could legitimately call their own. As the Shawnees said, the Delawares were "drinking their lands away."

In 1737 the Pennsylvania Colony perpetrated one of the most notorious land swindles in colonial history. In what has come to be called the Walking Purchase, the governor and his agents conspired to produce a fraudulent deed that supposedly proved the Delawares had transferred the land at the fork of the Delaware and Lehigh rivers to William Penn in 1686. Forbidden by the Iroquois from taking military action and without colonial allies, the Delawares were forced to recognize the deed. They further agreed that the boundary, which was specified as the line made in a day and one half's walk, had not been properly laid out and could be measured again.

This opened the way for the colonists to make a grab for as much land as they could get. In preparing for the walk, the Pennsylvania agents hired surveyors and mapmakers. They cut a path through the woods in advance, and trained three fast walkers whom they provided with horse-drawn supply wagons. On the day of the walk, what the Delawares understood as a daylight walk at a normal pace turned out to be a thirty-six-hour marathon. The strenuous pace set for the "walk" forced two of the walkers to drop out, but the third walker was able to pace off some sixty miles by the time he was finished. To add insult to injury, the line set from the end of the walk, which the Delawares understood to go straight back to the Delaware River, was surveyed at a right angle to cut off even more of the Indians' territory.

Aware that they had been cheated, the Delawares refused to accept this ruse and threatened violence if the colonists moved in. In response the governor and his agents called in the Iroquois. A delegation from the League of the Iroquois called a council with the Delawares. At the council, the Iroquois recognized the boundaries established in the Walking Purchase, and they upbraided the Delawares for assuming that they were empowered to sell land at all. "We conquer'd you," they said, "we made Women of you . . . and [you] can no more sell Land than Women. This land that you Claim is gone through Your Guts. . . . we charge You to remove instantly."

The Iroquois' cooperation in the colonists' fraud left the Delawares with no alternative. For Pennsylvania the "deed" extinguishing the Indian title had been obtained, and the farmers and other settlers moved in. The proprietors' participation in this purchase would come back to haunt them. It was one of the complaints that Teedyuscung brought up again and again during the treaty councils at Easton.

Following the humiliation and mistreatment of the Walking Purchase, many of the Delawares migrated west to the Ohio River. There they lived on the edge of the Iroquois' orbit, and regrouped to become an important military and political force on the frontier. The remaining eastern Delawares moved to the settlements of Shamokin and Wyoming. These are the two settlements represented on Teedyuscung's map, and it was to the latter that Teedyuscung and a group of his followers migrated in 1754.

Teedyuscung was a controversial leader of the Delawares. Christianized and without a hereditary claim to leadership, he nevertheless gathered a number of followers whom he spoke for and directed. Teedyuscung's skills at organizing would be needed as Wyoming became one of the stages on which the colonial powers played out their conflicting ambitions.

To the Iroquois, who had already ceded much of their land west of the Susquehanna, Wyoming provided an important buffer between themselves and the expanding colony. They maintained their title to the land and preferred to see the Delawares and their fellow Indians settle there. For the time being the Pennsylvania Proprietors also wanted the Delawares in Wyoming, both as a buffer between themselves and the Iroquois and as a deterrent to outside colonists who planned to settle the valley. In the scramble for colonial lands, the Connecticut Colony also laid claim to Wyoming, saying it had been deeded to them in a royal charter. In 1753 they formed the Susquehanna Company with the goal of acquiring the lands along the Susquehanna for themselves. For these three powers the Delawares served as a pawn upon which their rival ambitions were delicately balanced.

The entrance of the French into this mixture upset the balance and temporarily freed the Delawares. In 1754 the French seized the forks of the Ohio River where the Monongahela and Allegheny rivers meet. There they erected Fort Duquesne, extending French control over the Ohio Valley, and effectively blocking the westward expansion of the English colonies. Colonel George Washington and the Virginia militia were sent to tell the French to leave. Their defeat at Fort Necessity cut off English trade in the region, and the western Delawares were brought closer to the French. One year later, the Indians of western Pennsylvania witnessed General Braddock's shocking defeat at the hands of the French and their Indian allies at Fort Duquesne. The balance of power was now broken; no longer were the English and their Iroquois allies an invincible power. The western Delawares "shed their petticoats." Declaring that they were no longer women, they joined the French and began terrorizing the outlying settlements of Pennsylvania.

Teedyuscung and the Delawares at Wyoming at first resisted the urgings of their western cousins to take up the hatchet and drive out the English. But young Delaware braves could not resist asserting their manhood and cutting the strings of the petticoats that tied them to the Iroquois. One by one they joined the western Delawares in raiding Pennsylvania. When both the Pennsylvanians and the Iroquois showed themselves incapable of controlling this uprising, Teedyuscung went on the warpath as well. Calling himself a "war chief" and embodying the Delawares' anger over their years of abuse, Teedyuscung organized his followers for a series of bloody raids on the Pennsylvania frontier. Teedyuscung fulfilled the Delawares' need for leadership in these chaotic times. He quickly became recognized as the leader of the eastern Delawares.

Pennsylvania responded to the uprising by declaring war on the Delawares. By the autumn of 1756, Teedyuscung took it upon himself to enter a peace treaty with the colony. At the first treaty council Teedyuscung called himself king of the Delawares and claimed that he represented the Iroquois League and its Indian dependents. He declared that the Delawares were no longer under the direction of the League of the Iroquois, that "formerly we were Accounted women . . . but now they have made men of us." At the time, the Iroquois were not in a position to deal with the upstart "king." Teedyuscung made peace with Pennsylvania and drank in the gifts and attention the leaders of the colony lavished upon him.

Teedyuscung was wily, boastful, arrogant, and vain. Although conversant in English, he used a translator in his councils with the English and demanded that he be given the services of a clerk. Claiming a perk that had previously been the sole preserve of the English, a court appointed scribe recorded the minutes for the Delawares and copied the map that Teedyuscung presented. Teedyuscung's fondness for alcohol gave those who wished to turn him to their purposes an easy handle, and his drinking bouts were the cause of numerous delays and postponed proceedings. Still, Teedyuscung was the "king" that the Pennsylvanians were looking for. He could deliver peace where the Iroquois could not. From the first treaty council at Easton through 1758, Teedyuscung was treated as the leader of the Indians on the Susquehanna, and various colonial groups began to pressure him into furthering their agendas.

To the Quakers, no longer in power in Pennsylvania, Teedyuscung and the Delawares offered an opportunity to challenge the power of the proprietors. If they could use Teedyuscung to charge that the proprietors had cheated in the Walking Purchase, they could obtain a royal investigation. The proprietors, in turn, wanted Teedyuscung to accept the questionable deeds and drop the Delawares' claims against the colony. They also wanted the Delawares in place as allies at Wyoming, while the Iroquois, wishing to retain their preeminent position in the region, needed to assert their authority over the Delawares.

Through this labyrinth Teedyuscung blundered and bluffed on behalf of the Delawares. In subsequent councils, he sometimes followed the Quakers' instructions and raised the Delawares' complaint over the Walking Purchase. In the same council of 1757, when Teedyuscung presented this map, he voiced the Delawares' grievance that "lands had been brought by the Proprietors or his agents from Indians who had no a right to sell. . . . [and] when some lands have been sold . . . the Proprietors have . . . taken in more lands then they ought to have done, and lands that belonged to others." The Pennsylvania governor and his agents were equally determined to get Teedyuscung to release his claims against the colony. To this end they devoted most evenings of the council to getting Teedyuscung drunk, and through the use of

Shanawdithit (Nancy)

"Last survivor of The Beothucks so far as is known." Reproduced *from* The Beothucks or Red Indians, The Aboriginal Inhabitants of Newfoundland. *James P. Howley, 1915.*

Maps and drawings by Shanawdithit, 1829. Collection of the Newfoundland Museum.

gifts and trade goods endeavored to demonstrate that Teedyuscung's fortunes lay with the Proprietors and not the Quakers.

Teedyuscung's performances——the boasts, accusations, and "U"-turns he made in first trying to please one side and then the other——can be seen as part of a larger plan. It was Teedyuscung's aim to secure Wyoming for his people, to have a "Country fixed for our use and the use of our Children for ever," and he was willing to play one side off the other in order to get the title, just as the Delawares had been manipulated by the colonists' and the Iroquois' machinations.

Following the 1757 council, Teedyuscung continued to ask the Pennsylvania governors for the deed to Wyoming. But Wyoming was the property of the Iroquois, and although the Proprietors were happy to have the Delawares living there, title was not theirs to grant. For this Teedyuscung had to humble himself to the Iroquois.

In 1758 the Iroquois called a council with Pennsylvania declaring that they had something to say about Teedyuscung. At this point the English relationship with the Iroquois was once again essential. They needed the League of the Iroquois as an ally in the continued war with France, and that meant that the English had to support their preeminent position over the Indians on the

Another America

Susquehanna. The Iroquois were calling in their chips, and Teedyuscung was to be taught a lesson. Except for his ability to maintain himself in his strategic position, Teedyuscung had not endeared himself to either his fellow Indians or the white man. His insults and drunken boasts had put off potential allies on both sides and he arrived at the 1758 council without supporters.

For several days Teedyuscung's drunkenness and rude behavior further alienated those he would have to deal with. Still sticking to his goal, Teedyuscung tried once more to make Wyoming the price of Delaware peace and cooperation. Addressing the Iroquois he said:

> Uncles, you may remember that you placed us at Wyoming and Shamokin, places where Indians had lived before. Now, I hear since that you have sold that land to the English. Let the matter now be cleared up in the presence of our brothers, the English. I sit here as a bird on a bough. I look about and do not know where to go. Let me therefore come down upon the ground and make that my own by a good deed, and I shall then have a home forever; for if you, my uncles, or I, die, our brethren, the English, will say they bought it from you, and so wrong my posterity out of it.

Despite Teedyuscung's plea, the Iroquois would not grant the title to Wyoming. Instead, they told Teedyuscung that he and his followers were free to live and plant there without title or exclusive right. The Pennsylvania Colony supported the Delawares settling there as well, hoping they would continue to chase off the Connecticut farmers. As a show of support the Pennsylvanians sent carpenters, laborers, and building supplies to help build the Delawares homes and get their fields started. Although these plans never reached their full intentions, a number of Delaware houses were built at Wyoming.

It was in his home at Wyoming that Teedyuscung died on the night of April 19, 1763. He died in his bed, possibly sleeping off his latest drinking binge when his house was set on fire from the outside. Immediately following the burning of Teedyuscung's house the other Delaware houses at Wyoming were set aflame. The surviving Delawares fled. Two weeks later, when the settlers from Connecticut started to stream into the valley, Teedyuscung's efforts to establish a homeland for the eastern Delawares lay in ashes.

Following the destruction of Wyoming the remaining Delawares migrated to their relatives in the Ohio Valley or affiliated with other Indian tribes in the region. Today Delawares live in Oklahoma, Kansas, Canada, and Wisconsin.

In the winter of 1823 Shanawdithit (Figure 32), a young Beothuk woman, camped with her family along the lakes and rivers of northeast Newfoundland. Cold, sick, and starving the Beothuks awaited their fate. The past two decades had stretched them to their limits. The English invaders had taken over their lands and clashed with the Beothuks at every turn. Food was scarce, and illnesses for which they had no cure plagued Shanawdithit's people. A hostile world was closing in upon the Beothuks. The way of life and the people Shanawdithit had known were rapidly disappearing. In desperation Shanawdithit, her mother, and her sister went out to the bay to gather mussels. There they were found by several white hunters. Too weak to run or resist, the three women let themselves be taken captive. Although her mother and sister died soon after their capture, Shanawdithit lived for the next six years among the colonists of Newfoundland. During the final year of her life she drew an amazing series of maps that tell the story of the end of her people: the Beothuks of Newfoundland.

The Beothuks' extinction represents perhaps the cruelest fate suffered by Native Americans caught in the conflicting forces of the European encounter. Shanawdithit's record of their demise has helped to fuel theories on why the Beothuk Indians, a strong and well-developed culture at the beginning of European contact, did not survive into the second half of the nineteenth century. Everything from tragic errors to deliberate genocide have been cited as the reason for the Beothuks' extinction. Regardless of the role cultural factors may have played, it can be argued that the Beothuks would very probably continue to exist today were it not for the European colonization of North America. Shanawdithit's intricate maps and the notes supplied by her English translator provide a unique record of a people's extinction. Her drawings are eloquent testimony to the tragic history that followed the Beothuks' encounter with western civilization.

The Beothuk Indians' homeland was on the Island of Newfoundland. From there they would cross the Straits of Belle Isle to hunt on Labrador. Because of their early extinction, and their habit of avoiding contact with Europeans, little is known of Beothuk culture. They are assumed to be an Algonquian-speaking group with many of the same traditions and cultural systems as their Micmac and Abenaki neighbors to the south. They lived in bands that came together in the fall and early winter to gather food and hunt migrating herds of caribou, and then dispersed into smaller groups to fish and hunt on their island. Each band appears to have had a recognized leader, like Shanawdithit's uncle Nonosgawut who was the leader of the band composed of Shanawdithit's extended family and her relatives by marriage.

The Beothuks may have been among those Indians visited by the Norsemen in their brief period of settlement on Newfoundland. Cartier encountered Beothuks during his voyage of 1534. He described their practice of rubbing red ocher mixed with grease or oil over their hair, their bodies, their clothing, equipment, and many other items. This habit resulted in the Beothuks being called the "Red Indians." Pre-contact and early-contact estimates of the Beothuks' population are not available. Living as they did near the rich North Atlantic fishery it is very probable that the Beothuks had contact with, or at least exposure to, Europeans from the late-sixteenth century onwards. The fisherman who used the island no doubt brought European diseases with them, along with an ethnocentric attitude that saw nothing wrong with ridding the world of a savage or two whenever sport or the competition for the island's limited resources required it.

These early encounters left the seeds of disease and suspicion with the Beothuks. Unlike the Micmac and Montagnais Indians on the surrounding mainland, the Beothuks established no trading relations with the English or French invaders. They never obtained significant amounts of trade goods or adapted to the use of guns. This left the Beothuks at a disadvantage in inter-tribal wars and in their meetings with European trappers and colonists. It is also possible that the Beothuks' religious beliefs played a part in their rejection of European contact. While the colonists built their settlements along the coasts, the Beothuks retreated to the interior of their island.

By the 1700s several bands of Beothuks were reported to be inhabiting the island's interior. The only group for which there is a record of contact is the band living around Red Indian Lake and the River Exploits in north central Newfoundland. This is where the ancestors of Shanawdithit and her family were living in the 1760s when one English colonist estimated the population of Beothuks at around five hundred.

In addition to avoiding the colonist, the Beothuks were reported to be in the habit of stealing any property that was left unattended. In a land where scant supplies often meant one's meal was another's hunger, the Beothuks were seen as unentitled to the resources now needed by civilization, or as nuisances whose hands were to be kept out of the larder. The practice of indiscriminately shooting Beothuks became widespread on the island, with the rough-and-tumble trappers and farmers sometimes boasting of how many "Red Indians" they had bagged. Although stories of mass killings of Beothuks have not been substantiated, it is certain that the wanton murder of Beothuks was carried out by colonists and trappers.

In 1766, the continued persecution of Beothuks led the governor to proclaim that it was not British policy to exterminate the Beothuks and he outlawed the practice of indiscriminate killing. But the shooting of Beothuks continued. Around 1800 the colonists' desire to make contact and establish friendly relations with the Beothuks took on the misguided form of offering a £100 reward for the capture of a Beothuk. Several Beothuks are reported to have been brought in by colonists hoping to cash in on the reward, but relations with the Indians were not forthcoming.

The other strategy the English employed in their efforts to make contact with the Beothuks was to outfit expeditions into the interior to search for the tribe and establish positive relations with them. These expeditions did not usually result in contact——by then the Beothuks were well practiced in avoiding meetings with the white man——or they were spectacularly unsuccessful like Captain Buchan, whose visit in 1810 only served to further the Beothuks' alienation. It was not until 1823, when Shanawdithit let herself be captured, that prolonged contact with the Beothuks could be established. By then it was too late. As Shanawdithit's records show, there were not enough Beothuks left to find on Newfoundland.

Shanawdithit made her maps in 1829 while under the care of the Beothuck Institution. Founded by W. E. Cormack in 1827, the Beothuk Institution had the goal of "opening a communication with and promoting the civilization of the Red Indians of Newfoundland." Cormack brought a Victorian sensibility to the efforts to civilize the Beothuks, and having learned of Shanawdithit's existence he had her transferred to his care in St. John's. Cormack taught her to communicate, and during the several months that she lived under his care Shanawdithit provided him with "nearly all the information we possess regarding her tribe." Cormack notes that Shanawdithit "was of a most lively disposition. . . [and] had a natural talent for drawing, and being at all times supplied with paper and pencils of various colours, she was enabled to communicate what would otherwise have been lost."

Shanawdithit's maps, made under Cormack's care and annotated by him, tell the history of the last years of the Beothuks. Drawn in black and red pencil, Shanawdithit's sketches are very faint. Some of Cormack's redrawings of the maps are used here for illustration. Together, they relate the series of unsuccessful and often tragic contacts between the English and the Beothuks that both epitomized and hastened the Beothuks' fate.

In 1810 the governor of Newfoundland commissioned Captain David Buchan of the Royal Navy to lead an expedition up the Exploits River and establish relations with the Beothuks. The tragic consequences of this effort are recorded in Shanawdithit's sketch (Figure 33). The complex picture centers on the northeast end of Red Indian Lake. The Exploits River is represented flowing out of the lake as the diagonal going toward the lower right of the map. The map pictures several events occurring over three days and at different places around the lake. Indian encampments are

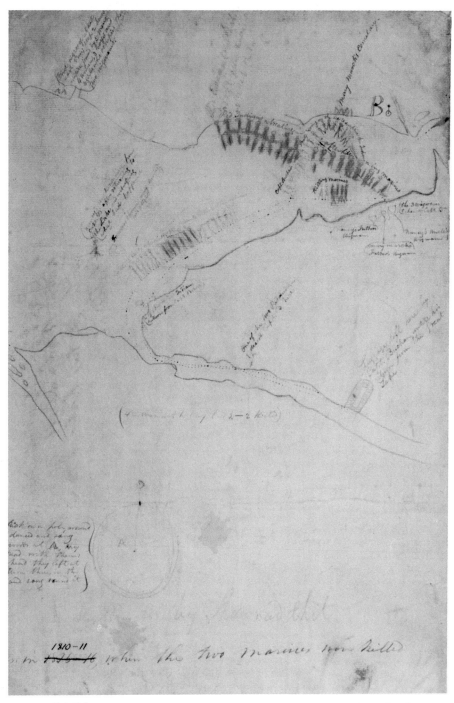

FIGURE 33. **Detail from** *Shanawdithit's Sketch I, "Captain Buchan's visit to the Red Indians in 1810–11 when the two marines were killed." Courtesy of the Newfoundland Museum.*

Another America

represented by teepee symbols, and on the original, Beothuks are marked in red (the darker figures) with soldiers and the geography shown in black outline.

The record of the event begins with Shanawdithit and her family camped in the three wigwams on the south side of the lake. The wigwams are shown on the right side of the map and labeled "Nancy's Uncle's wigwam," "Mary March's [Shanawdithit's aunt] Father's wigwam," and "Nancy's Father's wigwam." As Captain Buchan and his men came up the Exploits River they left their catch of trade goods and presents, represented by the horseshoe-shaped image, and then approached the Indians' camp. They surprised the Indians before they could flee, and may have threatened them with guns. Captain Buchan then coerced four of the Beothuks to accompany him and the soldiers back to the catch of trade goods that was to serve as a friendship offering. He left two marines to stay with the Indians. Captain Buchan, his marines, and the four Indians are shown returning to the catch as a line of figures approaching the Exploits River. In front of the campsite the two marines and four Beothuk Indians are pictured.

Captain Buchan's mistake was in not keeping all his men and all the Indians together. After years of being shot, hunted, and abused by the white men, the Beothuks were not content to wait for the soldiers to return. When three of the Indians who had gone with Captain Buchan returned by themselves, the Beothuks killed the two marines who had been left with them and fled across the lake (shown in the line of Indians going across the lake in the upper right). They made a new camp near the letter "B" on the map. Here they beheaded their victims and, in keeping with their custom, put the head of one of the marines on a ceremonial pole for dancing and celebrations. This event is pictured in the circle next to the "B," and enlarged in the lower half of the drawing.

The next day Captain Buchan and the marines returned to an empty village and found the bodies of their comrades. The Indian who had remained with them fled across the ice; he is shown with his dotted trail leading across the lake in the middle of the map. Fortunately, Captain Buchan had enough sense not to pursue the Indians. Instead he retreated to Exploits Bay on the Newfoundland coast where the expedition hoped to eventually make contact with the Beothuks. In the meantime, the Beothuks fled down along the lake, staying at the two camps represented by wigwams on the upper shore of the lake. Their journey continued across the lake where they set up a new camp (not represented in this detail). Here Cormack noted that, "The whole tribe encamp here and remain the winter." Shanawdithit gave Cormack a census of the Beothuks at the time of these events (1810): In the three winter camps she listed there were a total of seventy-two persons.

The annotations in the upper left of Shanawithit's second sketch (Figure 34) notes that it is "2 Different Scenes & Times." In the lower part of the map along the southern shore of Red Indian Lake, Shanawdithit again records the visit of Captain Buchan, showing the line of soldiers and the four Indians who accompanied them going along the lake towards the Exploits River in the lower left.

The other events being recorded are represented in the upper half of the map, and titled "The Taking of Mary March on the North side of the Lake." This drawing records an encounter between the Beothuks and whites that eventually resulted in the death of four Indians. Despite several versions of what took place, there is universal agreement on the series of events and their outcome. Shanawdithit's map records her perception of things she witnessed as a young adult when the Beothuks were once again visited by the white man.

The event began in 1818 when Beothuks raided the property of a local landowner, stealing

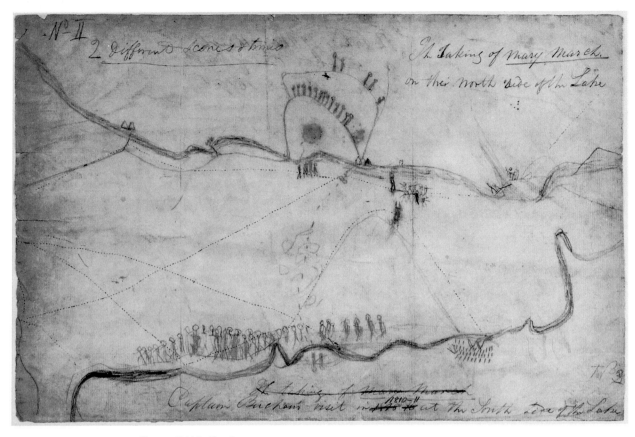

Within the sketch:
Nº II
2 different scenes & times
The Taking of Mary March.
on the North side of the Lake
Captain Buchan's visit in 1810–11 at the South side of the Lake

FIGURE 34. **Shanawdithit's Sketch** *Number II, "The Taking of Mary March on the North side of the Lake." Courtesy of the Newfoundland Museum.*

several items and cutting a boat loose. When the boat was recovered, part of its contents, including the sail, had been stolen. This prompted the landowner to go after the Indians to recover his property. The landowner asked the governor for authority to go after the Beothuks. The governor of Newfoundland had continued to offer a reward for the kidnapping of Beothuks, and he commissioned the landowner to capture some of the Indians and bring them in. The hope was to use a captive as a means of establishing friendly relations with the rest of these elusive people. With the governor's encouragement the landowner led a party of armed men up the Exploits River in the winter of 1818–1819.

In March of 1819 this party surprised the Beothuks camped along the north shore of the lake. Shanawdithit represents this encampment with the wigwams pictured along the top of the lake. She made one black——evidently to indicate that it had been covered by the sail stolen from the landowner's boat. At the arrival of the English, the surprised Beothuks fled into the woods; two lines extend from the camp in long semi-circles showing a number of Indians hidden in the woods. The white men succeeded in capturing one native, Shanawdithit's aunt, Demasduit——a young mother later given the name Mary March for the month in which she was captured.

Demasduit is pictured as the red (dark) figure among a number of white men (in faint outline) standing on the ice to the right of the wigwams.

When Demasduit was captured, two or more of the Indians who were fleeing stopped, turned around, and attempted to rescue her. One was Demasduit's husband——Shanawdithit's uncle, Nonosgawut——who was the chief of this band. He is shown as the lone red man standing in front of the white man on the ice. Unable to speak one another's language, the white men may not have understood Nonosgawut's demands, but it was clear that he did not want them to take Demasduit with them. The kidnappers insisted on their prize and at some point Nonosgawut pulled out his hatchet to stop them. Two or more of the white men then shot Nonosgawut; his body is shown lying prone on the ice in front of the little grouping. According to Shanawdithit, who pictures some of the Beothuks witnessing this event a little ways removed along the dotted line that follows the lakefront, the whites then shot the other Indian who tried to intervene. Before she was taken away, Demasduit bared her breasts to the captors, showing that they were full of milk and pleading that she had a baby nearby.

Resistance to the supposedly benevolent intentions of the white men was futile. Demasduit was taken to the settlements along the Newfoundland coast. There she contracted tuberculosis, and died before successful arrangements could be made to return her to her people. Shanawdithit also sketched a record of Captain Buchan's 1820 expedition returning the body of Mary March. They left Demasduit's body near the burial place of her husband, Nonosgawut, but encountered no Beothuks who, not surprisingly, remained hidden. On the map Shanawdithit records the death of the fourth Beothuk to die as a result of this encounter; she notes the site where "Mary March's child died . . . 2 days after its mother was taken."

In discussions with Cormack, Shanawdithit indicated that at the beginning of these events disease, hunger, and several unrecorded murders had reduced the remaining Beothuks to thirty-one. With the four deaths subsequent to the taking of Mary March, there were now only twenty-seven.

Shanawdithit's fourth map (Figure 36) records the last desperate winter of the Beothuks. The map represents the small lakes between the "River Exploits" in the lower left of the map, and Badger Bay on the coast of Newfoundland represented at the top of the map. Cormack's redrawing shows the copious notes that he added to the map, recording the number of the dead and living as it was told to him by Shanawdithit.

In the winter of 1822–1823 the remaining Beothuks camped first at a site between the first and second lakes north of the Exploits. It is marked by four wigwams in the center of the map. Cormack's figures count the individuals in each respective tent, adding up to the twenty-seven who remained after the events on the second map. Starvation and tuberculosis must have greatly weakened the band, Shanawdithit notes that six people died at this camp. Desperate for food, one of Shanawdithit's uncles and a cousin left the camp and went to the Badger Bay. They were shot by two trappers, with no reason given.

The nineteen remaining Beothuks moved to the end of the second lake. Their wigwams are pictured below the "A." Four more Beothuks died here (indicated by the "–4") from sickness and starvation. Shanawdithit, her mother, and her sister then left the camp and headed to Badger Bay along the route indicated by the dashed line. A note on the coastline indicates where Shanawdithit and the others were captured that April. Cormack's notes on the map repeatedly add the number of Beothuks remaining on the island: 5 men, 4 women, 1 lad, 2 children; only twelve out of a

FIGURE 35. **The capture** *of Mary March (Demasduit) as interpreted in a twentieth century painting by John L. Maunder. Courtesy of the Newfoundland Archives and Mr. Maunder.*

population that once exceeded five hundred. Shanawdithit's map is the last substantiated record of the Beothuk Indians of Newfoundland.

At the time of her capture, Shanawdithit is believed to have been between sixteen and twenty years old. Her mother and sister were suffering from advanced tuberculosis and died shortly after being taken prisoner. Shanawdithit was taken to live at the house of a wealthy landowner. There her lively disposition was noted and it was recorded that when "a black-lead pencil was put into her hand, and a piece of white paper laid upon the table, she was in raptures."

Despite these observations no attempt was made to educate Shanawdithit during the five years in which she lived as a servant in this household. She was considered a good worker, though she suffered from bouts of melancholy and she would periodically spend a day and a night in the woods "talking with her mother and sister."

Another America

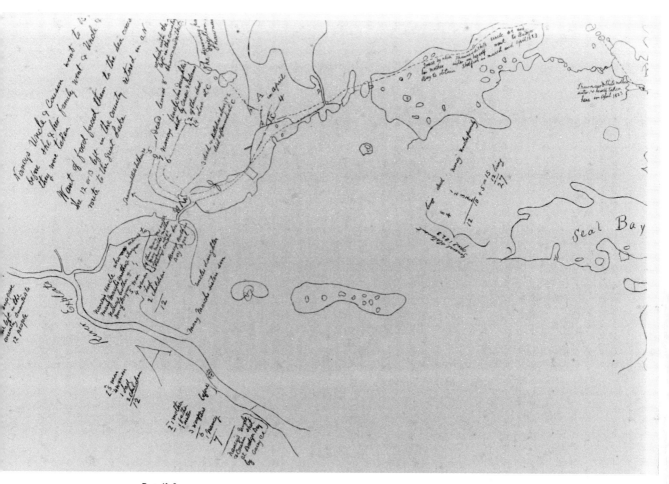

FIGURE 36. **Detail from** *W. E. Cormack's redrawing of "Shanawdithit's Sketch Number IV,"* from The Beothucks or Red Indians, The Aboriginal Inhabitants of Newfoundland. *James P. Howley, 1915.*

  In 1828 Shanawdithit was made a ward of the Beothuk Institution where Cormack undertook her education and encouraged her drawings. In the winter of 1829 she made the maps and drawings that record the last days of the Beothuks. At the time, Shanawdithit herself was beginning her final decline. Suffering from tuberculosis, Shanawdithit died at St. Johns', Newfoundland, on June 6, 1829. Among the obituaries was one that appeared in the London *Times* reporting that Shanawdithit, "supposed to be the last of the Red Indians or Beothicks" had died. The obituary described the Beothuks as "the Aborigines of Newfoundland," and noted how they "presents an anomaly in the history of man. . . . a primitive nation, once claiming rank as a portion of the human race, who have lived, flourished, and become extinct in their orbit. They have been dislodged, and disappeared from the earth in their native independence in 1829, in as primitive a condition as they were before the discover of the New World."

  In addition to her maps, Shanawdithit made several drawings of Beothuk artifacts and

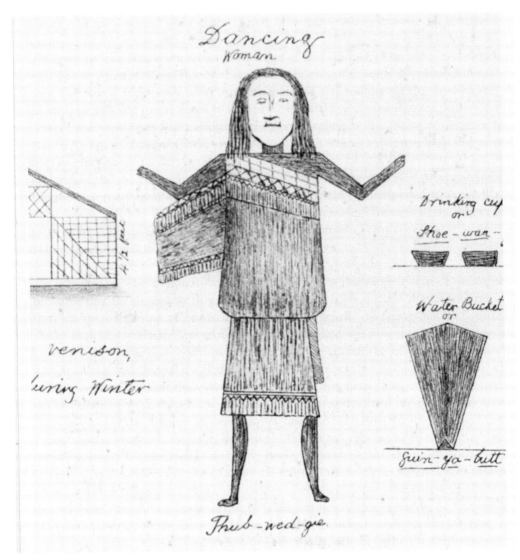

The handwritten labels on the figure read:

Dancing
Woman

Drinking cup
or
Shoe — wan —

Water Bucket
or

4 ½ feet

venison,
during Winter

Guin — ya — butt

Thub — ned — gie.

FIGURE 37. **W. E. Cormack's** *redrawing of "Dancing Woman," a detail from sketch VIII by Shanawdithit, 1829, from* The Beothucks or Red Indians, The Aboriginal Inhabitants of Newfoundland. *James P. Howley, 1915.*

aspects of life. This picture of a woman dancing (Figure 37) exhibits some of Shanawdithit's artistic abilities and is of ethnographic interest for the information it provides on Beothuk clothing. It is most moving, however, as a reflection of the life and culture of a people who's extinction became final upon the artist's death.

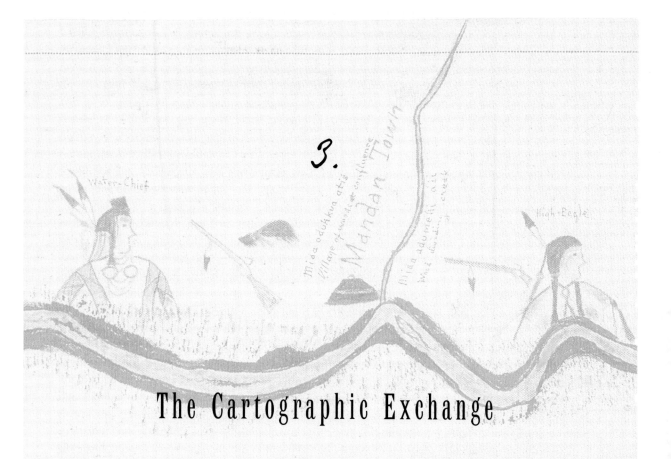

The Cartographic Exchange

T HE "CARTOGRAPHIC EXCHANGE" CONNOTES THE exchange of geographic information, trade goods, and military or political assistance that took place between Native American societies and the Europeans. Historically, this interchange was often a lopsided confiscation or acquisition of Native American land by the Europeans. But, in the middle of the eighteenth century, the exchange entered a phase of co-dependence and equality that culminated with the French and Indian War. This period was brought about by the need of France and England for Indian allies in their struggle for control of the eastern half of the continent. As the two colonial powers competed to gain the land, furs, and resources of the continent, Native

Americans used the conflict to gain political advantage for themselves. The maps presented here reveal the shifting allegiances and the military prowess with which Native Americans bartered their way to a position of power.

Native Americans are traditionally viewed as minor players in the European struggle for empire. Like the kneeling Indians bearing witness to the nobility of English arms in Benjamin West's painting of *The Death of General Wolfe,* Native Americans have been portrayed as suppliants and assistants in the inevitable hegemony of Great Britain. These maps, however, document more than the military reconnaissance Native Americans provided to the European allies; they hint at a Native American agenda, a well thought out sophisticated response to machinations of the colonial powers. Rooted in the traditions of Native American societies, this response differed from European strategies most markedly in it's individuality. Instead of the European kingdoms' monolithic drive for empire, Native American societies responded as individual groups, each seeking its own advantage. This disunity of purpose was only seldom overcome; more often it worked to the Native Americans' disadvantage as their tribal animosities brought them into conflict with each other and prevented the unified response necessary to repel the European invaders.

The maps Native Americans made for Europeans before and during the French and Indian War portray the conflict from their perspective. For the European powers, North America was only one theater in a global struggle for power. For Native Americans the outcome of this conflict was of crucial importance. Throughout the 1700s Native American participation in the international conflict made it a three-party struggle, with American Indians playing a central role in the battle over North America. Native American alliances and exchanges with the representatives of Great Britain and France were crucial to the success of each one's colonial enterprise. And Native American scouts and geographic information were essential for both the British and French military campaigns. Similarly, Native American fighters and their warrior traditions of pillage and torture were effectively used by both sides.

The American Indians' choice of whom they would form alliances with often shifted the balance of power in a region, and their involvement in military conflicts helped to determine the outcome of important battles. By exploiting the Europeans' desire for North America's natural resources, and their need for military allies and fighting men, native nations were able to insure their own survival. The introduction of European trade goods had created a dependence upon manufactured products among Native Americans, but they were far from naive or unsophisticated in their trading agreements. In the Southeast the Chickasaw Indians used their strategic location, and the English desire to have them serve as a counter to France's influence, to keep themselves well armed and unconquered. The League of the Iroquois used its diplomatic skills and trading empire to remain nominally neutral throughout the conflict while gaining advantages from both sides. Other tribes regularly switched sides to take advantage of European military protection or to get a better deal on trade goods.

The contest for North America took place along the borders of the European empires, and those Indians living in these regions were most closely involved in the struggle. In the Southeast, the area between the English colonies on the Atlantic and the French settlements east of the Mississippi River was home to tribes that allied themselves with both sides. In the Northeast, the Iroquois and their allies attempted to manage the conflict between the French in Canada and the English in their American colonies. In the interior of the continent, the conflict was for possession of the Ohio River Valley. It was here that the Native Americans' political agenda is most revealed. While Indians from the western Great Lakes knew only the intrusions of French traders and voyageurs, those living in the Ohio River Valley had experienced the takeover of their lands by the colonists. The question of who would control the land was of crucial importance, and the actions of the Native American nations reveal their strategies and concerns.

During the conflict, Native American groups asked both the English and French to keep their settlements out of the Ohio valley. And a guarantee of respect for the Native Americans' lands was often a condition of alliance. Without it, the Indian warriors would withdraw, resulting in drastic consequences for the both the English and the French. Finally, the English entered a treaty with many of the participating tribes that promised to divide the land between that belonging to the British colonies and that belonging to the Indians. According to this understanding, a line would be mapped down the Appalachian Mountains allocating the land to the west to the Indians. The cartographic exchange became an exchange of territory, a virtual redrawing of the North American map with two different traditions sharing the landscape. With this guarantee, the Native Americans withdrew from the conflict and allowed the superior numbers of English arms to take Canada from the French.

But the leaders of Britain and France felt no obligation to keep their word or respect the treaties they had written. Once the international conflict was settled and the cooperation of the native nations was no longer necessary, the political landscape of North America was once again transformed. The equal status Native Americans had enjoyed while their services were needed was no longer granted, and the promise of respect for the Native Americans' right to the land quickly gave way to policies that lead to the modern relationships between native nations and the United States.

In the century following the French and Indian War a similar exchange was conducted between Europeans and the peoples of the North American Arctic. During the sixteenth and seventeenth centuries the harsh and barren climate of the Arctic had discouraged European exploration and settlement. This protected the Eskimo and Inuit peoples through much of the first three centuries of the encounter. In the 1800s the newly triumphant British empire resumed the search for the Northwest Passage, once again sending European explorers to this region. Parry, Ross, and Franklin all made voyages of Arctic exploration. The knowledge and skills of the "Esquimaux," the Inuit-Inupiaq-speaking peoples of the central Arctic, contributed greatly to these voyages. The Eskimos' maps, based upon generations of thriving in the Arctic environment, helped to familiarize the explorers with the unknown land and fill in the blanks on the European map of the continent.

This exchange took place on two levels. At one level the Eskimos exchanged skins, furs, geographic information, and their labor for European trade goods and alcohol. At another level this nineteenth-century encounter set the stage for an intellectual transition. Because there was little immediate European desire for the lands or resources of the Arctic, there was no need to project a savage image upon the native inhabitants. Consequently, Eskimos were viewed benignly as a different, albeit primitive, culture that could be observed and studied. And, while the early-nineteenth-century explorers suffered from the ethnocentrism that is still too common in western culture, they nevertheless cataloged and inventoried the Eskimo cultures with a thoroughness and curiosity that was absent in earlier records of the encounter. Parry's description of the Iglulik peoples he encountered still provides basic information on Eskimo culture and the ingenious ways in which they exploited their environment.

Through the balance of the century, Eskimos continued to acquire European goods, but neither in the abundance nor in the form of technologies that fundamentally changed their way of life. By 1883, when Franz Boas conducted his study of the Baffinland Eskimos, nearly all the peoples of the Arctic had probably had some exposure——if only in the form of disease——to the whalers and traders who regularly visited the region, but they maintained their lives in much the same way as they had for centuries. The exchange between these people and the fledgling anthropologist helped to establish a new paradigm for the study of other cultures. The Baffinland Eskimos provided Boas with a detailed picture of their culture, an exchange in which they probably did not receive goods of equal value. But Boas's subsequent description of Eskimo culture helped to establish some of the central tenets of modern anthropology. Together Boas and his Native American informants charted an intellectual map that would transform the way in which we look at other peoples. In freely giving this cultural information, the Baffinland Eskimos, and many other Native American societies, have contributed to our understanding of cultural variability as an essential part of the human condition.

(Figure 38) is a copy of a map made by an unidentified southeast Indian Cacique or head man. Like the Catawba map (Figure 30) the original was painted on a deer skin and presented to Francis Nicholson when he was governor of the South Carolina Colony. The map is now in the North American Colonies collection of the Public Records Office in London.

The map is a highly complex picture of the political landscape of southeastern North America as Native Americans, French, Spanish, and English powers began nearly a century of struggle. Covering over seven hundred thousand square miles, the map uses Native American cartographic symbols to represent an area extending from the southeastern Atlantic and Gulf coasts to west of the Mississippi River and north to the Ohio River Valley and western New York State. For centuries Indian trade and diplomatic missions had crisscrossed this area. By the beginning of the eighteenth century, traders from both the English and French colonies were also selling their wares to many of the Indians in this region. Their European goods were exchanged for skins, slaves, and the loyalty of Indian allies. As these manufactured trade goods made their way through the native economic network, they helped to transform the native cultures, who developed a dependency on the goods and the good will of the European invaders just as surely as the Europeans depended upon the skills and good will of the Native Americans.

The map is a significant cultural document. The native mapmaker employed an indigenous graphic system of circles, lines, and alternating scales to portray his knowledge of the physical and social geography of nearly a quarter of the continent. It paints an American Indian picture of the politics of colonial North America. Because the language used on the map is from a Muskhogean dialect similar to that spoken by the Chickasaws and Choctaws, and because the "Chickasaw Nation" is pictured in the middle of the map, the map is believed to be of Chickasaw origin. By the time the map was made, the Chickasaws had firmly established themselves along the watershed of the Tombigbee River in what is now northeastern Mississippi and northern Alabama. They were central figures in the network of trade and communications that is pictured on the map and maintained contacts as far apart as Nebraska and the Carolina coast. The Chickasaws' com-

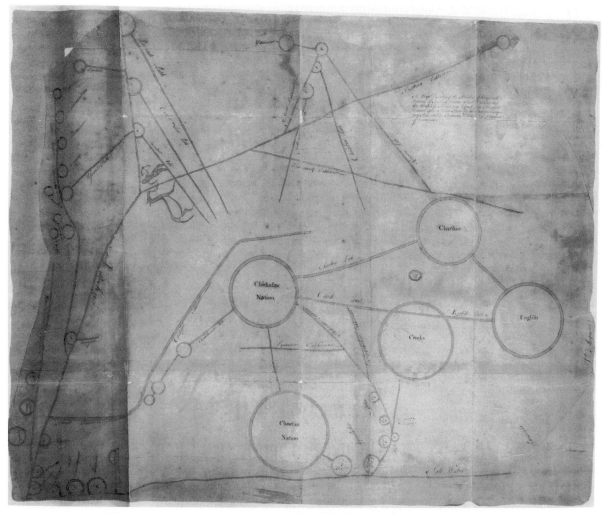

FIGURE 38. **A Map** *describing the Situation of the several Nations of Indians between South Carolina and the Massisipi; was Copied from a Draught Drawn upon a Deer Skin by an Indian Cacique and Presented to Francis Nicholson Esqr. Governour of Carolina, c. 1723. Size of the original 45 x 57 inches (114 x 145 cm). Courtesy of the Public Record Office, London [CO 700/6(2)].*

munication with the South Carolina Colony is noted in the circle labeled "English" and the "Creek and English Path." It was in their outposts along the Savannah River that the Chickasaws were visited by Governor Nicholson when he wished to establish diplomatic relations. And, it may have been at one of these villages that the original of this map was presented. It was also in these villages that trade and economic agreements were made between the English and the Chickasaws. The Chickasaws would bring skins and Indian slaves to the Charleston markets to exchange for English guns and trade goods.

According to Chickasaw mythology, they first came to this region in response to a religious vision. Strategically located along the trading and communications routes that connected the South, the Northeast, the Great Lakes, and the Mississippi River, the Chickasaws became an important power in the region. Though smaller than their powerful neighbors, the Choctaws and the Cherokees, Chickasaw warriors were known as the best and fiercest fighters, relentlessly exacting a toll on anyone who attacked them. In 1541 they drove de Soto's men out of the Southeast, and for the next two-and-a-half centuries they remained an unconquered people, defeating the Indians, French, and Spanish forces that attempted to subdue them.

The map can be read on several levels. First, its geographic content is testimony to the extensive Native American networks. Beginning at the bottom of the map is the Gulf Coast of the United States, indicated by "Salt Water," from the mouth of the Mississippi to the Spanish settlement at Pensacola in the lower right corner. The South Carolina Colony with its capital of Charleston is represented by the "English" circle, and the circle in the upper right represents the Seneca Indians in western New York. The river routes and paths connecting these far flung points are shown, beginning with the Mississippi River on the left side of the map. The confluence of the Ohio is represented near the figure of an Indian hunting and leading a horse. The Ohio River continues across the top of the map to its source in the east while the Tennessee River is represented as a diagonal extending southeast to the territory of the Cherokees ("Charikee"). The Wabash River is shown joining the Ohio from the northeast providing access to the Miami Indians who are represented by the circle in the center at the top of the map.

The Mississippi River and several tributaries are spread out across the left side of the map. At the very top a circle represents the Peoria Indians along the upper Illinois River, and the Mississippi, labeled "Massasippe River," continues down to the Gulf where several of the smaller tribes living in French Louisiana are noted. Extending west (up, on the map) from the Mississippi are first the Red River, on which some of the Caddo tribes of Oklahoma and Texas are represented, and the Arkansas River showing the Chickasaws' regular contacts with Plains Indian tribes like the Comanches and Whichitas. Chickasaw traders and warriors were known to range beyond the bounds of this map, with Chickasaw contacts recorded among Pacific Coast tribes and the Indians of Mexico.

In the center and lower right of the map, and at a much larger scale, the mapmaker portrayed the Chickasaws' strategic position in the Southeast. The Yazoo River extends towards the center from the Mississippi, and the Chickasaws' connections to the English in South Carolina, the Cherokees in Tennessee, the Creeks in Alabama, and the Choctaws ("Choctau") south of them in Mississippi are depicted with the paths and communications routes. The political landscape is also emphasized. The Tombigbee River extends from the Chickasaws' territory southeast between the Creeks and the Choctaws, and down to the Mobile River where it joins the Gulf. The French had established their colonial center at Mobile and the Choctaws were allied with the French, as were many of the tribes along the lower Tombigbee and Mobile rivers. The mapmaker indicated their allegiance with an "F" in the circles that represent these tribes.

The French had hoped to keep the Chickasaws within their network of Indian alliances, but the Chickasaws turned towards the cheaper and more plentiful goods offered by the English traders. The politics of the European powers required loyalty in military as well as economic matters, and the Chickasaws' change of trading allegiance meant that they were now the enemies of New France. The circles with the "F"s that indicate French allies continue to the south and across to the Mississippi River, and they extend up the Mississippi, Illinois, and Wabash rivers and their tributaries. The map effectively portrays the independent Chickasaws as a nation surrounded on three sides by the enemy.

Religion and the spiritual life permeated Chickasaw culture. Their customs required the strict observance of rituals that helped bring cohesion to Chickasaw life. Chickasaw clan structure, agricultural practices, the rituals of the hunt, and most of all the rituals of war and raiding parties were part of how the Chickasaws kept themselves and their people in balance. The warrior's life was the highest calling for Chickasaw males. Their military prowess, readiness to fight, and dogged insistence upon revenge made Chickasaw warriors respected and feared throughout the region. It was their warrior traditions that kept the Chickasaws an unconquered people, and the decline of the Chickasaws only came when the warriors' continuum was broken. At the time of this map, however, and for the rest of the eighteenth century, the Chickasaws were at the height of their power, a proud and independent people afraid of no one.

In 1702 the Governor of French Louisiana met with the Chickasaws and urged them to end their war with the Choctaws and reject the influence of the English. If not, the French threatened to arm the Chickasaws' enemies. In return for agreeing to these conditions the French offered the Chickasaws protection, French trade goods, and missionaries. The Chickasaws agreed to the French-imposed peace, and to trade with the French, but they wanted nothing to do with the Bishop of Quebec and his missionaries.

But the French did not build the forts they had promised and only a few traders visited the Chickasaw. English traders rushed in to fill the void and quickly built up a brisk business with the Chickasaws. While the French took them for granted, the English were making a concerted attempt to win the Chickasaws over, and the tribe moved closer to the English. The final straw came when the French proved unable to prevent the Choctaws from attacking Chickasaw trading parties. The Choctaw attacks cut the Chickasaws off from the French trading center at Mobile, and in 1711 the Chickasaws formally excused themselves from their agreement with the French and officially began trading with the English.

Despite the split, the first formal conflicts between the French and the Chickasaw did not occur for nearly a decade. In the intervening years the Chickasaws and English intermingled and some of the English traders married into the tribe. These mixed-blood families had an advantage in trading with the Europeans. As the Chickasaws became more and more dependent on European goods, these families gained power outside the traditional Chickasaw hierarchy. In addition, the Chickasaws' growing reliance on trade goods began to change their subsistence patterns. Hunters had to search farther and farther afield for skins and slaves to trade with the English. Inter-tribal warfare increased as the Chickasaws fought to gain larger hunting grounds and more captives. To get their slaves, the Chickasaws began to raid among the smaller tribes under the French domain. They struck up into Illinois country and among the Weas and Piankasaws on the Wabash River, and they raided west of the Mississippi along the Red and Arkansas rivers.

The Chickasaws brought their captives to be sold in the slave markets of Charleston, where they were shipped off to the West Indies. The English engaged in this human traffic with the reasoning that every Indian slave was just one less Indian the French could arm and send against them. The French responded by offering a bounty for Chickasaw captives and selling them in turn to the French West Indies.

The first French–Chickasaw war began when the Chickasaws executed a Frenchman who had been living among them as a spy. They subsequently attacked French settlements and French supply boats coming down the Mississippi. For nearly four years the Chickasaws effectively cut the French lifeline to Louisiana and captured many French prisoners in the process——prisoners that the Chickasaws exchanged at the price of a good horse for each European. The French struck back with their Choctaw mercenaries, but this only slowed the Chickasaws' trade with the English. Consequently the English, who wanted to keep their profitable commerce with the Chickasaws and who had an eye for expanding their trade to the Choctaws, initiated a peace between the tribes.

This English diplomatic effort, in which both the English and the Chickasaws attempted to turn the Choctaws from their allegiance to the French, struck at the very heart of France's control of Louisiana. In order to stop the spread of English influence the French also made peace with the Chickasaws. Around this time the original of this map (Figure 38) was presented to the English governor. The Chickasaws' strategic position, pictured on the map, was not lost on the English. Chickasaw diplomatic and military skills were crucial to the British goal of gaining control of the Ohio and Mississippi river valleys. A contemporary British military report noted the Chickasaws' ability to control the water routes between New Orleans and Canada, and that they were "expert Horsemen . . . the best Hunters; and without Exception . . . the best Warriors." In the political maneuvering of the 1720s the Chickasaw continued to upset French shipping on the Mississippi, and they worked with the English to entice "French" Indians over to the British side.

In 1729 the Natchez Indians, encouraged by the Chickasaw, attacked two French garrisons. The outraged French enlisted their Choctaw allies to help them retaliate with a campaign of extermination against the Natchez. They attacked the Natchez villages, killing several times more of the Natchez than the number of French killed in the Natchez raids. The surviving Natchez fled to the Chickasaws. The French demanded that the Natchez be surrendered, but the Chickasaws refused. A standoff ensued, the French and the Choctaws blockading the Chickasaw towns while Chickasaw and Natchez warriors harassed the French trade.

Between 1732 and 1736 these raids and counterraids made the Chickasaws an unwelcome presence among the French and their Indian allies. In 1736 the French governor assembled two armies in a campaign to wipe out the Chickasaws. One army of over twelve hundred moved up the Tombigbee from Mobile. Another, composed partly of Illinois, Miami, and Iroquois Indians came down from Illinois territory. When this northern group attacked the Chickasaws' palisaded town of Chocolissa, the Chickasaws cut the French to pieces. The Indian fighters fled and most of the French soldiers were killed or captured and executed. The victorious Chickasaws captured the abandoned French military supplies and quickly turned them against the French army advancing from the south.

The southern army attempted to capture the Chickasaw towns west of the Tombigbee River. Here the Chickasaws caught the French in a crossfire and drove them back with heavy losses. The French blamed their defeat on the Chickasaw marksmen, whom the French Governor wrote, "have the advantage of shooting more accurately than perhaps any other nation."

This defeat only strengthened the French desire to eliminate the Chickasaws. In 1739 the French Governor, Bienville, once again attempted to restore the honor of France by destroying the Chickasaws. The French had prepared for the battle ever since their defeat three years earlier. They built roads and forts to bring in their armies and weapons, and they sent Alabama Indian scouts to observe the Chickasaws' defenses. Finally, in the autumn of 1739, the French assembled 3,600 men above the Chickasaw towns, where a stalemate ensued when the routes proved impassable. To end the impasse Governor Bienville called a council with the Chickasaws, where they ended hostilities and exchanged prisoners. The Chickasaws claimed that the surviving Natchez Indians had fled and the French did not press the point. Subsequently the French commanders decided that they could not march against the Chickasaw towns without exposing the King's honor to defeat. To the disdain of the Chickasaw warriors, the French withdrew. The sight of such a large force giving up without a fight reverberated through France's Indian allies. One officer wrote, "Now they will treat us as women, and in a way they will be right."

Following this defeat, Bienville lost his job as governor of Louisiana. And for the next twenty years, until the French lost their North American colonies at the end of the Seven Years War, a small core of Chickasaw and Natchez warriors continued to harass the French and their Indian allies. In the treaty of Paris the French turned over Louisiana to the Spanish, who nominally administered the region until after the American Revolution. During the Revolutionary War, the Chickasaws again benefited from their warrior traditions. As allies of the British, they fought against both Spanish and colonial American forces. By 1780 the Spanish had captured all of the British settlements in the Southeast except the unconquerable Chickasaws.

After the Revolution, the Chickasaws made peace with the United States and lived under their protection. Their homelands were whittled away to just a small section of northern Mississippi and Alabama, and the Chickasaws suffered a loss of traditions and cultural identity similar to that of many Native American groups who attempted to live with the white man. In 1837, as part of the policy of Indian removal, they marched west to the territory they were given in Oklahoma, one of the last tribes to be removed from their southeastern homeland.

(Figure 39) This map is a copy of one made by the Alabama Indian identified as the Captain of Pakana (an Alabama village). Following their disastrous defeat in 1736, the French entered a three-year stalemate with the Chickasaws. Surrounded by enemies, the Chickasaws continued to raid the French and their neighbors. The French retaliated with counterattacks by their Indian mercenaries. The Alabama Indians, who lived in the same region as the Chickasaws, were allied to the French and employed to serve both as emissaries and spies. In June of 1737, the French enlisted the Captain of Pakana to meet with the Chickasaw and negotiate the release of two French captives.

Upon his return to the French camp the Captain of Pakana is believed to have made the original of this map. Using cartographic conventions similar to those employed by the Chickasaws, the Alabama Indian's map provides a succinct picture of the Chickasaws' fortifications and positions. Circles are used to indicate the ten Chickasaw and one Natchez village the Indian observed and the connections between them are shown by the double-lined paths. Additional information includes the location of bayous, paths, and fields in the area of the Chickasaw towns, and the routes and encampments of the previous French campaign. Also noted are the number of warriors in each of the towns.

This information would have been crucial to the French as they planned to retaliate for their earlier defeat. The map is an example of the Europeans' dependence on Native American infor-

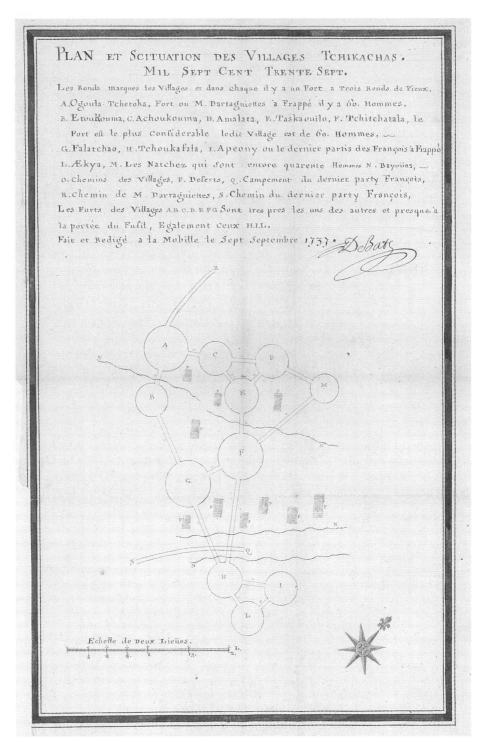

FIGURE 39. **Plan et** *Scituation des Villages Tchikachas, 1737. Courtesy of the Archives Nationales, Paris.*

Another America

mation, and of the Native Americans' willingness to exchange this information, regardless of whether it concerned white settlers or fellow Indians, for trade goods and military security. The importance of the map is indicated by its being redrawn and annotated by the French engineer Alexander de Batz, who then sent it back to France. It is de Batz's copy that has survived. This copy corresponds closely to the Indian account, and the map is probably accurate to the original except for the addition of the notes, scale, and compass point. The Chickasaws' fortifications, described as palisade forts surrounded by three rows of posts—and the Chickasaws' reputation as marksmen who would make their bullets count on any French or Indians approaching through the surrounding fields—proved too intimidating for Governor Bienville and the French forces when they prepared to attack once more in 1739. The French tactical retreat left the Chickasaws unconquered throughout the French and Indian war.

The story of the map also provides insight into the ambiguous nature of Native American–European relations in the eighteenth century. According to the Captain of Pakana, the Chickasaw war chief that he met with during his visit proposed that the Captain inform the French of the Chickasaws' desire for peace, and then that the two of them combine their forces to attack one of their smaller Indian neighbors. Whether this was a dodge used to further ingratiate the Alabamas with the French, or a true report of the Chickasaws' intentions cannot be verified. But the wariness with which Native Americans viewed their European allies may be reflected in the deadpan conclusion of the Captain of Pakana's report: "There is nothing left for me to do but to tell you about what their situation and their forces are, according to what I saw myself. I was in ten villages and I saw the one of the Natchez, which made an eleventh. The Chickasaws told me that there were two other forts. . . . but I did not see them. In each village there is a fort with three rows of posts and no earth in between."

(Figure 40) attributed to the Indian, Chegeree, presents a mixture of the Native American and European perceptions of what is now part of the northeast United States. The line work depicting the system of rivers and the location of settlements is very probably in the hand of the Indian identified as Chegeree. The notes, names, distances, and annotations on the map are in the hand of an unidentified English interlocutor who evidently hoped to obtain as much information as he could from Chegeree. The time, place, or circumstances of their exchange is not recorded, but its purpose can be found in the two pages of notes posted with the map on the right. These notes and the other English annotations concentrate on the locations and strengths of the French and their Indians allies. At the time, the area represented on the map was still Indian territory, although both the English and the French understood its strategic importance as they prepared to expand their North American empires.

The map begins on the left with the middle Mississippi River entering the map horizontally. A tributary extends toward the bottom of the map into the southeast where the settlements of the Chickasaws are noted. At the junction of the Mississippi and the Ohio rivers, the mapmaker turns the Mississippi abruptly to the right and continues it toward the top of the paper into Illinois territory. The Ohio River then continues across the map with Lake Erie represented to the northeast (upper right) where the English annotator added compass directions.

Continuing along the Ohio, the next major tributaries are the Tennessee, shown dipping down into the southeast, and the Wabash (called "Wowayoughtan" on the map), which forms a

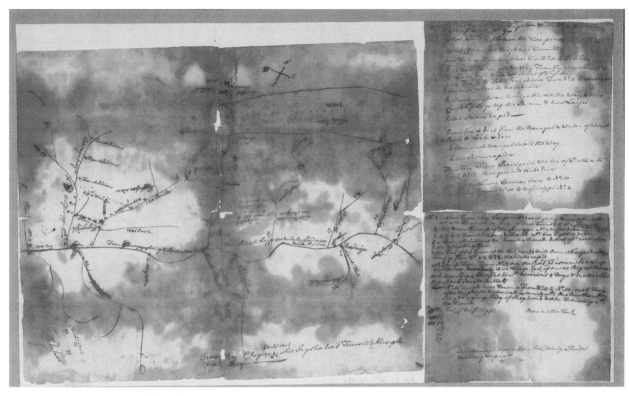

FIGURE 40. Map of *the Country about the Mississippi Drawn by Chegeree [the Indian] who Says he has Traveled through the Country, c. 1755. Size of the original 16 ¼ x 13 inches (41.3 x 33 cm). Courtesy of the Geography and Map Division, Library of Congress.*

northeast diagonal leading up to the unnamed Maumee River that flows into the western end of Lake Erie. Further east the Miami River joins the Ohio forming another link to Lake Erie. Two unidentified rivers enter from the north before the Ohio splits at what are labeled the "French Forks" and the Monongahela is depicted going towards the southeast, while the Allegheny continues north and east, its branches going towards Lake Erie and in the direction of Lake Ontario.

The map covers the northeast United States from the Middle Mississippi to what is now western Pennsylvania, and records the Native Americans' detailed knowledge of this region. Ethnographically, this area included Southeastern Indians, Illinois Indians, Miamis, Shawnees, Delawares, Iroquois, and the many others who were streaming into the region to escape the advancing colonies. All of these groups were being simultaneously courted by the French, who wished to maintain their control over Canada and the river systems that connected them to Louisiana; and by the English, who wished to expand their trade with these Indians, gain control of the rich fur trade coming in from the Northwest, and eventually expand their settlements into the Ohio Valley.

The forks of the Ohio served as the gateway to the lands west of the Appalachian mountains. The meeting of the Monongahela, Allegheny, and Ohio rivers would be the scene of repeat-

Another America

ed conflicts between the English and French. Chegeree not only gave his questioner this map but he also provided a picture of the political landscape with information that reveals a little of the Native American perceptions as well.

It is possible that Chegeree was a Miami, or Twightwee, Indian. The information on the map and the accompanying notes concentrate on the Twightwees, the English name for the Miamis, and the Miamis had a history of going back and forth between the French and the English trading posts. A knowledgeable Miami would be in a good position to give his English inquisitors the detailed information shown on the map. And one can easily imagine the Indian sitting with an earnest English officer going over the lines on the paper and confirming the names, distances and locations as the soldier put them down. The map can be related to the history of the Miami Indians and the part the French and the English colonial conflicts played in their lives.

Miami Indians migrated into the area of the Wabash and Maumee rivers around the beginning of the eighteenth century. They had been in contact with the French since the early 1700s, when the French sponsored a peace council between the Algonquian-speaking tribes in what is now Wisconsin and Illinois (including the Miamis) and the Iroquois. This French peace made it possible for the Miamis to migrate east. At the same time Shawnees, Delawares, and Wyandot Indians were moving west out of the areas controlled by the English and the Iroquois. Still tied to the English trading network, these eastern Indians established settlements along the Ohio and its tributaries south of Lake Erie. This put the Miamis on the edge of French influence in the Ohio valley and in touch with Indians who had ties to the English. The importance the French placed upon their alliance with the Miamis was such that they tried persuading the Miamis to move north to Fort Detroit. The Miamis refused and the French eventually built posts at Vincennes on the Wabash River and Fort Miami near the headwaters of the Maumee River to keep the Miamis supplied with French goods.

The Miamis consisted of three related groups; the Piankashaws who settled along the lower Wabash River, the Weas on the middle Wabash, and the Miamis who established their villages on the headwaters of the Maumee River. The Miami group kept the council fire at their village. Although each band maintained a certain amount of autonomy, there was a common tribal identity. Miami culture and technology included the planting of corn and other crops. They hunted, gathered, and fished, and led their warriors on raids as far south as the Chickasaw territory. The Miamis were a proud and independent people and they worked to their own advantage in the forthcoming international conflict. But they had also become dependent on European trade goods. The introduction of manufactured tools and clothing, of guns and alcohol, changed the Miami economy, and the intermarriage of Miamis and French Canadians upset the Miami traditions.

The English term for the Miamis, "Twightwee," was an interpretation of the Miamis' word for themselves which is the cry of the crane. The Twightwee towns were located at the head of the Maumee River (located southwest of Lake Erie) and down the Wabash to its junction with the Ohio (at number "10" on the map). The notes accompanying the map relate that there are six Twightwee towns. "All in Amity with each other they are a Very Large Body of People and not in Friendship with the French." This may refer to the continued English effort to gain influence over the Miamis, thereby gaining their trade and allegiance in the struggle for the Ohio valley.

The map shows the Miamis' strategic location. To the west of them on the Mississippi and along the Illinois rivers (labeled "Cahtagahaga") are the towns of "French Indians," probably the

Cahokias, Kaskaskias, Peorias, and other Illinois Indians who remained firmly within the French influence. The notes accompanying the map reveal the English concern about this potential source of enemy warriors. Numbers "1" through "6" are described as towns of Indians and French and the number of fighting men in each one is assessed. To the east of the Miamis, near the junction of the Miami River (number "16") and the Ohio River were the Shawnee villages, an area frequented by English traders. This exposed the Miamis to the cheaper and better quality English goods. The area east of the Shawnee villages was claimed by both the English and French. The French built their forts around Lake Ontario and claimed the area as part of New France, while the English established a trading post at Cuyahoga along the southern shore of Lake Erie where Cleveland now stands. The English later extended their trade to Logstown ("Logs T" on the map) along the Ohio River just west of the "French Forks."

Within this contested territory the Miamis lived at the frontier of both imperial powers. From about 1720 on, the French were having a difficult time maintaining their control over the Ohio Valley and Louisiana. The Chickasaws successfully interrupted the French traffic on the Mississippi, and the French attempts to make allies of the Indians migrating into the Ohio valley from New England were only marginally successful. As the French ability to meet the Miamis' needs diminished, the Miamis began trading with the English. By the 1740s the Miami had been in contact with the English for over a decade and found they no longer needed to wait for the French traders to get around to bringing the goods they desired. In 1747 la Demoiselle, a chief of the Piankashaw–Miamis, moved his village west of the Miami River to the proximity of the Shawnees, where he set up regular trade with the English. Pickawillany, as the village came to be called, quickly expanded to become a major trading center in the Ohio Valley. The British recognized la Demoiselle as the "Great King of the Miamis" threatening the French relationship with the tribe.

In 1748 the Miamis at Pickawillany sent a delegation to an English treaty council in Lancaster, Pennsylvania. There, under the sponsorship of the Shawnees and with the consent of the Iroquois, the Miamis allied themselves with the English and joined the Covenant Chain. Alliance with the English meant alliance with the Iroquois and accepting the condition of their supposed dominance over the Covenant Chain——although in reality this meant little to the Miami who, along with the other western tribes, now outnumbered the League of the Iroquois. Joining the Covenant Chain also meant embracing the treaties and land claims that the English recognized, including the treaty between the English and the Iroquois that would later be used as proof of the English claim for all of the Ohio Valley.

In exchange for the Miamis' and Shawnees' promise to protect their pack trains, the English promised to send traders to the western tribes. Pickawillany grew and Indians from other Miami bands migrated to the village. This English incursion infuriated the French, who tried first diplomacy and then military action to regain their influence over the Miamis. Hostilities grew over the next few years with raids and counterraids. But the Miamis held their own, maintaining Pickawillany as an important trading center and helping to spread the English influence among the Indians living along the Wabash River. In 1752 a party of Nipissing Indians led by a mixed-blood French trader successfully captured Pickawillany, killing and capturing both Miami Indians and British traders. In the battle, la Demoiselle was killed and the victorious French Indians feasted on his remains. The destruction of Pickawillany is an example of the effect the brewing

Another America

French–British conflict had on the Native American nations. After Pickawillany, the British were once again cut off from trading on the western Ohio, while the Miami, still in need of European trade goods, turned their allegiance back to the French.

This map was probably made sometime after the destruction of Pickawillany. It is not pictured near the Shawnee towns on the Ohio. Following this incident the French continued to exert their authority over the region, building forts towards the eastern end of Lake Erie in what is now Pennsylvania (indicated on the map with "French" along the southeastern shore of Lake Erie). In 1754, the English moved to reassert their influence by building a fort at the forks of the Ohio. When the French heard of this they immediately marched on the fort and accepted the English surrender. The French promptly began building their own fort in place of the English one. They erected Fort Duquesne at the forks of the Ohio and Monongahela rivers——the "French Forks" on Chegeree's map, and the site of the next major battle between the French and the English as they built toward the Seven Years War.

The Miamis no longer played an important role in the conflicts between the English and the French, but by the war's end they had been changed forever. The Miamis had decreased to less than half their numbers, and intermarriage with Europeans and their growing dependence on European goods had changed the structure of their tribe. By the middle of the next century the Miamis had sold most of their land in Indiana and Illinois and migrated first to Kansas and then Oklahoma. There the Wea and Piankashaw bands of Miamis lost their identities when they merged with the Peoria. The Miamis confederated with the Peoria into the tribal organization that is recognized today. Other of the Miamis remained in Indiana where they still maintain a tribal identity.

An endorsement at the bottom of the notes accompanying Chegeree's map reveals the callous attitude of both the English and the French toward their so-called Indian allies. Regardless of what economic advantage or military service the Indians might provide, they were only important in so far as they furthered the imperial aims of the European powers. Below the notes the annotator has written, "Christianize Indians their Friendship – Trade Extending Empire –"

"A Draft of the Ohio From an Indian Account" (Figure 41) is from the papers of Lieutenant Colonel Thomas Gage, who would go on to become the commander of British forces during the Revolutionary War. Like Chegeree's map, this map was probably part of the British reconnaissance of the Ohio Valley. The map concentrates on the Ohio River south of Lake Erie. From east to west the settlements of Delawares, Shawnees ("Shawanese"), and members of the League of the Iroquois are shown. Along the left side of the map the Twightwees (Miamis) are noted at the site that had been Pickawillany. The explanation accompanying it notes that the village had been "destroyed 3 years ago by the French."

By the middle of the eighteenth century the Ohio Valley was the focus of both French and English attentions. Although still largely Indian country, the two imperial powers saw this area as key to expanding their trade with the Indians and controlling the influx of furs and other goods from the interior. To the land-hungry British colonists this was also the area where their settlements could expand, and they could gain access to the fertile farm lands of North America's interior.

From a strategic point of view, whoever controlled the junction of the Monongahela and

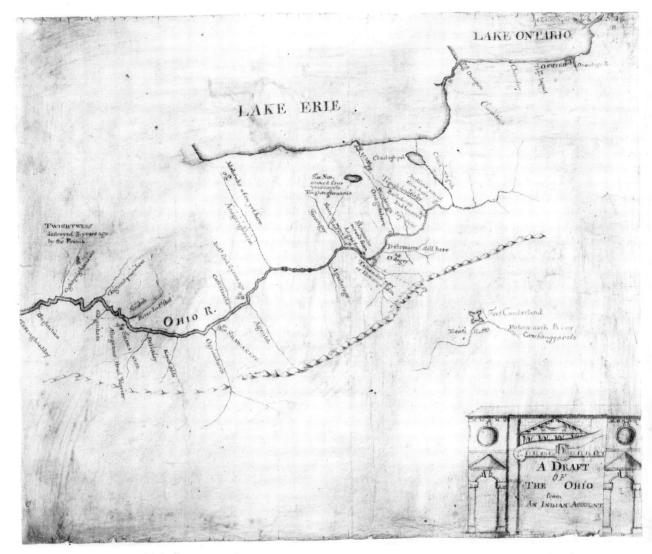

FIGURE 41. "A Draft *of the Ohio From an Indian Account*" *c. 1755. Size of the original 17 x 14 inches (42.5 x 34.9 cm). Gage Papers, Courtesy of the William L. Clements Library, University of Michigan.*

Allegheny rivers could control the entire Ohio Valley. The French wanted this control as a vital link between their colonies in Canada and Louisiana. The English wanted this control as a means of enforcing their claim on the continent's interior. The forks of the Ohio, shown on the "Copy of a sketch of the Monongahela" (Figure 43), with Fort Duquesne, built by the French in 1754, snuggled between the Ohio and Monongahela, was the site of several battles for control of the region. This map, by an unidentified mapmaker and based upon the report of an Indian who scouted for the British, records General Edward Braddock's defeat when he attacked Fort Duquesne in 1755. Braddock's defeat has gone down in history, and much has been written about

Another America

FIGURE 42.
"Paccane, a *Miami Man,*" a *western etching representing a Miami Indian with the traditional roach haircut and decorations. The etching was done between 1790 and 1796 by Elizabeth Simcoe, wife of the Lieutenant Governor of upper Canada. (Simcoe Family papers F47-11-1-0-287) Archives of Ontario, Toronto.*

the mistakes and twists of fate that lead to the failure of British arms on this occasion. The battle served as a proving ground for several Revolutionary War heroes including George Washington and Thomas Gage, and Benjamin Franklin gave his diplomatic career a spur when he helped to organize supplies for the campaign. But the actions of another group has been little recorded. The Native Americans who participated in the battle and those who decided to stay out and let the imperialists do their own fighting, were central to the outcome. Their actions reflect the policies of the third American presence that participated in the colonial wars of England and France.

The map shows the Ohio River on the left (actually the junction of the Ohio and the Allegheny) with the Monongahela flowing into it from across the page. The twists and turns of

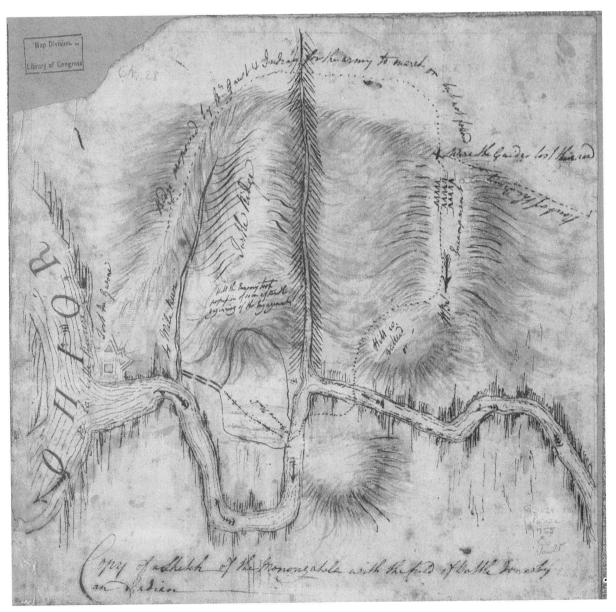

FIGURE 43. Copy of *a sketch of the Monongahela, with the field of battle, done by an Indian, c. 1755. Size of the original 10.6 x 10.2 inches (27 x 26 cm). Courtesy of the Geography and Map Division, Library of Congress.*

the Monongahela are noted. The small river flowing into the Monongahela near the center of the map is Turtle Creek. On the far right the "Route of the Army" is represented as a dashed line approaching the area. This "route" was the road Braddock's forces built to transport the supplies and artillery with which he planned to besiege Fort Duquesne. On July 8, 1755, the army camped within ten miles of the fort and their encampment is represented with tents. According to a survivor's memoirs the general had been informed of the dangerous narrows surrounding Turtle Creek, and the track of the army, continued as a dotted line going south, can be seen crossing the river twice in order to avoid this dangerous defile. By the afternoon of July 9, two detachments of British soldiers had crossed the river and the general ordered them to advance. They encountered the French and their Indian allies along the narrow road. The battle began with volleys exchanged, and the Indians, using tactics they had honed through years of forest warfare, quickly dispersed to the surrounding hills and trees, symbolized on the map by the "Hill the Enemy took possession of soon after the beginning of the engagement." From the surrounding forest the Indians poured their fire on the soldiers, and the British went down to a bitter defeat.

The Indians who participated with the French in this battle were largely "Far Indians"——Potawatomis and Ottawas from west of the Great Lakes who had yet to perceive the threat posed by the ambitions of the English and the French. Fighting for the French kept them in favor as trading partners, and in keeping with their warrior traditions they were given free reign to plunder the supplies, possessions, and even bodies of the enemies they defeated. These "Far Indians" were joined at the last minute by parties of Ohio Indians, Shawnees, Delawares, Mingos (a western mixture of some of the Iroquois tribes) and Miamis who were fighting to keep their land. To them the British, whom they had previously offered to help, presented a great enough threat that they were willing to enter the battle on the side of the French and stop the English advance.

For the British and French the events leading to the Seven Years War in America were about who controlled the land. For the Indians the vital issue was who would respect *their* rights to the land. In 1744 the Iroquois had ceded all claims to any lands within the colony of Virginia and recognized the right and title of "our sovereign the King of Great Britain to all the lands within the said colony as it is now or hereafter may be peopled and bounded by his said Majesty . . . his heirs and successors." The colonists did not explain that this included all the land as it was described in Virginia's royal charter, with boundaries extending from sea to sea. The British intentions had always been to expand throughout the continent, and shortly after this treaty the Virginia colony began to plan settlements on the other side of the Appalachian Mountains.

English and French traders had already been active in the Ohio Valley for several decades, and while their wares were welcome, the settlements and colonists that followed in the wake of the trading posts were not. When the French started erecting their forts along the southern shore of Lake Erie, the Mingo Iroquois living at Cuyahoga came to ask them to leave. Tanaghrisson, leading the Mingo warriors, laid claim to the Ohio Valley and forbade the French to advance, telling them, "I desire you to withdraw, as I have done our Brothers the English; for I will keep you at Arms length: I lay this down as a Trial for both, to see which will have the greatest Regard to it, and that Side we will stand by, and make equal Sharers with us."

But Tanaghrisson's demands were diluted by the disunity among the Indian tribes. Where one group may wish to drive the Europeans out, the other welcomed their presence and the advantages in trade that good relations brought. The French countered that the Ohio Valley belonged to the French king by the right of discovery. They continued to build their forts. The English responded to this French move by beginning to build their own fort at the forks of the Ohio. In the spring of 1754 the French attacked the unfinished English fort, took possession, and completed it as Fort Duquesne pictured on the map.

The French remained at Fort Duquesne and in control of the Ohio Valley when General Braddock arrived in North America the following February. He had been appointed commander in chief of the British forces in North America. His aim was to assert British authority over the Ohio Valley and the other territories it claimed. Braddock declared that he would personally lead the assault on Fort Duquesne and he was determined to enlist the colonies' help, both financial and material, to further the empire's aims. Braddock's cavalier attitude towards the colonial governments may have helped set the stage for their later rebellion, but it was his disregard for the abilities and interests of the American Indians that led to his downfall. Braddock commissioned William Johnson of New York as the Superintendent of Indian Affairs and requested that he supply Indians to help in the wilderness campaign. Johnson sent Mingo warriors, who brought their families with them to Braddock's camp. The Indian women quickly proved too popular with the officers and enlisted men for Braddock's puritanical blood. He ordered the women home, and the Mingo warriors went with them.

A chief of the Mingos described Braddock as full of "pride and ignorance . . . he looked upon us as dogs, and would never hear anything what was said to him." Braddock's disdain for the Indians and his refusal to understand their ways, both cultural and military, were fatal flaws. When some of the colonial supporters cautioned Braddock against ambushes by the Indians he replied, "these Savages may indeed be a formidable Enemy to your raw American Militia; but upon the King's regular and disciplined Troops, Sir, it is impossible they should make an impression."

Braddock's lack of respect for the Indians left him without allies in the upcoming battle, and his frankness concerning imperialist ambitions turned the Indians against him. The Shawnees and Delawares living along the Ohio had not committed to one side or the other. They wanted to preserve their homes from both the British and the French, and they were willing to fight with whichever side would guarantee the lands for them. A delegation of Delaware Indians met with Braddock to see if their objectives could be wedded together. Unlike Washington or Johnson, Braddock had not learned that it was useful to make a pretense of fighting to get back the Indians' land from the French. When he was asked what he intended to do with the land if he drove the French and their Indians away, Braddock said that the English should inhabit and inherit the land. The leader of the Delawares then asked if the Indians who were friends with the English might not be permitted to live and trade among the English and have a hunting ground sufficient to support themselves and their families. To this Braddock replied that "No Savages should inherit the land." The next day the Indians approached Braddock again, asking the same question and getting the same answer. The chiefs then replied that "if they might not have Liberty to Live on the Land they would not Fight for it." Braddock replied that he did not need the Indians' help and that he would drive out the French and their Indian allies without them. Braddock's hubris sealed his fate. In the days before the battle many of the Delaware and Shawnee warriors joined the French out of anger at Braddock's words. The rest stayed out of the battle, only coming to witness the English defeat.

Braddock's army advanced upon Fort Duquesne over a specially improved road that followed an Indian trail across the Appalachians. With a force of two thousand men, wagons, and heavy guns the campaign was easily observed by Indians scouting for the French. As they approached the fort a British Officer who kept a journal of the campaign noted how on July 7 the guides lost their way. This spot is marked with an "X" in the upper right of the map and noted "Where the Guides lost their road." The encampment of July 8 is represented below this point, along the route showing where the detachments crossed the Monongahela as they advanced upon the fort.

By the afternoon of July 9 a force of twelve hundred men had assembled on the fort side of the Monongahela River. Braddock, thinking the danger had passed, ordered the army to advance in military formation, a long file of soldiers four deep.

The French force of two hundred soldiers and over six hundred Indians encountered the British on this narrow road. The Indians quickly took to the woods and surrounded the advanced party. A military engineer who witnessed the battle recalled how, "As soon as the Enemys Indians perceiv'd our Grenadiers, they Divided themselves & Run along our right & Left flanks. . . [they] fell upon the flank partys, which only consisted of an officer & 20 men, who were very soon Cut off . . ." Braddock, hearing the sounds of battle, charged to the aid of his advanced men bringing the columns together in a mass of confusion and gunfire that resulted in a panic.

The British soldiers tried to break ranks, and some of the officers even suggested that the men be allowed to take cover and fight frontier fashion, but General Braddock would have none of that. Using the tactics and traditions of another continent he continually forced his men into military formation and attempted to advance, thereby keeping the soldiers huddled together in a clearing where they could be picked off by the warriors.

A surviving British officer recalled the battle, noting how, "The Indians . . . kept an incessant fire on the Guns & killed the Men very fast. . . . The men from what storys they had heard of the Indians in regard to their scalping and Mawhawking were so pannick struck that their Officers had little or no command over them, & if any got a shot at one the fire imediatley ran through ye whole line though they saw nothing but trees; the whole Body was frequently divided into several parties, & then they were sure to fire on one another. The greatest part of the Men who were behind trees were either killed or wounded by our own people, even one or two Officers were killed by the own Plattoon. Such was the confusion . . . during all this time the Enemy kept a continual fire & every shot took place."

Despite the confusion, the British officers held their troops together for more then two hours. Over four hundred fifty men were massacred, including nearly two thirds of the officers. Braddock himself received a wound from which he would die several days later. Refusing to heed the advice of sympathetic Indians and colonists, and without sufficient Indian scouts or warriors, Braddock had walked his men into a battle for which all the general's military training had not prepared them. A dotted line, extending over the top of the map from the spot where the guides lost their way to Fort Duquesne, is labeled, "Ridge proposed by Mr. Guest & Indians for the army to march on but not followed." It is perhaps symbolic of the advice given by Indian scouts that Braddock refused to take.

Braddock's defeat, before the war had been officially declared, reverberated through France and England. The French victory gave them the upper hand in the Ohio Valley, an advantage they would maintain, with the help of their Indian fighters, for three more years. The behavior of the Indian warriors, encouraged by both the French and the English when it served their aims, was taken as proof of their "savage" nature. The defeat turned the tide for many of the Indians as well. The Ohio Indians went over to the French and began their raids on the Pennsylvania and Virginia frontiers. The Iroquois, still practicing neutrality in the Europeans' war, prudently expanded their dealings with Montreal. And the British learned a lesson in tactics and policy. No longer would

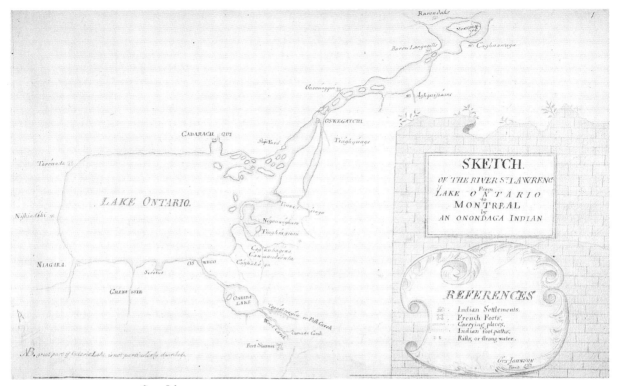

FIGURE 44. Guy Johnson, *Sketch of the River St. Lawrence from Lake Ontario to Montreal by an Onondaga Indian, 1759. Size of the original 12 ½ x 19 inches (29.5 x 48 cm). By permission of the British Library, Additional Ms. 57707 f.1.*

they openly disenfranchise the Indians; instead they would use the promise of guaranteeing Indians the use of lands taken from the French to insure Britain's ultimate victory.

(Figure 44) is an English copy of a map made by an Onondaga Indian. The copy is by Guy Johnson, the nephew, secretary, and later son-in-law to Sir William Johnson, the superintendent of Indian affairs for the Northern department. The map was made during the French and Indian War at a time when the English, having suffered a string of defeats, began to turn their fortunes around and were moving towards victory. The Onondaga Indian who made the original map was probably providing military intelligence for the British, practicing the Iroquois policy of playing the British and French off against each other while benefiting their own agendas. Despite its Indian origin the map has a very western appearance, as though the cartographer had taken the Indian information and translated it to a more familiar image of the landscape. This is not the first time the landscapes of the American Indian and those of the European invaders were melded together during the course of the French and Indian War. At some of the sites located on this map American Indians played a pivotal role in the political and military fortunes of the two European powers. The decisions made by these native nations in an effort to retain their sovereign status were crucial to the eventual British victory.

Another America

Guy Johnson, who would succeed his uncle as superintendent of Indian affairs, centered the map on the area to the east and north of Onondaga territory in what is now New York, Ontario, and Quebec. The French forts, named and pictured in the four-sided symbols that circle Lake Ontario, expand the map to include many of the strategic sites that the British needed to take in order to win the war and control the continent. From the Iroquois perspective these forts were a European incursion that they needed to restrain and control. By 1759, when the map was made, the Onondaga and the other Iroquois members had used their diplomatic skills to remain at least nominally neutral in the international conflict; they had kept their lands; and they continued to dominate the fur trade.

The map begins in the upper right with Montreal on its island in the Saint Lawrence. The governors of New France ruled from here. Below Montreal is Caghnawaga, a Mohawk settlement allied to the French. Further up the St. Lawrence is Garounggui, the site of a French fort. Oswegatchi, located where the river narrows near the site of present day Ogdensburg, New York, is the site of La Presentation. A French mission established in 1748, La Presentation attracted Onondaga and other Iroquois Indians to its site. The Onondaga Indians living at Oswegatchi were allied with the French, while those in the Onondagas' traditional territory remained neutral and moved closer to the English during the course of the war. In some interpretations this split in the Onondagas foreshadows later splits among the members of the Iroquois federation. In other interpretations it is seen as an example of the Iroquois strategy of playing to both sides and preserving the tribes' important position.

Black Lake extends below Oswegatchi, and the area east of Lake Ontario is shown in detail down to Oswego and Oneida Lake. Much of this area was the home of the Oneida Indians. One of the "younger brothers" of the Iroquois league, the Oneida lived in the area between the Onondagas and the Mohawks. The map shows the major portages and paths leading down to Oneida Lake. North of Oneida Lake, at the junction of the river with Lake Ontario, is Oswego. This was one of the first British trading posts built in Iroquois territory. Established in 1725, Oswego was in direct competition with the French trading post at Niagara (pictured at the southwest end of Lake Ontario). By allowing both British and French trading posts in their territory, the Iroquois were able to maintain relations with both the European powers and gain leverage in making deals and setting conditions.

Following Braddock's defeat at Fort Duquesne, the French moved to consolidate their hold over the territory west of the Appalachian mountains. The movement of Onondagas and other Indians to Oswegatchi helped to strengthen the French hold on the St. Lawrence, and Fort Duquesne at the forks of the Ohio protected French access to the Mississippi River and their Louisiana colony. In the meantime the British, having now declared war on France, planned to strike back by attacking Fort Niagara from Oswego. If the English took Niagara it would upset the Iroquois' strategic advantage. The Iroquois informed Vaudreuil, the French ruler in Montreal, that he could carry the war to Oswego but no farther. With this strategy the Iroquois let the French do the fighting needed to maintain the balance of power while preserving their own neutrality. The Iroquois were then prepared to sit out the next round of British and French hostilities. Besides, both sides had threatened the Iroquois with retaliation should they drop their neutral stance.

The French general, Montcalm, recruited a force to take Oswego by offering plunder to all those Indians who would come and fight for the French. When the British at Oswego surrendered, Montcalm could not keep both his promise to his Indian fighters and the guarantee of a safe retreat he had promised the English. A massacre occurred as the Indians took their plunder, killing and scalping soldiers and civilians alike. To the Indians this was the traditional method of warfare, plunder and the torture of captives being part of the long history of their warrior societies and the way in which one gained glory in battle. Such Indian tactics were abhorred in writing by the English and the French, although both were guilty of encouraging and condoning such Indian attacks whenever it served their purposes.

The essential question to be decided during the Seven Years War in America was who controlled the land. For the Iroquois and the other Indians who had been displaced by the growing presence of the European colonies, the war was a struggle to maintain their territories. That the Iroquois federation was particularly successful is a testament to the flexibility of the league they had established and to their diplomatic skills as one of America's sovereign powers.

The Iroquois League was brought into being sometime between the fifteenth and seventeenth centuries. By the time of sustained European contact, the league had evolved a structure of rituals, councils, diplomacy, and flexibility that enabled the members to maintain themselves against Indian enemies and the competing ambitions of imperial powers. The "eastern door" of the league was guarded by the Mohawks near the river that bears their name. The Mohawks turned this location to their advantage, controlling the trade in furs to both the French and to the Dutch and later to English administrators at Albany. The "western door" of the league was guarded by the Seneca Indians living between Lake Ontario and Lake Erie. They had access to the furs coming from the west and kept contact with the French at Fort Niagara. The Onondagas resided at the center of the league, with the Cayugas and the Oneidas on either side. The league was a confederacy that allowed the five nations to both act together and to pursue their own self interests.

Within the league the Onondagas were the fire keepers; they convened the councils and kept the records of treaties and meetings. During the seventeenth century the League of the Iroquois came to dominate the fur trade by acting as middleman between the other Indian nations and the Europeans. In the eighteenth century they used their diplomatic skills to maintain peace, trade, and neutrality with both the English and the French, and, through agreements such as the Covenant Chain, to gain a position of power over other tribes. The Onondagas, as the council keepers and spokespersons for the league, represented the capital of the Iroquois, and diplomatic missions from the European powers came there to petition the council and seek its favor.

Among the members of the league, factions within some of the tribes led to splits, such as the Onondagas who went to Oswegatchi or the Mohawks to Caghnawaga where they officially allied themselves with the French. But the league itself remained neutral. It tried to stay out of the overall conflict and would tilt towards whichever European power offered the greatest advantage. After the defeat of Braddock and the fall of Oswego, the Iroquois diplomats occupied themselves with the powers in Canada and did not invite the English to their councils at Onondaga.

By 1759, when the Onandagan Indian map was made, the tide of the war in North America had started to turn. In 1758 the British held a council with the Iroquois, the Delawares, and Indians of the Susquehanna and Ohio river valleys. They promised to recognize the Indians' territories in exchange for Indian neutrality in the British fight with the French. The British promised that after the war they would draw a line between themselves and the Indians' territory and prevent settlers from crossing this boundary. The council brought peace and neutrality among these tribes, and the British were able to apply their superior numbers of men and arms to do battle with the French.

The loss of their Indian allies meant defeat to the French. After the French victories over Braddock and Oswego some of the "Far Indians" began to take their plunder and go home. They could no longer be depended upon to supply the French with fighters. With peace among the eastern tribes and no western Indian allies for the French, the British quickly began their campaign, winning victories over the French forts.

In 1758 the British built Fort Stanwix (represented in the lower right of the map) at the "Great Carrying Place" between the headwaters of the Mohawk River and Wood Creek leading to Lake Oneida. This gave the British communication from Albany to Oswego. From here the British forces gained access to Lake Ontario, and they sailed across to capture Fort Frontenac, "Cadarach" on the map, where Kingston, Ontario now stands. To the southwest General Forbes led the assault on Fort Duquesne, which he took and renamed Fort Pitt, founding the settlement that would become Pittsburgh. In 1759 Fort Niagara was surrendered to William Johnson and General Wolfe began his bombardment of Quebec. By the autumn of 1760 British forces were advancing on Montreal, and Governor Vaudreuil surrendered Canada to the British.

With the surrender of Canada the conflict between Britain and France over North America was effectively decided. But conflicts of the Seven Years War continued in other parts of the globe until the Treaty of Paris in 1763. In North America an uneasy peace existed between the British and the Native American "subjects" they inherited with the French surrender. The Iroquois had been able to use the war to maintain their advantageous position. But the British victory was actually to the disadvantage of the Iroquois. Without the French, there could be no "French" Indians to attack English traders. The English were now free to trade with anyone, and the Iroquois role as middleman was no longer essential.

The British promise to make a boundary between themselves and the Indians' jurisdiction continued on paper, while the reality was that the British were busy installing their soldiers in forts throughout the Indians' territory. The Indians of the Ohio Valley were particularly wary of the British intentions. Three days after General Forbes entered Fort Duquesne, one of the Delaware chiefs plainly spoke the Indians' desire: "Brother, I would tell you, in a most soft, loving and friendly manner, to go back over the mountain and stay there." Another noted that all the Indian nations had agreed to defend their hunting grounds along the Allegheny and would suffer no settlers there. They begged the English to draw back over the mountain. If they remained and settled, "all the nations would be against them; and . . . it would be a great war, and never come to peace again."

But the colonists planned to move west, with or without a treaty line. The political disunity of the Indian nations made it difficult for them to make a unified stand against these invaders. The Indians on the Ohio were distrustful of the Iroquois intentions and while accepting the Covenant Chain in order to make peace with the English, they did not wish to act as though the Iroquois had authority over them. The English, on the other hand, found it advantageous to recognize the Iroquois' claim to have conquered the Ohio Valley. They could confine their treaty-making to the Iroquois and make deals with them to obtain the land. These cross purposes left the Indians on the Ohio as much at odds with the Iroquois over land ownership as they were with the British.

FIGURE 45. Colonel Guy Johnson *by Benjamin West, 1776. © Board of Trustees, National Gallery of Art, Washington.*

Another America

Furthermore, the continued presence of British soldiers on what had been promised as Indian lands rankled the Indians on the Ohio, and the sudden appearance of British soldiers in forts west of Lake Huron alarmed the Indians of the western Great Lakes. In 1763 the Indians along the Ohio encouraged Pontiac, the Ottawa chief, to begin his resistance. Pontiac's War, as it came to be called, quickly spread to many of the Indians on the western frontier and they laid siege to the British forts and settlements at Detroit, Presque Isle, and Pittsburgh.

The Indian uprising temporarily drove many of the colonists back across the Appalachians and into the safety of the British colonies. To further appease the Indians, the British made good on their promise to draw a dividing line between their part of the continent and that under Indian jurisdiction. The Royal Proclamation of 1763 drew a boundary line from Nova Scotia to north-west Florida, following the line of the Appalachians. On paper the continent was divided, but in reality the boundary was only temporarily established. And the colonists seldom respected a line drawn by administrators in London as they pursued their fortunes in the New World. But the real change wrought by the French and Indian War was hidden in the *words* of the proclamation. Instead of making a boundary between themselves and the sovereign Indian nations, the British now assumed imperial authority over the American Indians. The proclamation ordered that "the several Nations or Tribes of Indians . . . who live under Our Protection should not be molested or disturbed in the Possession of such Parts of Our Dominions and Territories as . . . are reserved to them . . . as their Hunting Grounds." The invaders now claimed the continent while the Indians were allowed to live upon it at their grace and favor. This policy of having Indian territory within the bounds of the nation state would carry over after the Revolution, when the United States would establish Indian territory on the other side of the Mississippi and forcibly relocate Indians from the East.

From the beginnings of the French and Indian War, Native Americans, with their valuable knowledge of the social and political landscape of North America, their maps, were powers to be reckoned with. The French and English need for Native American knowledge, military capability, and diplomatic allegiance required them to form policies and make overtures to the Indian nations just as they would to a European ally. The eventual hegemony of the British on the continent signaled a change in these relations. With the assurance of superior arms and the lack of a rival requiring the assistance of American Indians to defeat, the British no longer needed to court American Indians. Even with their incomplete knowledge of the continent's geography, they knew that the landscape of North America had been fundamentally changed.

When this portrait (Figure 45) was painted, Colonel Guy Johnson had succeeded his deceased uncle as superintendent of Indian affairs for the British Crown. Pictured behind Johnson is an American Indian identified as Karonghyonte (Captain David). He is presented as an idealized version of an American Indian, holding the peace pipe, in contrast to Johnson's gun, and gazing with admiration at his English overlord.

From the beginning of the European encounter the temperate zones of North America presented the Europeans with an unknown but familiar landscape. To the French voyageurs and the English farmers the fertile lands and abundant animal life of North America were resources to be exploited. They offered fuel to feed the engine of empire and the possibility of enriching oneself

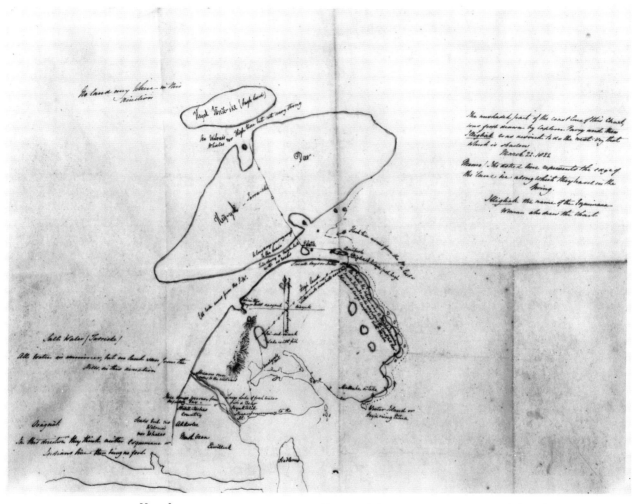

FIGURE 46. **Map of** *the Melville Peninsula and Baffin Island, by Captain W. E. Parry and the Eskimo woman, Illigliuk, March 22, 1822. Size of the original 17 ½ x 23 ½ inches (44.5 x 59.7 cm). Board of Trustees of the National Museums and Galleries on Merseyside [Liverpool Museum].*

in the process. The Arctic regions of North America presented an altogether different prospect. Here was a true terra incognita. The early European explorers found only a seemingly desolate and uninhabitable wasteland standing in the way of the much sought after Northwest Passage. Even the enterprising traders of the Hudson's Bay Company had only managed, with the help of Indians like Matonabbee, to sketch out two interior rivers leading to an unknown coast. The frustration of eighteenth-century Arctic explorers was epitomized in the name "Repulse Bay," which they gave to the northernmost point they had been able to chart in their search for the passage.

Because of these negative perceptions, the land and peoples of the Arctic remained largely unknown to the Europeans throughout the eighteenth century. By that time the peoples com-

Another America

monly known as Eskimos had been making the supposedly uninhabitable lands of the Arctic their home for over forty centuries. Distributed over a larger area than any other group of people in the world, the Eskimo, Inuit, Aleut, and Yupik peoples inhabit a region stretching from eastern Greenland to Siberia. They are distinguished linguistically, physically, and culturally from American Indians. Their Arctic cultures are the results of a later migration begun approximately six thousand years ago, when the ancestors of today's Eskimos came across the Bering Strait and spread along the northern expanse of the continent. Three language groups distinguish the Eskimo: Aleut, spoken by the people who occupy the islands that bear the name; Yupik, spoken by peoples in Siberia and western Alaska; and Inuit-Inupiaq, spoken by a continuum of peoples who occupy the Arctic from western Alaska to Greenland.

The Arctic region in which these people live is distinguished by its lack of heat energy, by limited vegetation, and by its harsh physical environment. Unlike hunters in more temperate zones, Arctic hunters cannot fall back on gathering foodstuffs when game is scarce or there is no luck. Consequently, Arctic peoples have developed extremely efficient hunting technologies and a unique relationship with the animals on which they depend. The long-term success of their cultures belies the popular notion that theirs is a bleak or marginal existence. The distribution of animal resources in the Arctic has affected Eskimo subsistence patterns, but it has not inhibited the range of human adaptations or expressions. Domestic life, sport, religion, oral traditions, and the essential role of the hunter were all fully developed and integrated within these cultures and expressed in the unique skills the Eskimos developed to exploit the Arctic environment. Among those skills, one of the most essential was the ability to navigate and orient oneself in what is often a trackless, windswept, and featureless landscape.

The area represented in (Figure 46)——the Melville Peninsula, and parts of Baffin and Devon islands in the Canadian Arctic——is the homeland of the Iglulik Eskimos. The lower part of the map (in plain line) represents the extent of the region known by Captain Parry and his fellow explorers. The shaded line that outlines the peninsula and two islands to the north is by the Eskimo woman Illigliuk. This was the homeland of the Iglulik Eskimos, and Illigliuk's giving this information to Parry and the English explorers was essential to their mission. The Igluliks' knowledge of the region was appreciated by Parry and his companions. Unfortunately it would be nearly a century before the complexity of the Iglulik culture would be appreciated for its accumulated wisdom and skills.

The Iglulik Eskimos regularly ranged across the area represented on this map; hunting inland caribou and fishing the freshwater lakes during the summer months; coming together for the social gatherings of the fall; moving out on to the winter ice to hunt the seals and walrus that gathered around breathing holes or at the edge of the ice floes; and pursuing seals and other marine mammals basking on the ice in the spring. During the winter of 1821–22 a group of about sixty Iglulik Eskimos set out across the ice from the mainland to set up their sealing camp along one of the bays of Winter Island (pictured in the lower right of the map). They brought with them their sleds and dogs, their array of specialized hunting tools, and all the domestic equipment needed to maintain their winter village. Out in the bay they saw two European ships frozen solid in the ice. The Eskimos knew these to be the same Europeans or "Kabloona" who had been mapping the mainland that fall. While bringing valuable metal and wood to trade, they had proven to be difficult, capricious, and almost vengeful when one of the more southerly Eskimos had tried to make off with some of their wares. The Igluliks constructed their winter village of interconnected snow houses or igloos and laid in a supply of seals, whose meat, oil, and skins supplied life's necessities. Curiosity and the desire to obtain iron, wood, and other trade goods led to the formation of a trading party and one morning the Iglulik set out to meet the strangers.

The ships the Iglulik saw were the *Fury* under the command of Captain William E. Parry and the *Hecla,* under the command of Parry's Co-captain, George Lyon. They had entered Hudson Bay in the autumn of 1821 on Parry's second attempt to find the Northwest Passage. When Britain emerged as the major world power of the nineteenth century, one of the missions picked up as the burden of empire was completing the search for the passage. Although it was no longer needed for the empire's economy, it was believed to be only proper that Englishmen should discover and name this long sought-after prize. Beginning in the nineteenth century official government expeditions were outfitted with ships, supplies, scientific equipment and the latest technology to sail the Arctic and find the Northwest Passage. By the 1820s they had only succeeded in finding that the northern route through the Davis Strait and Baffin Bay was an impassable maze of ice-bound islands. Parry's second expedition took the more southerly approach through Hudson Bay. That autumn he had mapped the coast a short way north of Repulse Bay and surveyed one inlet that proved to have no opening to the western sea. In November the ice began to form, making navigation dangerous. The *Fury* and *Hecla* cut their way into a bay on Winter Island, where they were quickly iced in and stuck fast as the snow and cold of the winter settled upon them.

The ships were equipped with all the latest that the science and industry of Great Britain had to offer. Heating stoves kept the men warm and dry below decks; a special building was erected on the ice to serve as an observatory and scientific lab; and a regime of baths, laundry, and regular rations was instituted for the health and well-being of the men. To help pass the long winter months a theater was improvised on the *Fury* and the crew put on fortnightly plays. Places of worship with regular Sunday services were established on both boats as were schools to teach the seamen the skills of reading and writing. With their English provisions and entertainments, Parry's ships must have seemed like the outposts of empire, the light of civilization in a dark and snowy wilderness.

On the morning of February 1, 1822, excitement ran through the ships when it was reported that a number of strange people were coming towards them from the west. Rather than let the strangers on to the ships Parry and Lyon organized a party and went out to meet the "Esquimaux." The twenty-five Igluliks approached the ships in a quiet and stately line. As Parry, Lyon, and the others came near, the Eskimos stopped and waited, showing the English some whalebones and other items they had brought to barter. Some minor exchanges took place and when Parry expressed interest in the highly decorated skins the women wore, they immediately began to strip them off despite the minus twenty-three-degree temperature. The English were at first distressed, until they discovered that each of the Eskimos wore two suits of deer-skin clothing that even to the Europeans looked warm and comfortable.

The Igluliks brought Parry and his men back to their village, after which Parry expressed his surprise that the combined crews of both ships had somehow missed the establishment of this fully outfitted Eskimo village erected within sight of their ship. Among those noted in this first encounter was Illigliuk, a woman estimated to be in her middle twenties. She showed a consider-

Another America

able ability to understand what the English wanted and quickly put her skills to work helping to translate the English questions and demands for her people. Illigliuk's intelligence and skills were much appreciated by Parry and his crew, and she was often called upon to help in the exchange between her people and the English. She was among the Eskimos who were regularly invited on the ships. Parry also noted Illigliuk's musical abilities; she sang for the English when they visited the Eskimo village and took a tremendous interest in the ship's organ.

Despite their admiration for the Eskimo's adaptations and skills, the journals of Parry and Lyon show a nineteenth-century myopia concerning Eskimo culture. Their major concern seemed to be about the Eskimos' honesty, and they repeatedly remarked upon this trait among the Iglulik. The Eskimos' lack of religion and the seeming absence of other western mores and values confirmed the English view that theirs was a primitive and underdeveloped culture. The British would dine with the Iglulik, both at their camp and on the ship, and they would exchange their trade goods for vital information, but they never seemed to transcend their paternalistic view of the Eskimos.

In the months that followed this first meeting, Parry and the members of his crew met with the Eskimos almost daily. At times they accompanied them on sealing hunts, observing the skill with which the Iglulik could read the ice and capture their prey. Parry recorded the myriad of specialized tools; snow knives, harpoons, lances, bows and arrows, darts and other highly sophisticated hunting devices and domestic implements that formed part of the Igluliks' material culture. He saw how they were able to trap wolves and foxes, catch birds, and successfully hunt large and dangerous marine animals. He continually noted the Igluliks' cheerful disposition and scrupulous honesty, as well as what he thought to be their tendencies towards such European vices as improvidence, ingratitude, envy, and selfishness. Although ethnocentric in their outlook, Parry's descriptions of Iglulik life give an impressive picture of their ability to survive and prosper in their native environment. While the English stayed on their heated ships and partook of the three-years supply of rations they had brought with them, the Iglulik almost daily had to obtain their food from the animal resources of the environment. This they did by traveling in nearly all weather to hunt wherever game could be found, and returning to share whatever food could be obtained with their families and kin. At night they would entertain the English with singing contests and games, giving Parry a glimpse of how the complex skills needed to survive and prosper in the Arctic were passed on in oral and cultural traditions.

Among the items the Iglulik exchanged for English trade goods was geographic information, and the Eskimo woman, Illigliuk, proved particularly adept at this. Captain Lyon, in his journal, records his respect for the Eskimos' ability to map and navigate their land in a climate that included several weeks each year of continuous night or day. His entry for March 1822 notes how they had spent a few days "agreeably employed in obtaining charts of the countries around us, from Ililgliak [Illigliuk] and Eewerat, who were our hydrographers, and appeared to enter into our ideas with great spirit and judgment."

Parry also records his reliance on the Eskimos' knowledge of the geography north of his present position. In his exchanges with the Eskimos, Parry would start by drawing the line of the coast as far as he had mapped it, and then ask his Eskimo informants to continue it. The Eskimos' portions of the maps, however, reflected their adaptations and methods of travel. Often they would make long journeys in the spring, traveling by sled before the coastal ice had broken up. The open water that Parry so desperately hoped to find was not what was important on their maps. Through gestures and translations the Eskimos made it clear that a sea lay to the north and west of their present position, but their maps continued as a vague northern coastline that showed none of the openings required by a western ship. Finally, Parry worked with Illigliuk, establishing the cardinal directions on the horizon and teaching her the basics of making a western map. Parry then drew the first part of this map (showing the coast up to Winter Island) and gave the pencil to Illigliuk.

As she made her portion of the map, which is shaded on the original, Parry had Illigliuk "box the compass" repeatedly to keep the relative positions of the land intact, and he requested that she make it *mikkee* or small. Illigliuk drew the coast of the Melville Peninsula lying north of Winter Island, showing the inlets and islands including Amitioke, where she was born, and Igloolik, where many of her people came from. But for Parry and his crew "the most important part still remained" and he records the anxiety and suspense with which they observed the tracings of her pencil. Their satisfaction may be imagined when, "without taking it from the paper, Illigliuk brought the continental coast short round to the westward, and afterwards S.S.W., so as to come within three or four days' journey of Repulse Bay."

Indeed, Illigliuk's map depicts the straits between the Melville Peninsula and Baffin Island that lead to the western sea. And Parry, who believed that Illigliuk's map showed the way to the passage he had been searching for, annotated the map with references to "Salt Water" and "No lands any Where in this direction." But Illigliuk's map is more than just a possible route to the West. Annotations on the map show that she and her fellow Eskimos provided a considerable amount of information about the world they lived in. The map includes numerous representations and references to the locations of rich sealing, walrus, and whale hunting sites and the lands where deer (caribou) can be taken. Lakes, the source of both fish and fresh water, are noted on the peninsula along with routes, features, and other landmarks essential to survival in the landscape Illigliuk knew. From Winter Island a dotted line shows the edge of the ice that Illigliuk and her people traveled on in their spring journeys north to Baffin Island (partially represented above the Melville Peninsula). There they joined the rest of her Iglulik band for the communal caribou hunts of summer.

As spring approached and Parry and his expedition waited for the ice to clear, the Iglulik Eskimos took their leave. When the ice finally broke up, Parry headed for the straits shown on Illigliuk's map. He named the strait after his two ships, the *Fury* and the *Hecla,* but Parry's western sailing vessels were not adapted to the Arctic environment——what was an easy crossing for the Eskimos' sleds proved an impassable ice-packed sea for the English. Parry and Lyon spent the winter of 1822–23 stuck in the ice off Igloolik Island and again met and traded with the Eskimos. The ice, harsh weather, and dangerous conditions in which the Iglulik flourished defeated the English, and Parry was forced to assess the results of his Arctic journeys as having "at least served the useful purpose of shewing where the passage is not to be effected."

At the end of his journal Parry wrote at length about the Eskimos he encountered. From his nineteenth-century viewpoint he commented on the character of the people whose hospitality and willingness to share their world had so enriched his journey. While praising their honesty and good nature, he felt pity for their improvidence and the difficulties of their existence. Parry resented the selfishness and self-importance that some, like Illigliuk, had shown when assuming themselves to be the equal of the Europeans. And he hinted, in disparaging the Eskimo women's chastity, at

Another America

other items that may have been exchanged for European goods. With the arrival of whalers and European traders in the nineteenth century, syphilis and other diseases were introduced into the Eskimos' culture, contributing to the tremendous decrease in population noted by Boas and other Arctic explorers at the end of the century.

(Figure 47) illustrates how little of the North American Arctic was known to the west at the beginning of the nineteenth century. No coastline is shown from north of Repulse Bay to the Bering Strait.

Like Parry's, the other British Arctic expeditions relied on Eskimos to help map the way. (Figure 48) shows the Eskimo Ikmalick, with his wife Apelagliu, making a chart for Sir John Ross on his second Arctic expedition aboard the *Victory*. The furnace used to heat the ship can be seen burning in the background.

Franz Boas collected the map (Figure 49) in 1883 before he found his vocation and went on to become one of the founding figures of American anthropology. He was a twenty-five-year-old geographer conducting a survey of the Eskimos living on Baffin Island. But his report, *The Central Eskimo,* published in 1888, marked a change in the methods of studying and describing other cultures. Like Nijuipa's map of southwestern Baffin Island, Boas's methods shed new light on a little known or understood territory. *The Central Eskimo* was the first of what would be his many important works in the emerging science of anthropology, setting a direction for an intellectual map that would bring us to a new way of perceiving and understanding human culture.

Prior to the work of Boas and others involved with the development of modern anthropology, ethnology or the study of so-called primitive societies was largely the province of dabblers or nineteenth-century "naturalists"——people who wished to classify and categorize all phenomena, including human behavior, in an "enlightened" or progressive model of the world. Armchair anthropologists of the eighteenth and nineteenth centuries developed elaborate theories of culture based solely in the history, experience, and ideology of western society. With the growing acceptance of the theory of evolution, human societies were labeled and ranked on a ladder of progress that curiously reached its pinnacle in nineteenth-century European culture. This ethnocentrism influenced even the best-intentioned of cultural observers, who, like Captain Parry in his descriptions of the Iglulik Eskimos, could not perceive the cultures of others except through the lens of their own values. Boas's work introduced concepts that changed the way one looks at other cultures. He helped to describe culture as a holistic configuration; a pattern of thought and behavior that is both adapted from and provides shape to a people's experience. The attendant values, ideologies, adaptations, and behaviors that evolve as part of a culture are entirely relative. There is no objective set of values or mores that can be used to judge the moral, human, or civilized attributes of any culture. This concept of cultural relativism implies that all cultures are of equal value, and its corollary concept of cultural pluralism implies that there are an infinite number of ways for human societies to organize and maintain themselves. Anthropology's third theoretical construct, functionalism, examines cultural behaviors in the light of their ability to meet society's and the individual's needs.

Following his survey of the Baffinland Eskimo, Boas went on to study Indians of the

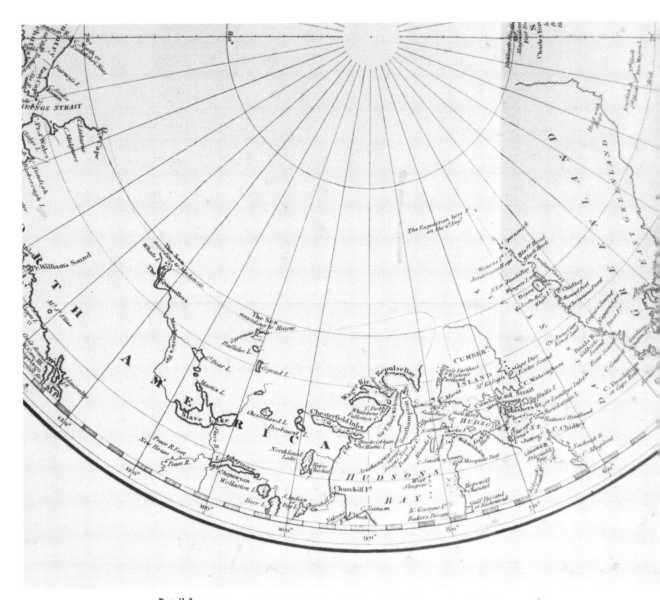

FIGURE 47. **Detail from** *"Map of the Arctic Regions" printed in* A Chronological History of Voyages Into the Arctic Regions, *by John Barrow F.R.S. London: John Murray, 1818. From the American Geographical Society Collection, University of Wisconsin–Milwaukee Library.*

Northwest Coast and to work at the American Museum of Natural History and Columbia University, where his efforts helped establish an "American School" of anthropology. The concepts of cultural relativism, pluralism, and functionalism that evolved in his work and that of his students became basic tenets of the emerging science. They continue to influence the way in which both scientists and the general public understand and perceive other cultures.

Another America

FIGURE 48. Ikmalick and *Apelagliu, from Sir John Ross's* Narrative of a second voyage in search of a North West Passage. *London: A. W. Webster, 1835. Courtesy of the Newberry Library, Chicago.*

The map by Nijuipa is just one of over fifty maps Boas collected from the Eskimos of Baffin Island. Nijuipa's map shows the southern coast of Baffin Island from the Foxe Peninsula to the Kingnait or Meta Incognita Peninsula in outline, while the offshore islands are drawn in black. Important features within Baffin Island are represented, such as lake Amadjuak ("Amakdjuak") which is partially outlined in the center, and Lake Nettilling towards the east with a representation of a seal or fish in its center. Boas's notes on the map include transliterations of the Eskimo place names for many significant locations. Reproducing the Eskimo place names shows in part Boas's recognition that the natives had already conceived and named this landscape.

Boas titled his study *The Central Eskimo* and attempted to include peoples from eastern Baffin Island to the west coast of Hudson Bay. His research, however, concentrated on the people known today as the Baffinland Eskimo. The Baffinland Eskimos inhabit the southern two thirds of Baffin Island across the Hudson Strait from Quebec. Within this region the Eskimos share a common culture of traditions and adaptations that enable them to survive in a shifting and difficult environment. The geography of the island includes coastal mountains and cliffs, deep fjords, nearly permanent ice, and extremes of temperature, wind, and tides. Except during winter, travel over the mountains is difficult and the quickly changing weather make it essential to know the

The Cartographic Exchange

133

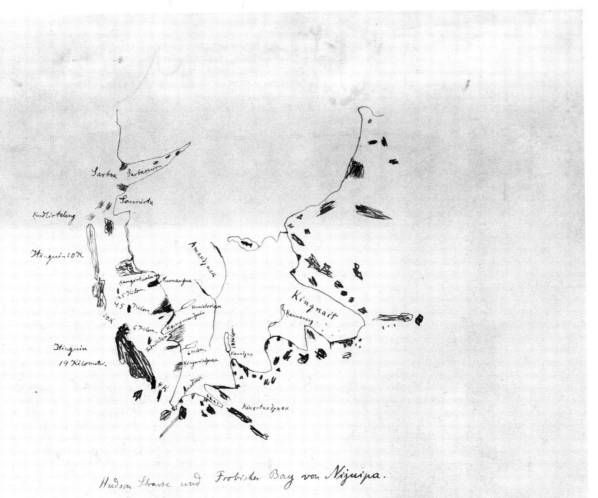

Hudson Strasse und Frobisher Bay von Nijuipa.

FIGURE 49. **Hudson Strasse** *und Frobisher Bay von Nijuipa (Hudson Strait and Frobisher Bay by the Eskimo Nijuipa), collected by Franz Boas 1883–1884. Size of the original 8 x 9 inches (20.3 x 22.8 cm). Courtesy of the National Anthropological Archives, Smithsonian Institution.*

details of geography, the name of every prominent place and its relative location, in case it becomes necessary to seek shelter. Boas's study relates several Eskimo stories about the way one travels through this environment, in which those who did not follow the traditions or take the required precautions perished in nature's indifference. The Baffinland Eskimos used the island's geography as a means of identification. The bands identify themselves with the suffix "miut" meaning "people of." Thus, those living on the Kingnait peninsula in Nijuipa's map are knows as the "Kingnaitmiut."

The record of Eskimo inhabitation on Baffin Island goes back over four thousand years. The first hunters to use the island were followed by peoples of the Dorset and Thule traditions, leading to the modern Eskimos encountered by Boas. These peoples ranged through the island in a seasonal cycle of fishing and hunting. With their specially adapted tools and highly developed understanding of animal behaviors, they harvested over twenty different species of marine and land animals. Boas describes and illustrates hundreds of their specialized tools in his monograph and explains the specific conditions under which they were used. He relates the Baffinland Eskimos' techniques of trapping, stalking, and killing to their material culture (tools) and their hunting traditions, demonstrating how their culture forms an integrated whole.

In the winter, the Eskimos would make their igloos or snow houses on the ice and hunt seals and walrus around the breathing holes or at the edge of the floe. In spring they would use their skills of mimicry and stalking to hunt seals basking on the ice. In the summer they would fish the mouths of the rivers for salmon and then move inland to hunt caribou. In the fall they would return to the coast to fish and hunt whales, walrus, and seals in the open sea, going back to the breathing holes and floe edge once the ice set in. Throughout the year they would cache food whenever possible, and, contrary to Parry's descriptions of Eskimo improvidence, they would store the extra meat so it could be used on the hunt or returned to in times of famine.

Prior to the coming of Europeans, Eskimo economic life was based on sharing. Game was divided among the hunters according to traditional formulas and brought back to feed their families and extended kin. Tools, clothing, and all the other aspects of material culture were taken from the environment, and the extensive network of kin relationships helped to establish one's identity and role in society. The arrival of Europeans affected this balance for both good and bad. Starting in the eighteenth century, whalers regularly visited this area helping to feed the Eskimos' desire for iron, wood, and other trade goods that made hunting and other tasks easier. At the same time, these new items created a continuing dependency on further trade goods; once the Eskimos acquired guns they had a continual need for ammunition. In the nineteenth century a number of whaling stations were established on the island, introducing more trade goods and the concept of wage labor. Previously, the Eskimos followed the seasonal cycle of hunting; now the invaders offered them a means of purchasing trade goods that took them away from the seasonal cycle. The introduction of European diseases and vices contributed to the Eskimos' decline, reducing the population from an estimated sixteen hundred in 1840 to a little over three hundred when Boas studied the population in 1883.

Unlike the earlier European view that condemned the Eskimos' lack of "chastity," Boas presented this and all other aspects of their behavior without judgment. It was the Eskimos' custom to periodically interrupt their usual practice of monogamy with the loan or exchange of wives. Religious custom even dictated this behavior during certain festivals, and some of the hunters

FIGURE 50. **Baffinland Eskimo** *adults and children, drawn by Aise'ang, a Nuvujenmiut. Reproduced in* "*The Central Eskimo,*" *by Franz Boas.*

Another America

practiced polygamy. Within Eskimo culture these traditions functioned as a normal part of society. It was only with the introduction of western influences such as venereal disease that the traditions resulted in unforeseen difficulties for the Eskimos.

Boas's inventory of Eskimo technologies and material culture——everything from hunting weapons to their techniques of house construction——speaks to the completeness and sophistication of their culture. He records a varied picture of Eskimo life, noting how when "All the work being finished . . . The men visit one another and spend the night in talking, singing, gambling, and telling stories. The events of the day are talked over, success in hunting is compared, the hunting tools requiring mending are set in order, and lines are dried and softened. Some busy themselves in cutting new ivory implements and seal lines or in carving. They never spend the nights quite alone, but meet for social entertainment. During these visits the host places a large lump of frozen meat and a knife on the side bench behind the lamp and every one is welcome to help himself to as much as he likes."

In the difficult and unpredictable environment of Baffin Island, Boas appreciated the Eskimos' ability to navigate and make maps. He notes that they had a thorough knowledge of the geography of their country; they knew the names of all the landscape features and measured distance in days' journey or sleeps. Some have described the Eskimo's mental map as a linear construction with journeys or destinations remembered as a series of landmarks linked together into routes. Boas contends that the Eskimos have a wider sense of geography and place. They orient themselves with the cardinal directions, which they determine by the sun or the stars or, when they are unavailable, they read the winds. Each wind is given a name and has a particular quality based upon the direction it comes from. During or after a storm the Eskimos navigate by reading the snow and the way it has drifted. After collecting so many Eskimo maps, Boas notes that they are excellent draftsmen and that if one Eskimo is going to visit a country he does not know, another one familiar with the area will draw a map in the snow, "so good that every point can be recognized." In his report he includes examples of Eskimo maps covering distances of nearly five hundred miles. His description of Eskimo life gives a glimpse of a culture in which all the questions, problems, and pleasure of human existence find expression.

Boas's visit to the Baffinland Eskimos occurred shortly before another major change was introduced into their lives by the Europeans. At the beginning of the twentieth century missionaries began to establish themselves in the region and the fur trade replaced whaling as the primary outside economic activity. Eskimos became even more involved with a cash culture, finding that they needed to both hunt and take jobs in order to support their families. As the Canadian government made its presence known on the island, the laws of Canada rather than Eskimo traditions began to dictate Eskimo life. With government bureaucrats came government programs that provided permanent housing, schools, and other institutions that benefited the Eskimos in one sense while taking them further away from their traditional life. Despite these changes the Baffinland Eskimos have proven to be a resilient people able to adapt in even this difficult social environment. Today the Eskimos remain deeply attached to their land and its resources. Hunting is still carried on in the traditional fashion, although with modern weapons, and indigenous political and cultural movements have involved the Eskimos in gaining control over their lives once again. Throughout this period Baffinland Eskimos have never abandoned their island and it remains central to their lives and their livelihoods. Today the Baffinland Eskimos call themselves "Nunatsiaqmiut, people of the beautiful land."

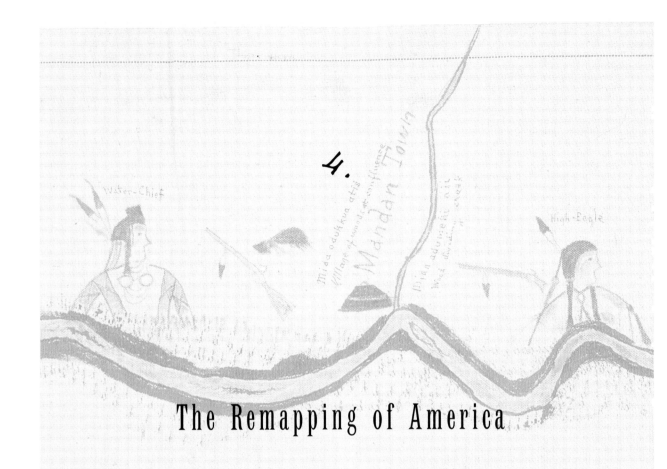

The Remapping of America

T HE REMAPPING OF AMERICA" DESCRIBES both the cartographic and the physical transformation of North America, from a continent that was conceived, experienced, and "mapped" within the traditions and cultures of Native Americans, to a continent owned, occupied, and pictured as part of western culture. Throughout this process western persons relied upon the geographic information they received from Native Americans. This information was often appropriated and then translated onto western maps where it was used to fill in the details of a land now claimed in the name of western empires and nation states. The maps presented here focus on the Native American experience of these events.

In the seventeenth and eighteenth centuries explorers and colonists took over the coasts and limited sections of the interior, displacing native populations with often devastating consequences. But it was not until the late eighteenth century that the wholesale transformation of the continent's interior began in earnest. Following the French and Indian War and the American Revolution, Great Britain and the United States were the major western presence on the continent. These two societies brought with them a world view that differed markedly from that of the Native Americans. Exclusive ownership, control, and exploitation of the land and its resources were central to the western world view. Native American societies also sought to exploit nature's abundance, but their technologies and economies evolved views of the land in which balance and non-exclusive use were central. The differences in these two perspectives on the land are reflected in the maps these two traditions produced. Western maps describe land as an object; their mapping systems use conventions like scale and the coordinate system to "accurately" picture the land and establish the boundaries of ownership that define it. Native American oral maps are fluid pictures of a dynamic landscape, a geography in which experience shapes the past and present of the land. By the end of the nineteenth century this indigenous conception of the landscape, along with many of the indigenous people who inhabited it, was replaced by the western view of nature as conquered, controlled, and exploited for the progress of civilization.

Ironically, the record of exploration contains numerous references to Native American participation in this process. From the Caribbean Natives who showed Columbus where he could find the gold he was seeking, to the Indian informants who supplied Lewis and Clark with maps that helped to open up the Louisiana Territory, western society has relied upon Native Americans to help fill in the details of its maps. While a few western maps recognize the Native American contribution, most simply used the information to fill in the picture of lands they claimed in the name of western kings, gods, and countries. Below the surface of these noble statements, there is a record of less glorious undertakings. The transformation of North America required that American Indians' land had to be appropriated, wars of extermination had to be waged, and entire populations had to be forcibly relocated. Far from simply adding westernized names to a paper landscape and tracing the course of exploration and development, the remapping of North America involved a path of conquest and repression.

The maps that accompanied these processes were made to show first a European and then an American audience the extent and character of the newly claimed landscape. They transformed the territory, giving it familiar names, noting the locations of important resources, and drawing in the boundaries and communications routes that reflected western inhabitation. For years these early maps have provided scholars and pedants with fodder for reconstructing the minutia of European exploration. But they are also a glimpse of the Native American geography. They offer insights into the territories occupied by American Indian groups, and a hint of the knowledge carried in their oral traditions.

Following the American Revolution, Great Britain and the United States accelerated their continental expansion. In the Province of Canada, England authorized the Hudson Bay Company to establish a network of trading posts to steer the riches of the fur trade into London's coffers. Trade was followed by mineral exploration and surveys to establish settlements. During the nineteenth century the Native Americans' lands were bought up in a series of treaties. By the end of the century Indian reserves replaced their previous dominance of the land.

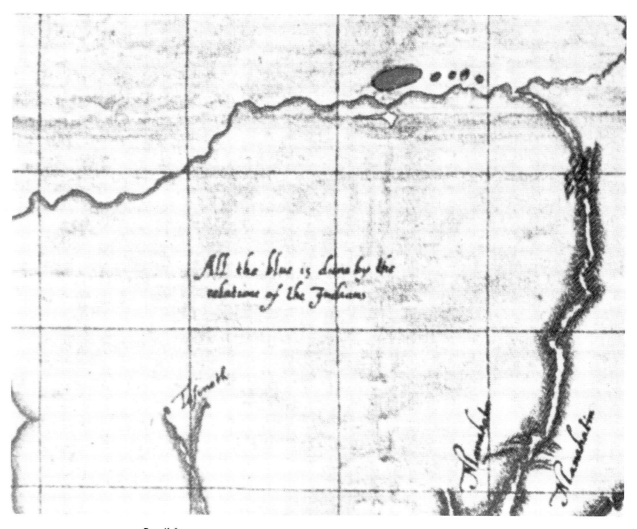

FIGURE 51. **Detail from** *the "Velasco" map of 1611. Courtesy of the Archivo General de Simancas, Valladolid, Spain. Often called the "Velasco" map because it was sent to Spain by Don Alonso de Velasco, the Spanish Ambassador to London, this is a Spanish copy of an English map. The entire map shows the coast of North America from Newfoundland to Cape Fear and a generalized interior indicating the limited extent of European knowledge. This detail shows that the mapmaker relied upon Indian information for some of the area shown. "All the blue is done by the relations of the Indians," has been written in the northeast. It is the oldest recorded map to acknowledge its Native American contribution. Within the land now claimed by Europeans, the areas depicted on the basis of native information include lakes Champlain and George, the upper St. Lawrence, the Susquehanna River, Lake Ontario, and unknown features to the west.*

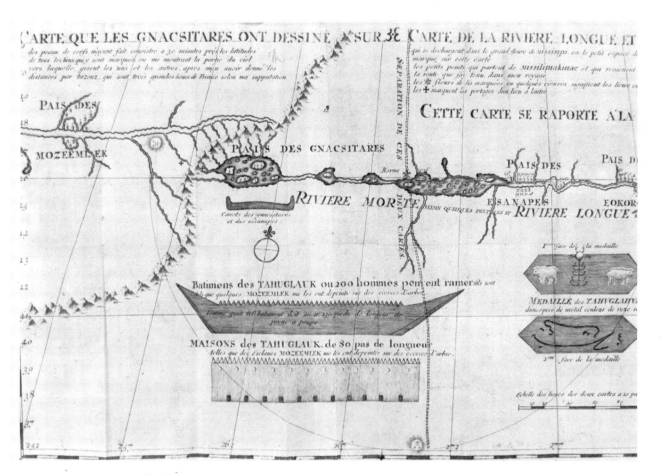

FIGURE 52. **Detail from** *the map printed in Baron Lahontan's,* New Voyages to North America, *London 1703. Courtesy of the American Geographical Society Collection, University of Wisconsin–Milwaukee, Library. Baron Lahontan, a French noble, visited New France between 1683 and 1692. He published his memoirs and included this map, said to contain information supplied by "Gnacsitares" and other Indians. The map shows a Long River ("Riviere Longue") extending west from Lake Superior to a mountain range, where it meets another river that flows to the western sea. The depiction of this mythical river fueled European speculation that a passage to the Orient could be found in North America. The Native American information that Lahontan misinterpreted may have reflected the Indians' knowledge of the river and portage routes that connected them to the Indians of the Plains and the Northwest.*

The Baron Lahontan's book was very popular and helped to create an exotic impression of Native Americans, including their lack of materialism. "Money is in use with none of them but those that are Christians," Lahontan wrote. "The others will not touch or so much as look upon Silver, but give it the odious Name of the French Serpent."

In the United States the economic impetus to take over the land was accompanied by a sense of national mission. Having won their freedom from the European powers, the citizens of the new nation were not about to recognize the sovereignty of the native inhabitants. Native American groups had to contend with both federal and state pressures on their lands. With the Louisiana Purchase the possibility of exporting the "Indian problem" west of the Mississippi became a viable solution. By the 1830s this possibility was turned into a policy, and the forced removal of Indians opened up great stretches of the eastern United States for farms and villages. But even the supposed haven of a permanent "Indian Territory" proved unacceptable to the land-hungry nation. By 1850 the concept of "Manifest Destiny" sent explorers, surveyors, miners, and settlers streaming across the west. The new nation would stretch from sea to sea. The Native Americans' way of life was to be changed and those who would not become "civilized" were to be confined to reservations. The remaining open lands were surveyed and mapped and the western infrastructure of railroads, telegraph lines, trails, and boundaries were laid down.

Maps were an integral part of the this process. Like the European explorers of three hundred years earlier, American explorers believed themselves to be entering an uncharted land, conquering nature, and opening up the wilderness for civilization. Once again the Native American presence and traditions were to be ignored and marginalized. The maps presented here document this process: All created for western explorers, surveyors, or treaty makers, they carry the traces of the Native American traditions that originally shaped the land. But they are also emblematic of the process of transformation. Accompanying the exploration and surveys were the diseases, trade goods, and wars that helped remove the indigenous inhabitants from the landscape.

When John Smith began his exploration of the Virginia Colony, he was entering a landscape in transition. Smith entered the lands inhabited by the Virginia Algonquians, a strong federation of Indian tribes under the leadership of Powhatan, the paramount chief. Powhatan was in the process of expanding his empire, and he formed an alliance with the English invaders to gain access to their trade goods and to exert some control over how they entered his lands. In exchange for the British goods and support, Powhatan provided corn, other foodstuffs, skins, and his knowledge of the region. Some of the geographic information that Powhatan gave to John Smith is no doubt reflected in this map (Figure 53). Even the self-aggrandizing English explorer had to admit he had not seen the entire area his map portrays. Smith notes that beyond a certain point the rest was "had by information of the *Savages*." Smith's admission that he used information obtained from his American Indian informants makes this one of the few maps of exploration to acknowledge its Native American contribution.

The map is a picture of the meeting of two worlds that was taking place in the tidewater region of Virginia. It projects British colonial ambitions through Anglicized names such as "Cape Charles," "Cape Henry," and the newly founded settlement of "Jamestowne" placed upon the map. It is also a reflection of the American Indian geography that defined this region. The "Powhatan flu"—now the James River—goes up to the fall line and into the area ruled by the emperor Powhatan. Powhatan's name, derived from his place of birth and given to all the groups of Indians over whom he held power, is written boldly across the territory he ruled. Other Indians—the Monacans, Mannahoacks, Massawomecks, and Susquehannocks—are also named, and representations of their settlements and houses fill the interior. Smith's map includes

FIGURE 53. John Smith, *A Map of Virginia With a Description of the Countrey, the Commodities, People, Government and Religion. Written by Captaine Smith, sometimes Governor of the Countrey. By W.S. at Oxford, Printed by Joseph Barnes, 1612. Size of the original 13 x 16.5 inches (33 x 42 cm). Edward E. Ayer Collection, The Newberry Library.*

the names and locations of nearly two hundred Indian settlements in a region where the only viable British presence was the struggling settlement of Jamestown. To claim that this land was "Discovered and Described by Captain John Smith . . ." as he does in the cartouche at the bottom of the map, and to place the words under the banner and seal of the chartered colony, is a misrepresentation. That the Indians who occupied this land were now considered inhabitants of Virginia is an example of the western concepts that would lead to so much conflict and tragedy as North America was transformed.

The area depicted on Smith's map, printed with "west" at the top, includes Chesapeake Bay and the eastern part of what is now Virginia, plus parts of Maryland, Delaware, and the Delmarva Peninsula that separates the Chesapeake Bay from the Atlantic. The rivers shown entering the bay include the Powhatan (now James), the Pamaunk (now York), the Rappahannock and the Patawomeck (Potomac). Smith had explored parts of this territory in 1607 and 1608, going up the various rivers and gathering information from the Algonquian- and Iroquoian-speaking Indians who inhabited this region. Smith's map reflects the European belief that North America was simply an isthmus separating the Atlantic from the western sea and the Orient. The Charter for Virginia granted the colony the right to expand "from sea to sea," and one of Smith's goals was to follow the rivers to the other side of America. One of the pieces of information he obtained from Indian informants was that a four or five days' journey would lead to "a great turning of salt water," and the body of water pictured in the upper right (northwest) of the map has been alternatively interpreted as a representation of the Pacific Ocean, or—more likely—Lake Erie. Powhatan himself is said to have tried to correct Smith by drawing a map on the ground showing that no "western ocean" lay within his domain regardless of how much the Englishman may have wished it.

On the map, Smith noted the extent of his explorations with a series of small Maltese crosses. The key in the upper right explains the "Significance of these marks, To the crosses has been discovered what beyond is by relation." And in his *Description of Virginia,* the book in which this map was printed, Smith explains "that as far as you see the little Crosses on rivers, mountains, or other places, has been discovered; the rest was had by information of the *Savages,* and set downe according to their instructions." Nearly half of the map lies outside the area delineated by the crosses and includes the course of rivers, the location of Indian settlements, and the territories of other tribes as communicated by American Indians. Even the area supposedly mapped by Smith is still largely a Native American landscape with the names and settlements of Virginian Algonquian Indians spread out along the rivers.

Much of this territory was part of the alliance or federation of tribes that made up the Powhatan empire. Around the beginning of the century Powhatan had inherited the paramount chiefdom that ruled over many of the Algonquian groups living along the James and York rivers. By the time Smith and the British arrived, Powhatan had succeeded in expanding his territory to north of the Potomac River, and at least twenty-seven villages paid tribute to him in a unique American Indian society that controlled much of the land and resources from the tidewater to the fall line and beyond.

As one of the first American Indian groups to encounter the Europeans, the Powhatans had the double misfortune of being early victims of imported diseases and of occupying the territory where the growing British colony would choose to expand. By the middle of the next century most of the tribes pictured on Smith's map would be gone. From the record that remains it is difficult to reconstruct Powhatan society without resorting to the terms and concepts of western culture; nevertheless, the Powhatan Indians provide a glimpse of the highly adapted complexity of Native American culture.

It is estimated that in 1600 between eight and ten thousand Indians were part of the Powhatan federation and that approximately twenty thousand Indians inhabited the region depicted on Smith's map. The Virginian Algonquians, as these groups are generally known, lived in small mobile villages along the rivers and streams. They practiced agriculture, growing corn and other crops, took fish and shellfish from the tidewaters and coastline, and hunted the deer and other game in the interior. Their social system included hereditary positions for the paramount chief and the other local chiefs or werowances. These chiefs received tribute from the villagers and had authority over some aspects of life. A priest class advised the chiefs and regulated the spiritual life of the community, and successful hunters and warriors obtained the position of counselor to the tribe. The economic aspects of the system, which concentrated wealth in the hands of a few, did not seem to affect the subsistence of the average commoner. Rather, the system has been interpreted as providing the military might and protection needed to hold the group together in the face of social and cultural changes. This interpretation is bolstered by the presence of independent groups living within the territory of Powhatan's empire, peoples who paid tribute and contributed to joint military ventures but were not part of the political system.

The political and military tensions of the region included a long tradition of warrior conflicts and revenge. From outside the Powhatan federation, Iroquoian tribes like the Massawomecks were pushing to expand the hunting territories. The Siouan-speaking tribes of the Southeast were traditional enemies of the Algonquians, and a nearly constant state of raids and war existed in the region where their territories overlapped. With the introduction of European diseases and the beginnings of colonization, new pressure threatened to tip the balance of power to one side or the other and may have motivated the Virginia Algonquians to strengthen their alliances. In his efforts to expand and secure his territory, Powhatan is said to have wiped out the Indians living at the southern entrance to the James River and to have forcibly relocated whole peoples to shore up his empire's defenses.

As chief steward of the Powhatans' lands it was Powhatan's responsibility to see that his people were unmolested by outsiders and to revenge any attack. He may have befriended the British to neutralize a potential enemy or to gain additional fighters. Whatever the reason, Powhatan's support for the colony is reported to have been meager. The corn and game the colonists needed was not always forthcoming, and the British deaths that resulted from these "starving times" may have been part of Powhatan's political and military maneuverings. During their period of alliance Powhatan spent time with John Smith, and both he and his assistants provided Smith with information that is included in this map. The famous story of the threat made on Smith's life, and his rescue by Pocahontas, may in fact have been part of a Powhatan adoption ritual. Following that episode Powhatan announced that he and Smith were friends, and he cemented the tie between the two peoples several years later by having his daughter, Pocahontas, marry John Rolfe of the Virginia Colony.

The British colonists proved not to be the best of friends. Although Powhatan was able to maintain a truce with the Jamestown colonist and share his lands, the British were less than sterling allies. They regularly stole the Indians' corn and expanded their farms onto Powhatan territory. And the British soldiers were of little use as military allies. The Virginia Algonquians had a highly developed warrior tradition. Young Powhatan men underwent a ritualized death to their boyhood and their family ties. The custom involved torture, isolation, and poisoning. Those who emerged from this initiation were born again and united in a warrior brotherhood, a brotherhood that prided itself on its prowess in battle and its readiness to protect the Powhatan people. When needed, Powhatan would rally these warriors to defend against enemy attack or to strike a blow to the land of his enemies. Part of their tradition called for the ritualized torture of captive fight-

FIGURE 54. **John Smith's** *map of Virginia with the part "had by information of the Savages" lightened to highlight the limited extent of the area actually seen by the explorer. Courtesy of Louis De Vorsey.*

ers, and the unflinching practice of "dying well." A captive Algonquian would taunt and belittle his torturers, stoically refusing to recognize the pain and dying. The British on the other hand did not "die well." In the eyes of the Powhatans, they humiliated themselves and their people with their screams under torture. A history of travels in the Virginia Colony, written in 1612, recorded the Powhatans' song ridiculing the "lamentation our people [the English] made when they killed them, saying how they would cry whe whe etc. which they mock't us for and cryed again. . . ."

During the period of their truce, both the Powhatans and the British tried to gain the upper hand. They signed various treaties, but could not come to an agreement on whom had rights to which land. In the meantime imported diseases and Indian wars continued to wear the Powhatans down. They could see the balance of power tilting towards the British, and in 1622 a band of

Another America

Powhatans and several of their Indian allies attacked the colony, killing nearly a quarter of the inhabitants. This did not shift the balance of power decidedly towards either side, but it did convince the British that it would be impossible for them to share the soil with the Powhatans, and a decade of intermittent wars began. In 1644 the Powhatans and their allies again attacked the English. This time the colonists responded with arms and enlisted other Indians in their campaign to smash the power of the Powhatan federation. The Indians' crops were burned and Powhatan warriors fell under the British guns. After two years of war a peace was concluded that reduced the Indians to tributary status and confiscated all their lands from the York River to the other side of the James, the very heart of Powhatan territory. The English soon occupied the remaining Indian lands, and by 1677 the remainder of the Indians who had once been part of Powhatan's empire were confined to a small reservation. There the warriors were forced to take up the humiliating work of farming, and the Indians paid tribute to the English for the use of what had once been their land.

The transformation of Virginia continued and the many tribes that are pictured along the rivers in John Smith's map were slowly obliterated, loosing their identity in the new landscape of America. When Robert Beverley published his *History and Present State of Virginia* in 1703, he listed only a handful of Indians remaining from the twenty-seven or more groups that had made up the Powhatan chiefdom, and he estimated the total population of Virginian Algonquians at less then five hundred. While some Indians continued at the fringes of white society or among the growing population of mixed Indians and African slaves, the world they had known was completely changed. The remapping begun by Smith in 1612 transformed Virginia into part of a large empire and a member of an emerging nation state. By 1900 only two of the more than forty bands of Virginian Algonquians remained as a continuous identity.

(Figure 55) a copy of a map from 1785 represents one of the first treaties between the United States and the Indian nations with whom the new nation found itself sharing the continent. Executed with the Cherokee Indians, it reflects an early stage in the formulation of national policies that led to the removal of the Cherokees and other southeastern Indians in the first part of the nineteenth century. The printed map is said to be a copy of the map made by Tassel, a headman of the Cherokee village of Chota, and added to by other Cherokee headmen and representatives. The treaty negotiations were held at Hopewell on the Keowee River, identified by number "8" on the map, a source of the Savannah River that formed the boundary of the new states of Georgia and South Carolina.

As was often the case in the western history of the continent, the American Indians were in the middle of a conflict between western political entities. The map was made to set a boundary between the Cherokees and American citizens, but the conflict was between the federal government and the states of Georgia and North Carolina—a conflict that would be settled at the expense of the Cherokees and their American Indian neighbors.

The conflicting visions of the landscape that are expressed on the map and in the record of the treaty negotiations have their roots in the different views of land and history held by the American Indians and the colonists, now citizens, who had recently invaded Indian territories. Tassel began his address to the treaty commissioners with a statement of the Cherokees' rights to the soil, "I am made of this earth," he said, "the great man made it for us to subsist upon. . . . I

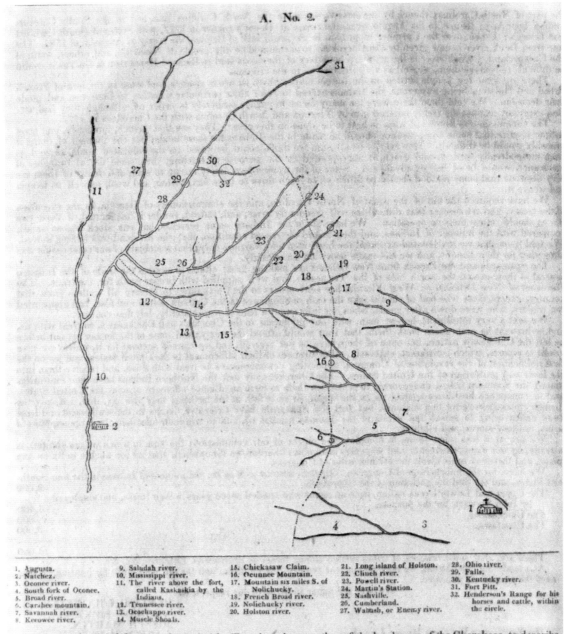

A. No. 2.

1. Augusta.
2. Natchez.
3. Oconee river.
4. South fork of Oconee.
5. Broad river.
6. Carahee mountain.
7. Savannah river.
8. Keowee river.

9. Saludah river.
10. Mississippi river.
11. The river above the fort, called Kaskaskia by the Indians.
12. Tennessee river.
13. Ocochappo river.
14. Muscle Shoals.

15. Chickasaw Claim.
16. Oconnee Mountain.
17. Mountain six miles S. of Nolichucky.
18. French Broad river.
19. Nolichucky river.
20. Holston river.

21. Long island of Holston.
22. Clinch river.
23. Powell river.
24. Martin's Station.
25. Nashville.
26. Cumberland.
27. Walnash, or Enemy river.

28. Ohio river.
29. Falls.
30. Kentucky river.
31. Fort Pitt.
32. Henderson's Range for his horses and cattle, within the circle.

This map is copied from one drawn by the Tassel, and some other of the head-men of the Cherokees, to describe their territorial claims. It is not known whether the line from the mountain, six miles south of Nolichucky, will touch the North Carolina line to the east or west of the South Carolina Indian boundary; but it is supposed to be to the west.

FIGURE 55. Map "copied *from one drawn by the Tassel, and some other head-men of the Cherokees." 1785.* American State Papers. Documents, Legislative and Executive of the Congress of the United States, Volume IV. *Washington: Gales and Seaton, 1832.*

am of the first stock . . . and a native of this land." But the Indians were also aware of the political and military powers they confronted, and Tassel continued his speech with a presentation of beads to the commissioners, "as a confirmation of our friendship."

The area represented on Tassel's map extends from Augusta, Georgia, represented by the symbol of a building at number "1" on the right, west to the lower Mississippi River, with Natchez represented by the building symbol at number "2" on the left. The Mississippi River extends up the left side with the Ohio branching off and extending diagonally towards the upper right where it ends with the forks of Ohio (number "31") and Fort Pitt or Pittsburgh. The Tennessee and Cumberland rivers occupy the center of the map, looping southeast from the Ohio and branching out to their Appalachian tributaries. The Saludah, Savannah, and Oconee rivers, represented going off the page to the right (east), mark the contemporary boundaries of South Carolina and Georgia. The dotted line extending from the Ohio River down to the south fork of the Oconee River (number "4") represents the eastern boundary of Cherokee territory as drawn by the Tassel and the other Cherokees.

The conflicts that followed the establishment of this boundary are based in colonial history and the recent war. Like many other American Indian groups, the Cherokees had seen the Revolutionary War as an opportunity to fight back against the farmers who were continuing to invade their territory, and they allied themselves with the British. The British, after all, had promised to respect the Indians' land and prevent their colonists from invading Indian territories. During the war British Indians raided white settlements throughout the Mississippi and Ohio River Valleys, sending their victims' scalps to Henry Hamilton, "the Hair Buyer," at Fort Detroit. He in turn kept the Indians supplied with weapons. In the Southeast, Cherokees fought against colonial militias several times, killing revolutionaries and subsequently having their towns and crops burned by the outraged citizens. The war created a legacy of animosity between the U.S. citizens and the Indians. Contrary to the British promise, when the war ended and Great Britain recognized U.S. independence, there were no provisions to protect the rights and territories of the American Indians included in the treaty.

Initially the United States looked upon those Indians who had fought with the British as having forfeited their rights to soil. If it chose, the new nation could simply confiscate their lands and order them to move. But the government espoused a magnanimous policy, while at the same time insisting that the Indians make the desired land cessions and pay war reparations. The treaty commissioners at the Hopewell council told the Indians that they "sincerely" wished the Cherokees "to live as happily as we do ourselves, and to promote that happiness as far as is in our power, regardless of any distinctions of color, or of any differences in our customs, our manners, or particular situation." And they reminded the Indians to hold this "humane and generous act" in grateful remembrance, "the more so, as many of your young men, and the greatest number of your warriors, during the late war, were our enemies, and assisted the King of Great Britain in his endeavors to conquer our country."

The record of the treaty was transmitted to Congress by Henry Knox. President Washington had appointed Knox the secretary of war, and together they helped to formulate United States Indian policies. For the purposes of making treaties, the nation was divided along the Ohio River into northern and southern districts. In the South the situation was complicated by the conflicting territorial claims of the states. Based upon their original charters both North Carolina and

Georgia claimed territories extending west to the Mississippi River, and they disliked the federal government meddling in what they considered their internal affairs. Local militias and volunteers had fought the Cherokees during the Revolutionary War and settlers had moved into the territory the Cherokees now claimed. Nashville, Cumberland, and Muscle Shoals (numbers "25", "26", and "14" respectively) were all established white settlements within Cherokee territory, and numerous farms and trading centers existed along the rivers and landmarks pictured on Tassel's map. In most cases these settlements had been established without a treaty or sale. Tassel complained to the commissioners that "the people of North Carolina, have taken our lands for no consideration and are now making their fortune out of them." He accused the settlers of "encroaching on our lands expressly against our inclination."

The U.S. objective was to settle the land question and get the Cherokees to accommodate the white settlers already living on their territory. The Cherokees and other Indians wanted a guarantee that would preserve their lands from future incursions and give them restitution for lands that had been taken. North Carolina had its view on the treaty as well. In his addendum to the treaty, the agent for North Carolina directed the commissioners to the North Carolina constitution, which incorporated the charter of King Charles and granted the state "all the territory, seas, waters, and harbors" lying between the borders of Virginia and South Carolina, including part of the territory on Tassel's map. The State of North Carolina had legislated its own boundary to the west of that proposed in the U.S. treaty. North Carolina protested that the treaty entered into by the federal government contained "stipulations which infringe and violate the legislative rights of the State." Similarly, Georgia claimed that the land to the west of Augusta was its territory, over which the federal government had no right to make treaties or set boundaries.

The Cherokees were in the middle of a dispute over states' rights versus federal authority. Tassel drew the boundary line on the map and accepted the commissioners' explanation that they could not move the white people out. The Cherokees would accommodate these whites (as indicated by the circles around the white settlements), but he pleaded for the removal of the whites living in the fertile land between the French Broad and Holston rivers (number "18" on the map). This, Tassel explained, was "a favorite spot of land" which the Cherokees prized highly. But the commissioners said they could not remove these people and asked why the British had not removed them previously. In the end the Cherokees had to accept the limited ability of the federal government to make and enforce treaties.

The boundary made between the Federal Treaty Commission and the Cherokees meant nothing to the citizens of North Carolina and Georgia. Settlers from North Carolina continued to move into what is now Tennessee, and Georgia began fixing its own treaties to appropriate the land of the Creeks. By 1786 hostilities between Indians and whites once again erupted in the Southeast. Creeks, Cherokees, and others made intermittent war against the southern states, and the states retaliated with raids on the Indian towns and the confiscation of Indians territories. By the end of the century the policies of the United States had proved a failure. The Government was unable to restrain the frontiersmen and Indian warfare was taking an increasing cost in military expenditure and national prestige.

The hostilities between Indians and whites created a deep division between the two societies. The federal policy of "civilizing" the Indians was an attempt to end this conflict by convincing the Indians to cede their hunting grounds and take up the white man's way of farming.

Another America

President Thomas Jefferson championed this policy. But his civilization program did not take into account the difficulties of changing the American Indians' long and successful cultural traditions, nor how the whites' desire for land and national expansion would override any considerations of equity and fair treatment. With the Louisiana Purchase, a new possibility arose of exporting the Indian problem to the West, and early in the nineteenth century some Indian groups voluntarily migrated across the Mississippi.

Ironically, the policy of "civilizing" the Indians had its greatest success among the tribes of the Southeast. A portion of the Cherokees in particular adopted the "American way of life," becoming successful and even wealthy farmers. Lesser numbers of the other "five civilized tribes"——the Choctaws, Chickasaws, Creeks, and Seminoles——adapted to agriculture as well, but the settlers' demands for more land continued to put pressure on the Indians. A series of treaties weakened the hold of the Cherokees on their lands and the state of Georgia refused to recognize the federal boundaries. Finally, in 1802, Georgia agreed to give up its claim to lands to its west in exchange for the federal government's promise to extinguish the Indians' title to all lands within the State. To the Georgians this meant that all Indians would be removed. Pressure was exerted on the Cherokees, so that by 1806 the settlements in eastern and western Tennessee, separated by the Indian lands on Tassel's map, were united. The Cherokees, however, remained in their towns and settlements, much to the resentment of the settlers streaming over the Appalachians into Tennessee.

Following the War of 1812, the Indians' rights and territories were once again overlooked in the treaty. The Native American presence was simply not recognized on the social or political map. Although U.S. policy nominally recognized the Indians' sovereign nations, the ultimate aim was to restrict American Indian sovereignty and confine native peoples to smaller and smaller areas of land. By the 1820s, the westward expansion of white settlement and the growth of agriculture reignited the desire to remove the Indians from the states' lands. In the Southeast, the five civilized tribes still held large tracts of land and had organized themselves as viable political and economic entities. They refused to give up more of their lands and intended to stay where they were with the lands and the rights guaranteed them in their treaties.

At the same time Georgia demanded that the federal government live up to its promise to extinguish the Indians' claim to all land within its boundaries. President James Monroe proposed exchanging the Indians' lands for comparable lands in the West. While the federal government struggled to form a policy that would induce the Indians to accept removal, Georgia acted to extend its jurisdiction over the Cherokees' territory. Georgia denied the Cherokees their own constitution and the right to exercise tribal authority. This systematic repression of Indian rights led to a ban on the Indians' ability to bring charges against white citizens in the state's courts, a provision that left the Cherokees without recourse when their lands and property were looted or confiscated. Georgia was bolstered in its policies by the election of President Andrew Jackson. He supported Indian removal and told the Cherokees that he could not help them in their fight with Georgia. He urged them to sell their lands and remove themselves west.

In 1830 Indian removal became official U.S. policy and the Jackson administration moved quickly to negotiate removal treaties. The Choctaws and Chickasaws signed treaties of removal in 1830 and 1832. The Creek Indians delayed removal, and in 1836 the hostilities called the Creek War led to their forced removal. The Seminole Indians did not accept the removal treaties and a war between the Seminoles and federal troops was carried on in Florida until 1842. The Cherokees refused to make a treaty and move. The tragedies of removal, from the loss of property and ancestral territories to the deaths by disease and hardship on the journey west, were felt by all the tribes. That the Cherokees' experience of removal was not unique only makes it that much more compelling.

The pressure for removal caused a schism in the Cherokee tribe. One faction signed the Treaty of New Echota in 1835 and agreed to migrate to the lands allotted them west of Arkansas. Although this faction represented only a small portion of the seventeen thousand Cherokees, the president and senate quickly accepted and ratified the treaty. They informed the eastern Cherokees that their government in Tennessee was no longer recognized and that the treaty was to be carried out without further discussion. In 1837 forced removal of the Cherokees began.

Under the leadership of John Ross, the Cherokees continued to protest their removal, hoping that the courts would give them justice. But Georgia asserted its right to block every Cherokee appeal. On May 23, 1838, the time set for the Cherokees' departure, nearly fifteen thousand remained on their ancestral territory. While white settlers moved in to take over their lands and confiscate their belongings, the Cherokees were systematically rounded up and put in concentration camps to await their removal.

Under military escort and with the help of four thousand militia and volunteers, the Cherokee were forcibly removed to the West on boats, in wagons, and on foot. The government having no experience in such an undertaking, the removal was under-supplied and badly planned. Several waves of migration took place with each one facing the difficulties of disease, lack of food and supplies, and inhospitable conditions on the Trail of Tears. Deaths occurred on every migration and no accurate count of the number of Indians who died in the removal is possible. It is estimated that an average of forty or more Cherokee were lost in every migration, with some reporting more than a hundred fatalities. The leader of the last party to begin the migration reported that they were about to leave "our native land, the country that the great spirit gave out Fathers . . . forced by the authority of the white man to quit the scenes of our childhood. . . ." A traveler, observing part of the Cherokees' forced migration through Kentucky, described "the road literally filled with the procession for about three miles in length. The sick and the feeble were carried in wagons . . . a great many ride on horseback and multitudes go on foot. We learned from the inhabitants on the road where the Indians passed, that they buried fourteen or fifteen at every stopping place. When I thought . . . that my native countrymen had thus expelled them from their native soil and their much loved homes . . . I turned from the site. [and] When I read in the President's Message that he was happy to inform the Senate that the Cherokees were peaceably and without reluctance removed . . . I thought I wished the President could have been there that very day in Kentucky with myself, and have seen the comfort and willingness with which the Cherokees were making their journey."

The Cherokees, Choctaws, and other southeastern tribes survived the trauma of their removal. While their ancestral lands were remade in the image of the new nation, the Indians made a new home for themselves in Indian territory. The tribal organizations of the Choctaws, Chickasaws, Creeks, and Seminoles continue today, and over forty-five thousand Cherokees are registered with the tribe in Oklahoma. Other branches of the Cherokee people continue in Alabama, Georgia, Missouri, North Carolina, Oregon, and Tennessee.

Another America

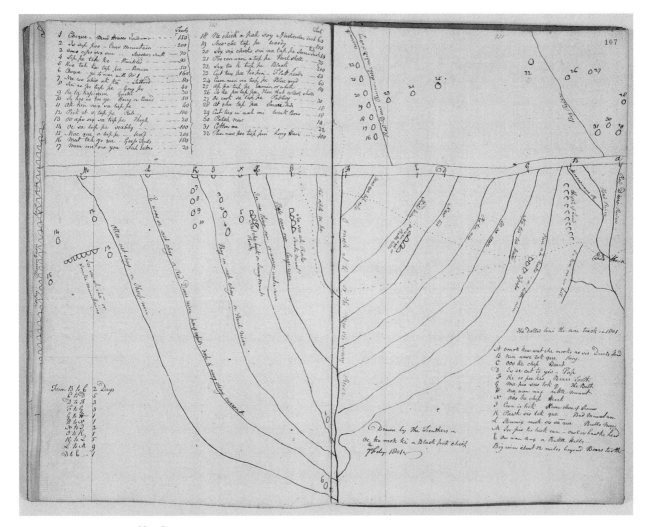

FIGURE 56. **Map Drawn** *by the Feathers or Ac ko mok ki a Black foot chief 7 Feby 1801. Size of the original 18 ½ x 15 inches (47 x 38 cm). Courtesy of the Hudson's Bay Company Archives, Provincial Archives of Manitoba.*

*   *   *

In 1800 the vast interior of North America remained an unknown and unexplored territory to the Americans and Europeans who claimed it. Traders and frontiersmen had followed a few routes and trails, and Indian guides had assisted explorers to map the Coppermine and Mackenzie rivers, but the bulk of the Plains and Northwest were still not portrayed on the western map. It was a Native American landscape, a world where American Indians hunted, traded, migrated, and raided one anothers' territories according to their own traditions. By the end of the century this frontier was declared closed and the Native Americans were no longer free to roam it. The West was transformed into part of the new nations of Canada and the United States. This map (Figure

56) by the Blackfoot chief Ac ko mok ki is one of the more important documents of this process. The map portrays the territory known to the Blackfoot and other Indians of the Plains and gives a glimpse of their life. It is the first map to fill in for western explorers details of the Missouri River drainage and Rocky Mountains.

Ac ko mok ki made the map for Peter Fidler, a Hudson's Bay Company trader whom he met at the company's trading post on the Saskatchewan River. As the Hudson's Bay Company extended its trading empire west it was dependent upon the assistance of American Indians. American Indians provided information on routes and geography, they filled the company's coffers with furs and skins, and they taught the white men the skills and adaptations that helped insure their survival. None of the western trading interests, from the early Spanish and French traders to the Hudson's Bay Company and Jacob Astor's American Fur Company, would have been successful had not an elaborate and highly efficient trade network already existed among Native Americans. Rather than view the building of posts and trading factories by Europeans as the creation of a trading economy in North America, it is more accurate to see the western outposts as tacked onto and taking advantage of the already sophisticated network of trade and travel that the American Indians had developed.

Ac ko mok ki's map is a good example of the appropriation and transformation of the Native American landscape by the Europeans. In 1800 the Hudson's Bay Company established Chesterfield House at the junction of the Red Deer and South Saskatchewan rivers. Shown in the lower right of Ac ko mok ki's map, Chesterfield House was one of the company's westernmost establishments. It represents the edge of European knowledge, and the map laid out from this point is essentially a Native American landscape. The area represented on the map extends five hundred miles south into what is now central Wyoming, and east and west from the confluence of the Missouri and Yellowstone rivers across the Rocky Mountains to the Pacific Ocean. The Rocky Mountains are represented as the double-lined feature going across the map. The lines flowing to the top represent the rivers forming the drainage of the Missouri River, which is drawn down the middle of the map. On the other side of the Rockies, Ac ko mok ki indicated two rivers flowing towards the coast. These have been interpreted as the Columbia and either the Fraser or the Snake. In addition to these previously unknown features of physical geography, Ac ko mok ki added a census of thirty-two Indian groups living in this region, showed their relative locations, and gave the number of tents for each one. Ac ko mok ki's map was the first to provide this amount of detail for the two hundred thousand square miles it portrays. It is a picture of territory previously unknown to western history. The surviving map is an annotated copy drawn in Peter Fidler's notebook. It is possible that Ac ko mok ki sketched the original of this oral landscape on the ground or snow outside the Hudson's Bay Company post that February.

Ac ko mok ki's map is a glimpse of the information retained in the Blackfoots' oral traditions. The physical landscape of rivers, landmarks, and geographic features is very succinctly drawn. It is also a picture of the Native trading and communications networks that had evolved on the Plains. With the introduction of the horse and the fur trade some of the points of exchange and the flow of trade may have altered to take advantage of the goods offered by the Europeans, but the map remains a portrait of a network that had evolved long before the Hudson's Bay Company and their predecessors invaded the country. The Blackfeet controlled an important part of the northwest Plains. They lived east of the Rocky Mountains, although their trade and raid-

Another America

ing parties went to the west as well. They migrated across their territory, hunting buffalo and gathering foods in an annual round that could involve as much as twenty different camps in a year. They had developed an efficient economic system in which they broke up into smaller bands to corral and trap groups of Buffalo that they would kill and butcher to create a surplus of meat and hides. Having seen to their needs, or having temporarily exhausted the game in an area, they would move to the next hunting or gathering site. In summer, when the great herds of buffalo would gather on the plains, the Blackfeet would come together in the thousands to exchange news and goods between the bands. They traded with outside groups who would visit their rendezvous, and they reaffirmed their cultural identity and the control they exerted over a great extent of the prairie. This coming together was an essential part of the Blackfoot culture. The summer rendezvous of the Plains Indian tribes has been compared to the temporary erection of a city state; a polis or grand place of meeting and exchange that provided continuity to the Plains cultures and reaffirmed their political, religious, and social institutions. It compares to the Mesoamerican cities built by Aztec and Mayan Indians, to the great trading and agricultural center of Cahokia, and to the trading cities of Europe and the East.

In North America the efficient hunting technologies of the Plains Indians and the trade network that supplemented their diets and material culture, had evolved as part of this complex cultural system. Although these were often dismissed as nomadic or foraging peoples, the trade network reflected in Ac ko mok ki's map shows that their economic and cultural life transcended the misinformed image of isolated bands surviving with primitive technologies. The Blackfeet and their neighbors were part of a continental network. Ac ko mok ki's map includes routes from the Blackfoot territory in western Canada down along the Rockies to the land of the Shoshone and central Plains Indians in Wyoming, and east to the trading villages of the Mandan and Arikara along the Missouri. The Rocky Mountain route follows the promontories and landmark Ac ko mok ki made on the map, and he supplied Fidler with a scale of the number of days' journey between each one. Crossing the area from north to south was a thirty-three-day journey. But the Blackfeet were familiar with Indians and trading centers far beyond the confines of this map. In 1905 the Blackfoot Indian, Brings-Down-the-Sun, described the trail running north and south from the area where Calgary, Alberta now stands. The north fork ran up into the Barren Lands of the Northwest Territory and the Yukon, "as far as people live," while the southern trail followed the mountains "south into the country inhabited by a people with dark skins, and long hair falling over their faces (Mexico)." This journey was said to take many months and was the source of pipes and other specialty products from the Southwest.

The summer rendezvous on the Plains helped to move ideas and goods (including horses) north and south throughout the plains and east and west across the mountains and towards the trading centers on the Missouri. These centers were, in turn, tied in to the Mississippi and Ohio rivers, thus linking Indians from both east and west of the Mississippi. Cahokia, the largest permanent city north of Mexico, flourished between one thousand and six hundred years ago and rivaled many European cities in its size and economic activity. Situated below the confluence of the Missouri and Mississippi rivers and above the mouth of the Ohio, many have interpreted it as the ancient center of the American Indian trade network, a hub for the spread of agriculture, technologies, and ideas throughout the Native American continent.

By the time of Ac ko mok ki's map, Cahokia was no longer an important trading center. It

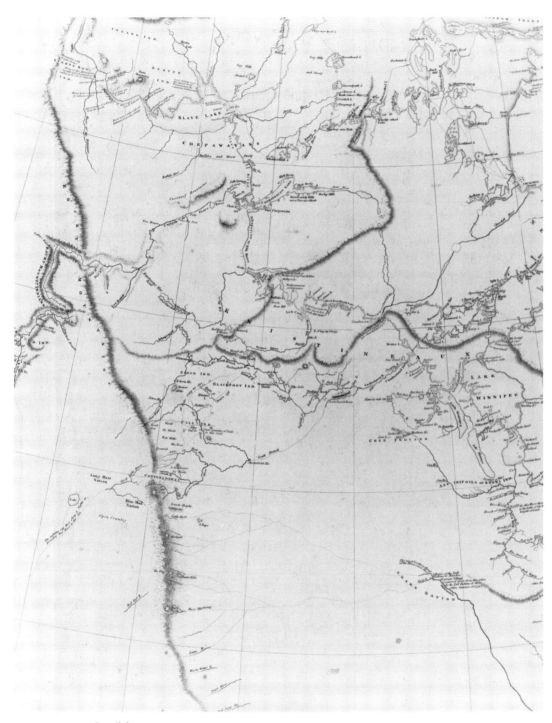

FIGURE 57. **Detail from** *A. N. Arrowsmith's map exhibiting all the New Discoveries in the Interior Parts of North America, January 1st 1795 additions to 1802. Courtesy of the Newberry Library, Chicago.*

Another America

had been replaced by the new trading posts where Indians exchanged their products for the guns and goods of the white man. The white traders' indiscriminate relations with the Indians upset the balance of power on the Plains. The Blackfeet suddenly found themselves besieged by newly armed Indian enemies, and weakened from within by alcohol and disease. A few years after Ac ko mok ki's meeting with Fidler, the Blackfeet responded to these unwanted changes by isolating themselves from the white traders. They spent much of the next twenty-five years fighting both Indians and the white intruders on their territory. But it was too late to stop the white advance; Ac ko mok ki's map had given the competing western powers a glimpse of the rich land that lay before them.

Peter Fidler copied Ac ko mok ki's map and those of several other Indian informants. From these he compiled a map of the Northwest that he sent to the masters of the Hudson's Bay Company in London. There this information was passed on to the mapmaker, Aaron Arrowsmith, who considered it important in ascertaining, "with some degree of certainty," the sources of the Missouri, [and] much curious Information respecting the face of many Countries hitherto unknown to Europeans." Arrowsmith used this information to fill in the landscape on his updated map of North America published in 1802. Arrowsmith's map (Figure 57) uses many of the same names for the rivers and mountain peaks as given on Ac ko mok ki's map, and his is the first western map to extend the Missouri beyond the great bend in what is North Dakota and to begin filling in the blank space of what would become Alberta, Saskatchewan, Montana, and Wyoming.

Arrowsmith's map did more than redefine this previously unknown territory. Following the Louisiana Purchase in 1803, Arrowsmith's map offered a glimpse of where the United States could now expand. In 1804 President Jefferson sent Lewis and Clark along the route first delineated by Ac ko mok ki. In planning and executing their expedition, Lewis and Clark were familiar with both Arrowsmith's and Fidler's maps. The Indian geography, translated by Fidler and Arrowsmith, came from an oral tradition in which scale and orientation had little graphic meaning. Consequently, many of the features from Ac ko mok ki's map had been placed too far to the south on the western maps. In June 1805, while at the confluence of the Missouri and Marias rivers, Clark records how he was beginning to "suspect the veracity of Mr. Fidler or the correctness of his instruments." Clark concluded that the Missouri turned sharply to the south at this point, entering the Rockies on the other side of the Salmon River and the Clark Fork, the beginnings of the river systems that would complete their journey to the Northwest. Until Lewis and Clarks's map, published in 1814, Ac ko mok ki's map would remain the most accurate map of this region.

(Figure 57) This detail from the 1802 edition of Arrowsmith's map shows the information Ac ko mok ki provided now incorporated into a western map. Many of the same promontories of the Rocky Mountains are now articulated, and the beginnings of the rivers featured on Ac ko mok ki's map have been tentatively added to the British map.

Lake Nipigon, spelled Neepigon on the map (Figure 58), lies north of Lake Superior in the Canadian Province of Ontario. This area was home to bands of Ojibwa Indians, part of the Chippewa/Ojibwa peoples who occupied the region from Lake Ontario to the west of Lake Superior. By the time this map was made, the European transformation of North America had already changed this landscape. A boundary between the western nations of Canada and the United States now existed, where there had been none in the Native American landscape, and the

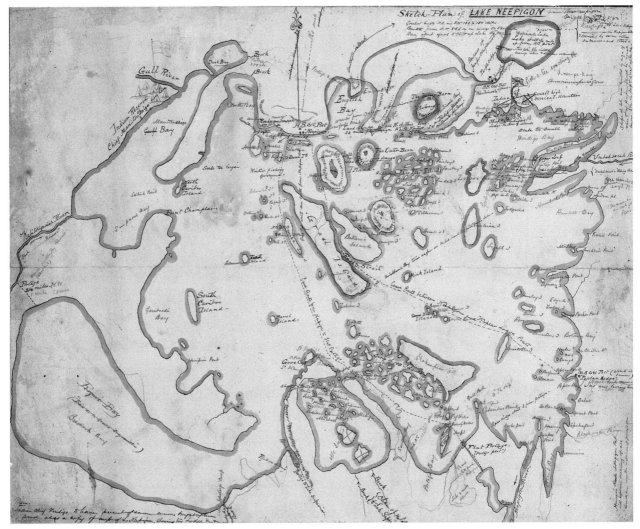

FIGURE 58. **Sketch-Plan** *of Lake Neepigon, [1869]. Size of the original 21 x 25 ½ inches (53 x 65.5 cm). Courtesy of the National Archives of Canada, NMC 21734.*

Anishinawbeg peoples no longer moved throughout the region but lived on reservations under separate government policies and different names: Chippewas in the United States and Ojibwas in Canada. Their traditional ways of life were restricted to defined areas and they were changing from hunters and gatherers to agriculturists. Some of the bands, like those represented on this map, retained their right to hunt and fish across their traditional territories. But the landscape was ultimately transformed, changed from the way it had been inhabited and exploited by Native Americans to a western European model of individual land ownership and economies based on resource extraction.

The nineteenth-century British and Canadian Indian policies, with their goals of protecting

Another America

and enfranchising the Canadian Indians, resulted in an overall peaceful transformation of the Canadian landscape. Nonetheless, by the end of the century the lands of Canada had been alienated from their original inhabitants and the Canadian Indians had become wards of the new nation. This map of Lake Nipigon reflects this process. The features of the landscape, drawn by Native Americans, have been renamed in the traditions and language of the western nation-state.

The area represented on the map was drawn by the Indians living around the lake, with the annotations, directions, and place names added by Canadian surveyors. The map is thought to have been solicited from the Ojibwas in 1869 as part of the Canadian Geological Survey's effort to map the mineral resources of the area and plan the Trans-Canadian railroad. The note in the upper right gives the "former" Indian name for the lake as "Am-neepigon" and identifies the map contributors as Windigo (Chief) for the northeast side of the lake, and another unidentified "Neepigon Indian." Their sketch is said to have been "corrected by seven other Indians and others." The contributions of this panel of informants may be reflected in the several hands that are evident in the differing outlines and the crossed out and changed place names. The map has taken on a western character, probably because it was compiled by Canadian surveyors asking the Indian inhabitants to add to or verify the contributions of others. It is not so much a picture of the process of transformation as the image of an area that has been transformed.

The Indian presence in the region has been reduced to "Chief Windigo's lodge," located in his band's reserve and marked with a British flag in the upper right, and "Indian Reserve Chief Manitouchaize lives here," also marked with a British flag along the Gull River in the upper left. Both of these Ojibwa bands had been assigned to reservations in the Robinson Treaty of 1850.

Great Britain obtained the bulk of Canada from the French in 1763. Having learned the importance of Indian allies in the French and Indian War, Britain formalized its policy towards the Indians with the Royal Proclamation of 1763. This proclamation set up a vast Indian territory within North America. In what became the United States, the boundary between the British colonies and Indian territory was established along the Appalachian Mountains. But this proved impossible to enforce and the incursions of soldiers, settlers, and unscrupulous traders led to further Indian–White hostilities. In Canada the boundary line extended from the settlements north of the St. Lawrence River into the interior above the eastern Great Lakes. By the first part of the nineteenth century, much of the unclaimed area from Lake Ontario to Lake Huron had been ceded to or purchased by Great Britain. But those Indians living north of Lake Superior remained largely untouched by Canadian society.

The Hudson's Bay Company had spread its post through the interior, bringing trade goods to the Indians and involving them in the economics of the fur trade——two of the Hudson's Bay Company posts, abbreviated "H.B. Co Post," are noted on the map of Lake Nipigon. The Wabinosh ("Waubinosh") House established in 1786 is pictured north of Windigo's lodge, and the Nipigon ("Neepigon") House is noted along the north shore of the lake. These posts and the trade they engendered affected the Ojibwas' material culture and way of life, but they did not transform the Native Americans' world like the changes that came with the nineteenth century. In 1830 the British adopted a policy of civilizing the Indians, and missionaries, agents, teachers, and instructors were sent to the Indian settlements. At the same time the process of purchasing Indian lands was extended to the West and the Indians of Western Canada soon found their lands ceded and their territories confined by reservations.

The means of obtaining the Canadian Indians' lands had been established in the Royal Proclamation of 1763. It served, with some modifications, throughout the next century. A formal council was called where the two sides would meet and come to an agreement on the terms of the land sale. These terms would then be recorded in a treaty. Early treaties involved a simple payment in money or trade goods, but as pressure for the land increased and the Indians became more sophisticated in the ways of the Europeans, new provisions and rights were written into the treaty. By the time the area around Lake Nipigon was purchased, it was the custom for treaties to include provisions formally establishing the Indians' reserve, granting them hunting and fishing rights, and setting up annual annuities.

The treaty purchasing the lands north of Lake Superior was made in 1850. The British Crown and its Canadian colonists wanted the lands for mineral explorations; in fact some mining operations had already begun in the Indians' territory. They sent in Special Commissioner William Benjamin Robinson to negotiate a treaty and legitimate the mining activity. Known as the Robinson–Superior Treaty it purchased the area from the eastern end of Lake Superior to the Pigeon River (the boundary of Canada and Minnesota), and north to the height of land that separates the Lake Superior drainage from the rivers draining into Hudson Bay. This area includes Lake Nipigon; and Manitouchaize, who's reserve is shown on the map, is one of the "principal men" who signed the treaty. For the sum of two thousand pounds and a perpetual annuity of five hundred pounds the Indians "freely, fully, and voluntarily surrender, cede, grant, and convey unto Her Majesty, Her heirs and successors forever, all their right, title and interest in the whole of the territory above described, save and except the reservations set forth in the schedule hereunto annexed . . ."

On the reservation the Indians were supposed to be guided by the policy called "enfranchisement." Aimed at integrating the Indians into Canadian society, the goal of enfranchisement was to remove all legal rights and distinctions between Indians and regular citizens. A male Indian, if literate, over 21, of good moral character, and free from debt, could be sponsored by the local missionary and Indian agent for enfranchisement, the result being that he "shall no longer be deemed an Indian within the meaning thereof." In pursuit of this policy Indian agents and government officials intruded into much of the Indians' lives. Traditional ceremonies were outlawed, Indians were discouraged from supporting themselves with hunting and trapping and induced to take up farming, and laws such as compulsory schooling and fish and game regulations were extended over the reserves in an effort to make the Indian live like the white man. The policy led to abuses of power and resulted in few successes; by 1920 fewer than three hundred Indians had obtained enfranchisement.

Despite the goal of enfranchisement, the majority of Indians retained their status as tribal members on their newly established reserves, and the treaty process was updated to deal with this aspect of the Indians' dispossession from their lands. The Ojibwa bands that signed the Robinson treaty were promised annual annuity payments, and the treaty spells out that these are to be paid at one of the nearby Hudson Bay Company Posts. This practice became a regular feature of Canadian–Indian relations, with the distribution of "treaty money" becoming an annual event. Manitouchaize and Windigo, both named on the Lake Nipigon map, are listed on the annual paylists for the annuities resulting from the Robinson Treaty. After 1871, "Windigo's widow" continued to receive his payments. The treaty also protects the full and free privilege of the chiefs and

their tribes "to hunt over the territory now ceded by them, and to fish in the waters thereof . . . "
But they were restricted from selling, leasing, or otherwise disposing of any portion of their reserve
and they were further restricted from hindering or preventing "persons from exploring or searching for mineral or other valuable productions" in any part of the ceded territory. Finally, the treaty
sets up reservations including "Four miles square on Gull River, near Lake Nipigon." This is the
Gull River reservation pictured in the upper left of the map, where Manitouchaize is named as the
chief.

In addition to confining the Indians to reservations and purchasing the rights to the land
and its wealth, the treaties marked a change in the way the Canadian and North American lands
were conceived. The map reflects this change in the excess of Anglicized place-names. Not content to use the Indians' place names to map and measure the land, the surveyors appear to have
made a sport of transforming its very meaning. A few transliterated Indian names are retained, but
a clever homage to European arts and science has been mapped in the names of islands and other
features. Along the east shoreline scientists and explorers of the nineteenth century are honored
with Humboldt Bay, Franklin Point, Huxley Island, Botany Bay, and Linnaeus Island. And the
islands in the southeast part of the lake have been transformed into a literary anthology.
Shakespeare is appropriately given the largest island, and he is surrounded by the likes of Scott,
Burns, Milton, and Chaucer. It is not known if Windigo or Manitouchaize saw the map after it
was completed, but one can only wonder at their reaction to finding themselves in a landscape
that was now described with such unintelligible and meaningless foreign words.

The original of this map (Figure 59) was made by the chief of the Chemehuevi band of
Indians living along the banks of the Colorado River. The chief made the map for Lieutenant
Amiel Weeks Whipple of the U.S. Army who was surveying the area as a possible route for the
transcontinental railroad. Although settlers had been streaming through this region ever since gold
had been found in California, the course of the Colorado River was still Indian territory. The
names of the inhabitants and the places are all Native American. Within thirty years these
American Indians would be confined to reservations and white settlers would be building towns
and farms on what had been the Indians' land. "Manifest Destiny" was fulfilling itself in the conquest of the West.

Represented on the map is the Colorado River from its southern bend at the west end of
the Grand Canyon. From there the River runs through the valleys and bottomlands along what is
now the border of Arizona with Nevada and California. Included are the Bill Williams River ("Bill
Wms Fork"), the Gila River ("Rio Gila") and the Gulf of California. Along this route different
tribes of Yuman-speaking Indians and Southern Paiute bands are represented in their ancestral territories. The ancestors of these tribes had inhabited this region for many centuries. They were pivotal members of the indigenous trade and information network that linked the Indians of the
Northwest Coast to the pueblos of the Southwest and the hunters of the Plains. by the middle of
the nineteenth century this Native American network was in the process of being replaced. Over
the Native American landscape, Whipple and the other surveyors would propose the making of a
new network, one composed of railroads to link the products, trade, and peoples of the rapidly
expanding United States.

While the first half of the nineteenth century saw the American exploration of the west, the

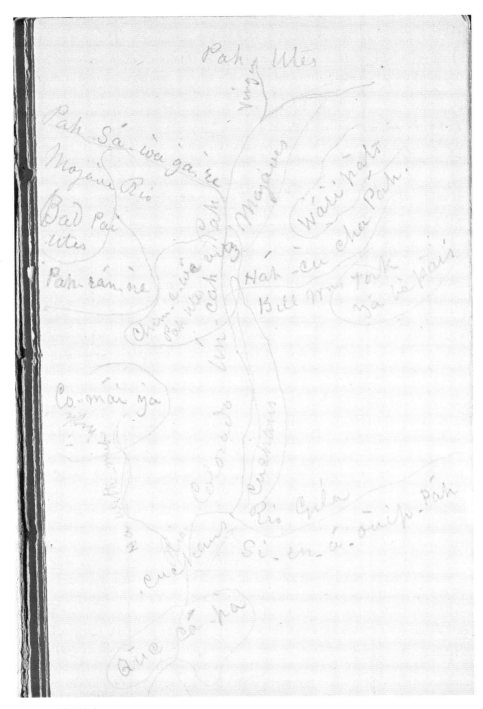

FIGURE 59. **Untitled map** *of the Colorado River, giving the names and positions of various tribes and tributaries. From the notebook of Lt. Amiel W. Whipple, February 22, 1854. Size of the original 6 x 4 inches (15.2 x 10 cm). Courtesy of the Oklahoma Historical Society.*

second half saw the region mapped, surveyed, divided, reallocated, and exploited for the Euro-Americans who came flooding out on to the plains. Where Lewis and Clark had used Native American maps to help find their way, American Indians now unwittingly contributed to the end of their way of life by cooperating with the expanding trade, military outposts, and immigrant homesteaders pushing the boundaries of the nation westward. As always, the conflict was about who would control the land and its resources. The cultures and ways of life that had served American Indians for centuries were to be replaced by a new society that believed it was its destiny to own and inherit the continent. Along his survey route, Lieutenant Whipple could foresee the end of the buffalo herds and the coming of cattle ranches, settlements, farms, and railroads. And he understood that the passing of the buffalo would mean the end to the way of life practiced by the Kiowa and Comanche Indians he encountered. Even for the best intentioned of Americans, the question was not whether it was right to displace the Indians from their lands, but whether humanity required that they be provided for, protected, and taught the ways of civilization and Christianity.

With the discovery of gold in California and the fertile lands of the Northwest, the United States became a nation with two coasts. Settlers and prospectors clamored to get to the Pacific, and the vast unknown interior west of the Mississippi and Missouri rivers was charted, explored, traversed, and settled. Wagon routes were cut through the Plains, the Rockies, the Great Basin, and the Southwest. Settlers braved the difficulties of terrain, weather, and hostile Indians to fulfill their dreams in a new land. America's westward migration captured the world's imagination, and by 1850 the need to open up, control, and reap the riches of this vast interior had become a national obsession. Only the railroad, a symbol of the new technologies and industry of the nation, could adequately link the population centers of the East with the settlements of the West, and only the federal government had the means and resources to accomplish such a feat.

Although everyone agreed on the need for a transcontinental railroad, its implementation was far from a unified national mission. The regional factionalism that would lead to the Civil War turned the routing of the transcontinental railroad into a political issue. The money to be made off the trade and traffic flowing through the eastern terminus of the railroad pitted North against South, the center against the periphery, and cities like Chicago, St. Louis, Vicksburg, Memphis, and New Orleans against one another. Powerful political and business interests lobbied for the most advantageous routes, and proposals ranged from a northern route extending from St. Paul, Minnesota to Washington State, to a southern route through Texas to Los Angeles. The high stakes and regional infighting made it impossible for Congress to resolve the question. They sought refuge in the political expedient of a survey. In March 1853, Congress passed a bill authorizing the secretary of war to conduct a series of surveys. Within ten months he was to submit a full report on all the practicable routes for a railroad from the Mississippi River to the Pacific Ocean.

Jefferson Davis, who would go on to become president of the Confederacy, was the secretary of war and he initiated three transcontinental surveys: one between the 47th and 49th parallels across the northern plains; the second between the 38th and 39th parallels from the western Missouri to the Great Salt Lake; and the third along the 35th parallel from Fort Smith, Arkansas across Oklahoma and Texas to Albuquerque and west to the Colorado River and California. This third survey was under the command of Lieutenant Amiel Weeks Whipple, a West Point graduate from New England. In addition to surveying the land for its suitability as a railroad route, Whipple was ordered "to make scientific observations on the nature of the land . . . the plant and animal life, the availability of water, the products of the country, the white populations, and the location, character, habits, traditions, and languages of the Indian tribes."

These surveys were to provide a scientific solution to the political difficulties of locating the railroad. The expeditions were accordingly fitted out with the latest experts and equipment. Just as Manifest Destiny made the appropriation of the Indians' land part of the national mission, these Pacific railroad surveys were to establish the unique position of American science. The biological, geological, and zoological information to be gathered would put U.S. scientific institutions on a par with their European counterparts, and the specimens collected would fill museums and scientific reports for decades. Like the American businessmen who could see the profits to be made from the railroads, the scientific community could see the experiments to be conducted and the reputations to be made from the surveys. Scientists from around the world lobbied to be included. The recently founded Smithsonian Institution advised on the scientific personnel, the instruments to be used, and the range of observations to be made. Whipple's expedition was accompanied by a French geologist and the German naturalist-artist, H. B. Mollhausen, who had been sponsored for the task by Alexander von Humboldt himself. In July of 1853, accompanied by over one hundred men, fifteen wagons, a herd of mules, and enough cattle and sheep to sustain the party, the Whipple expedition started out from Fort Smith, Arkansas.

When Whipple crossed into Indian territory he was making his way into a land that was very unlike the New England landscape of his childhood. Crossing what is now Oklahoma, he observed the farms and settlements of the relocated Choctaw. Forcibly removed from their southeastern homelands in the 1830s, the Choctaws, Whipple reported, had adjusted to their removal excellently. From there the expedition followed the Canadian River, taking the reverse of the route Juan De Oñate had taken in his search for Quivira in 1601. Since that time settlers, prospectors, and traders had worn out any welcome the Indians may have had for the white man. Whipple kept his expedition in close formation to present an obstacle to attack. This show of force protected the expedition from outright hostilities, but the Indians let the white men know they were unwelcome. They set the prairie ablaze in front of the expedition, and for several days Whipple and his men had to struggle through smoke and parched ground and make detours around the fires. Whipple encountered Comanches and Kiowas moving onto the Plains for the summer hunts. He recorded meeting Mexican traders bringing in flour and sugar to trade for the Indians' buffalo robes and ponies.

The expedition then crossed the Pecos River to Albuquerque, and from there they headed across New Mexico into Zuni territory and the area that was most critical for the railroad route. Along the way the expedition picked up numerous plant and animal specimens and the geologist studied the rocks and mineral resources. Whipple noted the problems that the region's lack of water and fuel might pose for the railroad, but optimistically suggested that fuel could be shipped in from the Southeast. Mollhausen sketched and painted the Indians and their territory. His drawings accurately recorded some of the indigenous artifacts and features, but they also contributed to a mythologized view of the Indians as exotic savages.

In western Arizona the expedition picked up the valley of the Bill Williams Fork and entered the territory of the Yuman-speaking Indians represented on this map. These southwestern Indians;

Another America

the Walapai ("Wáli pàis"), also known as Hualapai, the Mohaves, the Cuchan or Yuma Indians, and the Que cá hà ("Cocopa") are all named in their ancestral territories along the Colorado River. Together they shared a number of unique cultural traits and an economic system that enabled them to flourish in this arid region. The southern Paiutes, also represented on the map, were Indians of the Great Basin and from a different tradition. But their relatives, the Chemehuevi Indians, represented in the middle of the map, had adapted to the Mohave way of life and the Mohaves allowed them to farm along the river in the area west of the Bill Williams Fork.

Together these Indians had occupied the valleys and bottomlands along the Colorado River for over a thousand years. The rich alluvial soils that covered the area following the springs floods, and the intense heat of the growing season, enabled these tribes to practice an efficient form of agriculture that included plantings of maize, beans, pumpkins, melons, and winter wheat. They supplemented this with hunting local game and gathering wild foods in a subsistence economy that supported a population estimated at 11,500 and a Native American way of life quite different from that soon to be imposed upon them.

The lay of the land and the Indians' method of farming produced a settlement pattern of spread-out rancheros rather then villages. Extended family groups would construct their open-sided dwellings on rises above the flood plain and clear the land for planting. Cleared plots were considered an individual's property, but anybody could clear and claim the unattended land. The abundance of fertile land is reflected in the Indians' tradition of abandoning a plot after the death of the owner, and in the Mohaves' practice of allowing the Chemehuevis to farm on part of their land, when they otherwise jealously guarded their territory. The material culture of these tribes was generally limited. Crops could be planted and harvested with simple planting and digging sticks, clothing was minimal in the heat of the region, and open-sided houses or shades sufficed for shelters throughout much of the year. Within these circumstances the Mohaves and their Yuman neighbors developed the custom of burning all the belongings of a dead person and leaving their lands to lie fallow. Funerals and the rituals of mourning were a unifying factor in these cultures, and professional orators would use the occasion to recite the tribal mythology in stories and song cycles. The rituals surrounding death were one of the few organized activities in these societies.

Overall, these Indian groups were very egalitarian. No organized political structure existed to place one person or group of persons in a position of power over another. One gained position and authority by the power of one's dreams. Dreams provided the basis of one's abilities and accomplishments. These Indians believed that the dream of one's fate was experienced in the mother's womb, only to be forgotten at birth and, with luck, found again through "great dreams" experienced as one entered adulthood. Dreams gave one the powers needed to be a warrior, a shaman, a leader, or an orator. Dreams enabled one to go back to the beginning of time and retell the past in the recitations and song cycles of tribal belief. But a dreamer's power could not simply be claimed; it must be validated in knowledge and deeds.

One of the primary means of validating one's dreams was through deeds of bravery in warfare. Warfare was another of the organizing principles in these societies. Despite their spread out settlement patterns and their lack of a political structure, these Indians possessed strong tribal identities——identities that were reaffirmed in the nearly continuous wars and raids that went on between themselves and the other Indian groups with whom they shared the region. The Yuman-speaking Indians represented on the map were not united in their opposition to outsiders, rather a ritualized form of warfare was often carried on between these groups. The Mohaves and their allies the Cuchans would war against the Walapais, Cocopas and others to the south and west. The Chemehuevis, though not of the Yuman tradition, sometimes joined the Mohaves in their raids while at other times they were warred upon by the Mohaves. Unlike the wars of extermination practiced by the whites, these Indian wars were a ritualized form of combat where deeds of valor and skill were realized and only a few scalps and other fatalities were taken. The warrior traditions that fed this enterprise permeated these societies. The Cuchans (Yumas) differentiated between "going to the enemy" in war parties, and "waking the enemy" in raids. In the latter the young warriors stirred up trouble by stealing horses or otherwise upsetting their enemies. Going to the enemy was a much more formal occasion. Often undertaken to revenge earlier losses, the sides would arrange to meet and wait for each other to prepare. Then, following ritualized insults, they would engage one another in formalized ranks and combat formations using clubs, spears, and bows and arrows. To the warriors this was the path to glory and honor. Although not usually costly in terms of losses, some disastrous defeats did occur. And if death did come in battle it was looked on as an acceptable way to enter the hereafter. The spoils of these wars were captives to work for the victor or to trade to the Spanish and other Indians for goods and horses.

The encounters between these Native Americans and the Europeans were seldom successful. In the eighteenth century the Spanish attempted to set up some missions, only to be wiped out. In the nineteenth century the Cuchans' land at the confluence of the Colorado and Gila rivers became the focus of military and civilian development. A popular crossing place for both Mexicans and Americans, opportunistic whites set up a ferry service to make money off the wagon trains making their way to California. The new immigrants helped themselves to the Indians' crops and attempted to appropriate their lands. The Cuchans retaliated by attacking the settlers, and in 1852 the United States Army established Fort Yuma to keep a military presence and enforce peace in the region. Further up the Colorado, settlers followed the Mormon road and crossed the Colorado at the Needles in the heart of Mohave territory.

In 1851 an army expedition to the region had been attacked by the Indians, but Whipple, proceeding with caution, was left undisturbed. As the expedition made its way north along the Colorado, picking its way over the Indian trails and leaving wagons and discarded supplies behind, it entered the Chemehuevi Valley. There Whipple records that the expedition suddenly found itself surrounded by Indians, some armed and others carrying equipment from the army's abandoned camp. These were the Chemehuevi Indians and they invited Whipple and his expedition to their camp. Going up to the Chemehuevis' camp, Whipple records that they crossed the Chemehuevis' planted fields and saw their main village and principal fields on the other side of the river. The Army bivouacked near the Chemehuevis' camp and the leader or chief came to pay his respects. He urged Whipple and his men to trade with his people. In exchange, Whipple relates how that night the chief gave him a vocabulary of the Chemehuevis' language, and made the original of this map: "[he] drew a sketch of this country, giving the Pai-Ute names of tribes, and the rivers where they dwell."

Following this encounter, Whipple continued up the Colorado and met with the Mohaves. They guided him across the river and through the pass that led to California. The results of Whipple's survey, and those of the other expeditions, were published in the following year. In the

Another America

Reports on the Pacific Railroad Surveys each of the proposed routes is described and the cost of building the railroad on each route estimated. But this scientific approach failed to settle the political issue of whom would profit from the railroads. While the argument could be made that the route Whipple surveyed held the greatest promise, it was not until nearly ten years later that the transcontinental railroad was finally built, and then on an altogether different route than any of those that had been surveyed.

The failure to determine the most practicable route notwithstanding, the *Reports on the Pacific Railroad Surveys* collected a veritable mountain of knowledge about the West. The *Reports* were published in several volumes and updated as new findings were added and analyzed. They comprise an illustrated catalog of the American West. In addition to the descriptions of the routes, there were volumes on the geology, plants, animal life, and natural resources of the region, each one abundantly illustrated from the specimens collected on the surveys and now filling the national collections. The Pacific Railroad reports helped to transform the native landscape into one pictured in the language of western science. The geological data and fossil specimens helped to prove the still theoretical concepts concerning the age of the earth. Coupled with the theories on natural selection and evolution published in Darwin's *The Origin of Species* in 1859, these scientific findings transformed the way people understood the world. By applying these concepts to the little-understood cultures and technologies of the American Indian, it was easy to assume that they were meant to pass from the earth. America's "vanishing Indians" were the victims of social evolution, and their disappearance was a natural part of the realization of the nation's destiny.

In keeping with his orders, Whipple published a "Report on the Indian Tribes" as part of his survey results. This report enumerates the peoples he observed, and provides information on population, environment, cultural practices and beliefs. Whipple attempted to show the Indians as having unique cultures and respectable traditions. But the popular image of the Indian as uncivilized savage, assisted by sensationalized reports of Indian raids and hostilities, proved more powerful and more effective for the growing nation. Indian hostilities were met with campaigns of extermination and enforced internment. In 1858 the Mohaves were warred upon by the U.S. Army and in 1859 soldiers used their rifles to mow down the Mohave warriors and end their resistance. Fort Mohave was established and became the basis of the Mohave reservation. In 1865 the Colorado Indian Reservation was established south of the Bill Williams Fork, and a band of Mohave that settled there was joined by the Chemehuevis and other tribes of the region. Further south, the Cuchans or Yuma Indians found work in the growing river town that bears their name. They were eventually moved to a reservation on the west side of the Colorado.

Whipple's "Report on the Indian Tribes" reflects much of the thinking and policies concerning Indians as the nation completed its nineteenth-century expansion. The national zeal for growth and progress left little time to be concerned with American Indians. In the introduction to his report, Whipple refers to his study of the Indians as a "collateral branch" of information that now "seems the most remotely connected with the main object of the exploration." He described the Indians as hemmed in upon every side "by descendants of a foreign race. Year by year their fertile valleys are appropriated by others, their hunting grounds invaded, and they themselves driven to narrower and more barren districts." The time had arrived, Whipple prophesied, "when we must decide whether they are to be exterminated: if not, the powerful arm of the law must be extended over them, to secure their right to the soil they occupy; to protect them from aggression;

Figure 60. Mohave Indians pictured by H. B. Mollhausen. Mollhausen was the naturalist–artist on Whipple's expedition, and his paintings provide basic information on the clothing and customs of the Indians they encountered. This sketch of Mohave Indians was published with the report of the Ives expedition to the Southwest in 1857–1858.

to afford facilities and aid in acquiring the arts of civilization, and the knowledge and humanizing influences of Christianity."

By the end of the century, the Native American landscape had been remade into the United States of America. From giving directions to the earliest explorers to acting as scouts for the army in its wars upon Indian peoples, Native Americans had participated in this transformation. In return for their contribution they were often removed, confined, and persecuted; denied the use of the lands their ancestors had occupied and restricted from practicing the ways of life that formed their identities. The "powerful arm of the law" was extended over them in the form of reservations and national Indian policies that sought to transform the Native Americans in the same way western society had remapped the land.

Another America

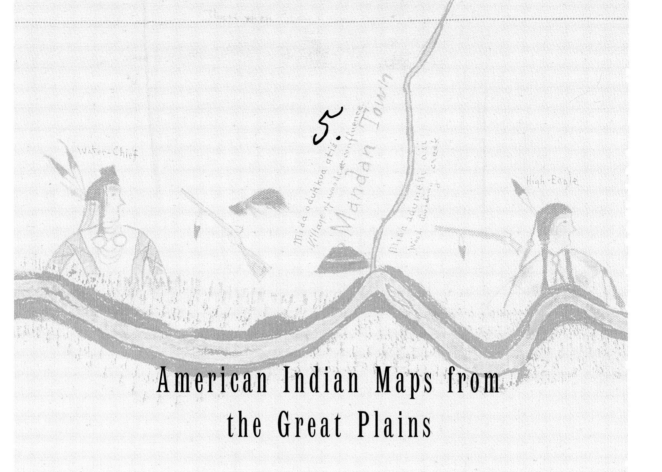

American Indian Maps from
the Great Plains

T HE NATIVE AMERICAN SOCIETIES THAT inhabited the Great Plains occupy a
unique position in American history. Of all the Indian groups encountered in western society's continental advance, the Sioux, Cheyennes, Blackfeet, Kiowas, Comanches, and other
Indians of the Plains are remembered for their role in forestalling the nation's westward expansion.
That these nomadic hunters with their warrior societies were able to delay the fulfillment of
Manifest Destiny for more than fifty years has brought them a place in American mythology. The
end of the Indians' resistance has been alternatively portrayed as the ultimate triumph of the light
of civilization over the forces of savage darkness, and the crushing of mankind's noble and natur-

al state by the juggernaut of western technology. Adding to the poignancy of this historical moment is its symbolism for the end of an era. The control of the Indians of the Plains signaled the "closing" of the western frontier. With it, North America was no longer a wild country and the century of the modern nation state had begun.

The roots of the war for the West lay in the history of the cultures that met near the beginning of the nineteenth century. Up until that time the plains of central North America had been largely a native place. Like Ac ko mok ki's map of 1801 (figure 56), from the bend of the Missouri River to the Rocky Mountains the Plains were unknown to western culture. But they had been named, traversed, and inhabited by Native American groups for centuries. Within the century before Ac ko mok ki's, these societies had adopted the horse and taken advantage of western trade to outfit themselves with the hardware needed for their mobile villages. They had grown in numbers and strength, extending their hunts and their hostilities across the Plains in a sophisticated and complex cultural system—a system that perceived itself and the land on which it lived in marked contrast to western society. These maps give a glimpse of the Native Americans' perception of and history on the land while at the same time recording their experience of the western invasion.

The Native American presence on the Plains goes back to the earliest North Americans. Archeological evidence shows that Neolithic bands of hunters pursued herds of mammoths and other ice age herbivores across the plains nearly thirty thousand years ago. As the climate moderated and the Plains became more arid, these animals died out, as did the cultures that relied upon them. At the beginning of the modern era the region between the Mississippi River and the Rocky Mountains evolved into a huge grassland covering 750,000 square miles. In this environment, the American bison or buffalo proliferated, taking over grasslands from the plateaus and passes of the Rockies to east of the Mississippi River. A thousand years ago, when the ancestors of the modern Plains Indians began to hunt, travel, and trade across the Plains, approximately thirty million bison filled the region. Additional millions of elk, antelope, deer, and other game lived on the Plains. The Native American societies that migrated into this region naturally organized themselves around these animal resources, and their abundance enabled the evolution of a unique way of life.

Before the acquisition of the horse, Plains Indian societies had successfully adapted themselves to the alternatively difficult and bountiful environment of the Plains. Some, like the Pawnees, Wichitas, and Mandans built semi-permanent villages along the river basins. There they grew corn, squash, and other vegetables to supplement their hunts and help them through times when there was no game. Native groups like the Apaches and Comanches adapted a more mobile lifestyle. They followed the buffalo herds, sometimes living alongside the herds and only taking animals as they were needed, at other times organizing kills in which considerable numbers of the beasts were taken, their meat and hides providing a temporary largess that could be traded for corn and other staples. Other Indian groups like the Sioux and Cheyennes, names that would become synonymous with the Plains, actually started out as farmers living in villages along the edge of the grasslands.

All three of these traditions were linked by the buffalo. In the Plains-village tradition of the Mandans and their neighbors, organized communal hunts were undertaken on a seasonal basis, with the buffalo providing an essential source of food and material goods. Those Indians living

Another America

along the edge of the Plains also organized hunts to go onto the grasslands and take the animals needed for their subsistence. And the nomadic Indians living among the buffalo regularly brought in their meat and hides to trade with the agriculturists. Within these traditions the buffalo and other animals of the Plains had a spiritual relationship to the tribes. They were a gift from the creator, a covenant that sustained existence.

Traveling on foot and using dogs to carry their possessions, members of these societies developed a unique interdependence that included both trade and conflict. The Plains trade network linked these Indians to the rest of Native American society. Nomadic hunters would trade in the Mandan and Arikara villages on the upper Missouri River and at the Shoshone and Blackfeet rendezvous. Southern Plains Indians regularly traded with the inhabitants of the Pueblos in the Southwest, and the Indians of the plateau and Northwest exchanged with the residents of the northern Plains. Goods moved back and forth from the Pacific Coast to the Mississippi valley and the Great Lakes, and on to the eastern half of the continent.

Along with the system of trade, a tradition of conflict and tribal animosity developed. In the difficult environment of the Plains, one tribe's gain was another's loss, and the goods that might be obtained through barter could, if one had sufficient strength, be just as easily taken. Plains societies adapted the Native Americans' warrior tradition to a level of ritual in which reciprocal raids and hostilities tied them to one another in nearly interminable warfare.

The value placed on these hostilities and warrior accomplishments was balanced with the social values of discipline and group responsibility. The traditions of the societies reinforced one's role and responsibilities to the group. Identity was forged and rewarded within a system of kin, social, and religious ties. This group identity and group discipline reflects the environment of the Plains. To successfully hunt the buffalo, a large, dangerous, and skittish beast, it was necessary to act in unison. A hunter acting on his own could stampede the herd and scatter the food needed by an entire tribe. Similarly, in a landscape in which raids and armed hostilities were a regular way of life, the need to close ranks and protect the group even at the expense of one's life was necessary to survival.

The other side of this coin was manifest in the celebration of bravery and reckless action in battle. Young Indian men were expected to prove themselves in battle before they were granted the privileges and responsibilities of adulthood. An elaborate system of military honors evolved. Counting coup, entering the battle to strike your opponent with a hand or a stick, humiliating your enemy by stealing his honor and his manhood and then turning away in disdain, were acts of the highest honor. Other deeds of bravery and methods of counting coup were awarded merit as well. Given such emphasis these honorable acts evolved into elaborate rituals and displays. The group reinforced these behaviors by celebrating successful raids and military victories and recording the warriors' honors into the tribal memory. The value placed on these deeds permeated Plains Indian society and is reflected in the maps that record raids and battles as the events that gave meaning to the landscape.

The emphasis on aggression came into conflict with the need to repress and control such behaviors within the group. To maintain social control, many of these societies adapted the tradition of Dog Soldiers, in which members of a warrior society were appointed to police tribal gatherings, settle disputes, keep the peace, and enforce the discipline of the hunt. These groups were often the most aggressive of warriors. In the campground their word was law and they had the authority to exact punishment on all who did not follow the peoples' way. The need to repress the aggressive tendencies that were cultivated and rewarded in other areas of life created very formal and strict societies with a strong identity and knowledge of what it meant to be Cheyenne, Lakota, or the thirty other identities that made their life on the Plains.

The introduction of the horse in the late 1600s spurred the development of these societies. Horses were introduced by Indians who left the Spanish settlements of the Southwest and took the Spaniards' horses with them. Following the Pueblo Revolt of 1680, large herds of domesticated horses came into Indian hands. The speed with which these animals and their offspring spread throughout the Plains is testimony to the efficiency of the Indians' trade network. By the middle of the next century, virtually all the Plains Indians possessed enough horses to practice the traditions of hunting and raiding that epitomizes the Native American cultures of the Plains.

As an economic tool the horse revolutionized Plains Indian life. Since one good horse could replace the work of several hunters, the supply of meat and hides increased. The mobility that the horse provided spurred the development of Plains society. A horse could carry much more than a dog. With the horse the Indians living in semi-permanent villages along the rivers could make longer hunting trips farther out on to the Plains. Those Indians living along the edge of the Plains began to increase their reliance on the buffalo and other game. By the end of the eighteenth century Indians like the Cheyennes and Dakotas could abandon their farming villages altogether and take up the nomadic life of the Plains. The increase in population and mobility that followed the acquisition of the horse was accompanied by a more elaborate expression of the warrior traditions of the Plains. Pageantry and elaborate ritual entered the preparations for war, and stealing your enemy's horses became the major means by which young warriors expressed their ambitions and proved their bravery.

The horse and the abundant buffalo were the resources that made these societies flourish. By 1780 more than thirteen thousand Native Americans filled the region, living a life in which there was no greater satisfaction than to hunt and fight on the Plains. The following year the first great epidemic of smallpox hit the Plains. It is estimated that the epidemic of 1781 cut the Native American populations in half; it went down in Plains Indian history as one of their first great plagues. This and subsequent epidemics changed the history of the Plains. Weakened by disease and reduced in number, tribes were forced to regroup. The Mandans moved their villages up the Missouri River to join the Hidatsa and seek strength in numbers; the Assiniboine moved south to put distance between themselves and their neighbors. Those who had suffered the least took advantage of the weaker tribes. The Dakotas and the Cheyennes used the opportunity to permanently establish themselves west of the Missouri River. Their constant raids took their toll on smaller tribes who sought protection by making alliances among themselves. By the first quarter of the nineteenth century the Indians of the Plains had begun to recover from the smallpox, when a new threat in the form of the United States government entered the region.

These maps record the Indian experience of this invasion. Beginning in 1825, when the first official "friendship" treaties were signed by the Indians of the upper Missouri, and continuing through the Battle of the Little Bighorn and the repression of Indians on the reservation, the maps record the epidemics, treaties, and military battles that shaped this history.

In 1837 the second great epidemic hit the Plains. The smallpox once again nearly halved the Indian population, and the subsequent economic and political restructuring took place within the

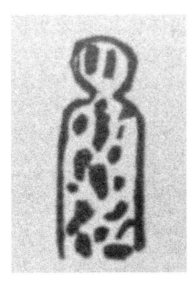

FIGURE 61.

The symbolic *representation of the small pox epidemic that struck the Yanktonais Dakotas in the winter of 1801–02.*

shadow of a growing western presence. In 1851 the government called a meeting of northern Plains tribes at Fort Laramie. The treaty that resulted attempted to assign tribes to specific territories and draw boundaries around the lands they could occupy. Though unsuccessful in controlling Indian–white hostilities, the treaty foreshadowed the later policy of confining Indians to reservations. During the 1850s and '60s similar treaties secured most of Kansas, Nebraska, and Colorado from the Plains tribes, and the army established fortified trails into the minefields of Colorado and Montana. The influx of settlers took over the Indians' traditional hunting grounds and sacred areas. More than a decade of hostilities resulted. Despite treaties and battles, many of the warrior societies of the Plains refused to submit to the anathema of reservation life, and insisted on continuing their traditions of raids, wars, and unrestricted hunting.

Following the Civil War the forces of the United States were focused on the Plains Indians, and the campaigns to shut down the Plains and confine the Indians to reservations were carried on in earnest. The Plains' riches of land, minerals, and animal hides were to be the nation's patrimony, and the debate over Indian policy centered on the best way to control or eliminate the threat the "savages" posed to white civilization. In 1874 the army began the Red River War, conducting an unrelenting series of raids and attacks that broke the Indians' resistance on the southern Plains. In 1876 the army declared war on the Dakota and their Indian allies on the northern Plains. This war reached its climax in the Battle of the Little Bighorn, but the Indians' massacre only brought a reinforced effort against the Dakotas and their resistance was ended by the next spring.

The maps made during the course of these events document the persistence of Indian identity. They are testimony to the strength of the American Indian cultures and to the unique place that warfare, hostilities and the warrior ethic assumed in these societies. While at the same time they celebrate the traditional way of life, the maps record how the Plains Indians coped with, struggled against, and survived the western expansion of the United States.

The maps show the continuation of the graphic tradition of the Plains. They employ the same elements of picture writing that can be seen in prehistoric rock paintings. More than just

FIGURE 62. **Depiction of** *a buffalo hunt by the Cheyenne artist Howling Wolf, c. 1881. Courtesy of the Joslyn Art Museum, Omaha.*

pictures of territory, the maps tell the story of the events that give meaning to the land. Like the oral record, the picture writing of the Plains developed conventions or graphic shorthand to convey meaning. Tribal affiliation was noted by details of hairstyle or costume, and the action of counting coup, stealing horses, or fighting one's enemies was recorded as the objective of journeys and interactions. With the introduction of western goods, pencils, ink, colors, and papers were adapted to these ends, developing the ledger art that continues to influence Native American art today. Like the oral record of deeds and accomplishments, warriors used these ledgers to record their honors. These maps are a part of this record. Like graphic résumés they document both social history and individual achievements.

The Oto (Otto) Indians were one of several groups that evolved in the area of the western Great Lakes during the thirteenth and fourteenth centuries. Related to the Iowas and the Poncas, they planted corn and other crops and hunted and gathered in the woodlands and prairies. They also hunted the buffalos grazing in the grasslands east of the Mississippi River and followed the herds out onto the Plains. In the early 1700s the Otoes obtained horses and quickly adapted a more nomadic lifestyle. Their annual hunts went further and further out into the Plains where they pursued the vast herds of buffalo. On the Plains the young Oto men tested their bravery against roving bands of Sioux, Cheyenne, and other Indians, or earned their reputations stealing horses from the villages of the Wichitas and the Pawnees. They traded for horses and other goods in the rendezvous of the Plains and in the villages of the Arikaras and Mandans along the upper Missouri River.

By 1780 the Otoes had established their village east of the Missouri River with the Iowas and Poncas. Each of these smaller tribes numbered about one thousand when the small pox epidemic swept over the Plains in 1781. Exact losses are not known, but it is estimated that nearly half of the Otoes were wiped out in this epidemic, with consequent disruptions to their social and cultural patterns. Following the epidemic the Teton, Yankton, and Yanktonai band of the Dakota or Sioux began their push west towards the Missouri. The largest tribe of the Plains, the Dakotas, swept the smaller Otoes and their neighbors before them.

By the beginning of the nineteenth century the Otoes had moved west and established their village on the Platte River, above its confluence with the Missouri. This village is represented on Gero-Schunu-wy-ha's map (Figure 63) below the trading post at Council Bluffs, where the Otoes exchanged hides for western guns, alcohol, and manufactured items. The Otoes were an active part of the horse culture, warrior traditions, and buffalo hunting economy of the Plains. Gero-Schunu-wy-ha, an Oto brave, lived in this village; he recalls two of his exploits on this map. The first is his successful raid on the Arapahoes. The second is his participation in the expedition that marked the first official contacts between various Plains Indians and the government of the United States.

The area represented on Gero-Schunu-wy-ha's map extends from what is now western Iowa to Colorado and north to Montana. In keeping with the Plains picture-writing style, the emphasis is on information rather than on a western perspective of scale and orientation. Gero-Schunu-wy-ha fit the graphic account of his adventures into the available space, highlighting the places and events that shaped this landscape. The English language annotations on the map are believed to be in the hand of one of the members of the expedition that Gero-Schunu-wy-ha accompanied. The events recorded on part of this map correspond with the western historical record.

The Missouri River is represented on the right side of the map. It begins in the lower right at the confluence of the Platte River near what is now Omaha, Nebraska. The Missouri continues up the right side with the trading fort at Council Bluffs shown and several tributaries depicted in South and North Dakota. The Missouri is represented up to the Little Missouri River, which is named at the top center near the contemporary border of Montana and North Dakota. On the other side of the map the Arkansas River enters from the lower left in what is now western Kansas or eastern Colorado. It is represented going up the left side of the map skirting the Rocky Mountains in central Colorado. A white settlement, represented by the square in the upper left, has been interpreted as the Taos Pueblo, an important center for both Indian and Spanish trade. Gero-Schunu-wy-ha's map encompasses much of the central Plains. Next to his Oto ("Otto") village, pictured just to the west of the Platte River in the lower right, he represents the Iowa villages sit-

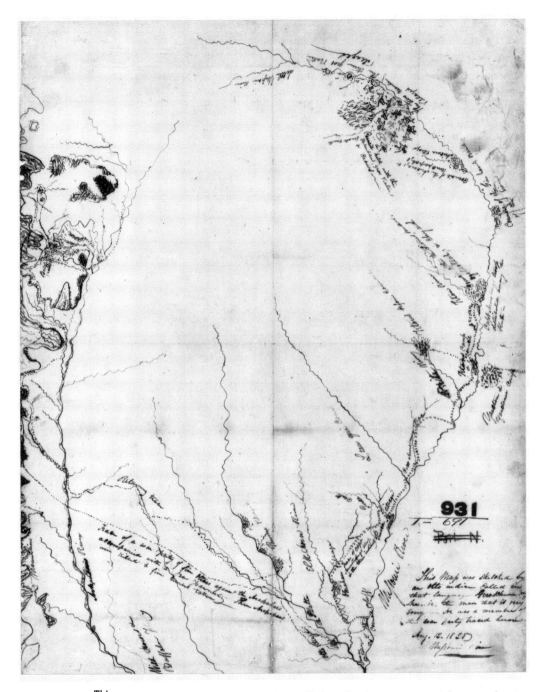

FIGURE 63. *This map was Sketched by an Otto Indian called in that language Gero-Schunu-wy-ha, ie. the man that is very sorry——he was a member of the war party traced hereon, August 12, 1825. Size of the original 21 x 16 inches (53 x 42 cm.). Courtesy of the National Archives and Records Administration, RG 75, Number 931.*

uated near the Platte–Missouri confluence. From here Gero-Schunu-wy-ha records events that occurred to the West and the Northwest in the Great Plains.

The first event Gero-Schunu-wy-ha portrays is his raid against the Arapahos. Far from being sorry, as the title of the map might imply, Gero-Schunu-wy-ha would have been very proud of his accomplishment. He records the raid with the dotted line that goes from the Oto village across the Plains to the Arkansas River. This line is labeled "Trace of a war party of five Ottoes against the Arapahoes . . ." It crosses into the Rocky Mountains where a chase and a fight are recorded. Gero-Schunu-wy-ha documents his success: "Three Arapahoes were killed & five horses taken," an outcome that would have earned him much honor among his people. The date of Gero-Schunu-wy-ha's raid is not known but it predates the other events recorded on the map, those having occurred when the map was dated. In 1825 Gero-Schunu-wy-ha evidently participated in the Atkinson-O'Fallen expedition, going up the river to make friendship treaties with the upper Missouri tribes. His experience is recorded on the right side of the map.

The Indian territory west of the Mississippi River was administered by the War Department. They established forts to control the area and to promote trade. By the 1820s fur traders and trappers were regularly entering this region to trade with the Indians and sometimes to deliberately bypass the Indians' trade network by getting the furs and hauling them to market themselves. This white intrusion into the economic system of the American Indians was not always welcome. In 1823 the Arikaras, who ran an important trading center on the Missouri River, struck back at a party of fur trappers killing twenty-four men. The United States retaliated with an expedition of over three hundred soldiers. They enlisted five hundred Sioux warriors, traditional enemies of the Arikaras, to help overrun the villages. This was the first major U. S. military action against the Indians of the Plains.

Two years later, in an effort to establish communications and trade, the War Department created a peace commission to deal with the Indians of the upper Missouri. In May of 1825 General Henry Atkinson and Major Benjamin O'Fallon led an expedition consisting of 476 men on eight specially designed paddle boats going up the river to make friendship treaties with the tribes. These treaties established official relations between the United States and these tribes; they arranged for the location of forts and rights of way, and they guaranteed the safety of soldiers and settlers entering Indian territory. By August of that year Atkinson reported that he had made treaties with seven branches of the Dakota nation, and with the Cheyennes, Arikaras, Mandans, Hidatsas, Crows, Osages, and Kansas. Although the Atkinson–O'Fallon expedition ascended the river by boat, it was shadowed by Captain Armstrong and a contingent of forty soldiers on horseback. This latter expedition was accompanied by three Indians, one of whom was Gero-Schunu-wy-ha. His map records the track of Captain Armstrong and the councils the Indians held with the white men that summer.

The expedition began at the trading fort of Council Bluffs, represented as a square along the Missouri River in the lower right. The "U"-shaped marks that signify the hoofprints of Captain Armstrong's horses begin here and extend up along the river as he followed the route of the river expedition. The hoofprints are labeled "Trace of Capt. Armstrong with the three indians." Gero-Schunu-wy-ha records the route and events of the expedition in the picture-writing language of the Plains. Earth lodges, like those made by the Pawnees and the Mandans, are represented by circles, while tipis are represented as upside down "V"s. The gatherings of people for councils is represented by the number of tipis and dots or lines to indicate people. Further up the river, Gero-Schunu-wy-ha has drawn mounted horsemen to represent a large council.

Captain Armstrong's route goes up the Elkhorn River to the Omaha villages. The Omahas had migrated west from the Ohio Valley in the seventeenth century. They shared a tradition of farming villages with the Kansas and Osages and, like them, had grown to depend upon the buffalo for food and materials. Captain Armstrong continues past the Ponca villages which are represented along the Missouri and past the "L'eau qui Courser" (Running Water)——probably the Niobrara River in northern Kansas——to the White River and the location of the "Tetons before Council."

The Teton Dakotas, also known as the Brules, are pictured on the west side of the Missouri, indicating that the Dakotas had established a village on that side of the river and begun their migration towards the Black Hills. A little further up the Yankton and Yanktonai Dakota camps are pictured on the east side of the River. A council is represented on the Missouri at what is probably Fort Lookout (established 1822) where it is recorded that the Brules, Yanktons, and Yanktonais signed a friendship treaty on June 22, 1825. Further up the Missouri the Teton River (now called the Bad River) is represented as the site of the "Council of Siones . . . , Ogallesh, & Chyand (Saones, Oglalas, and Cheyennes)" where another treaty was signed. On the east side of the Missouri it is noted that "Capt. Armstrong's troop distributed among the [Floats]," possibly indicating that they joined the eight riverboats ascending the river and no longer continued on horseback. This would explain why the hoofprints of Captain Armstrong's route end here but the information Gero-Schunu-wy-ha presents continues.

The next councils are with the Fire Heart Band of the Sione (a group that later divided itself into three brands of the Brule), and the Arikara & Huncpapah (Hunkpapa), represented on the east and west sides of the Missouri respectively. The Hunkpapa are a branch of the Dakotas living near the Arikaras at that time. The Arikaras, at the time of this map somewhat diminished because of the recent campaign against them, are represented by the circular earth lodges they inhabited. The next council is a large gathering represented with mounted Indians, earth lodges, and tipi villages centered around the Mandan and Hidatsa villages located near the Knife River. The image represents the council held with the Mandans, Gros Ventre (Hidatsas), and the Crows. Further up the river the earth lodges of the Gros Ventre villages are shown. Also known as the Hidatsas, the Gros Ventre had established their villages above the Mandans. The Hidatsas were related to the Crow Indians who lived to the west in the Powder River country. All three evidently came together for the council meeting that General Atkinson and his expedition were hosting. From the drawing, it appears that the council was the occasion for feasts and games in which the whites exchanged presents for the Indians' hospitality and their promise of friendly relations.

Gero-Schunu-wy-ha's map records these first friendship treaties between these Indians of the Plains and the United States. In 1825 this was still an untouched Indian territory with few of the trading forts and military installations that would be built along the river in the next decade. White society had yet to feel the need to invade the Plains Indians' territory; all the Atkinson expedition wanted was a guarantee of safety for the white fur traders and the right to establish trade and military infrastructure in the region. With the addition of the white trading posts in the 1830s, the trade networks and hunting practices of the American Indians would begin to shift to accommodate the growing markets of the east, but the Plains Indians would still have several years in which to practice their way of life undisturbed.

Another America

Following the small pox epidemic of 1837–38 the landscape Gero-Schunu-wy-ha portrayed was altered. The Mandans and their neighbors on the Missouri, the Arikara and Hidatsa, were greatly weakened. They were no longer able to pose a threat to the Dakota Indians who began to freely cross the river and move to the south and the west, displacing other tribes and rearranging the landscape of the Plains. At the same time white migration began to increase the traffic on the wagon routes that cut through the middle of the Indians' territory. Within twenty-six years of Gero-Schunu-wy-ha's map the first land cession treaty was signed by the Indians of the Plains.

This Assiniboine map (Figure 64) was made at the Fort Union trading post, established on the Upper Missouri River by the American Fur Company in 1829. Located at the mouth of the Yellowstone River near what is now the North Dakota–Montana border, Fort Union attracted Assiniboine hunters who would bring in their dressed buffalo robes to trade for guns, ammunition, and manufactured items. With the supplies from the fort and the horses they could obtain in raids or at the summer rendezvous, the Assiniboine enjoyed to the full their life of the Plains. Nomadic hunters, they pursued the buffalo and other game and enthusiastically participated in the rituals of wars and raids. Edwin Denig, who collected this map from an anonymous Assiniboine warrior, was a white man who had married into the tribe. He took an Assiniboine wife and lived among the tribe before he went on to become the superintendent of the American Fur Company's operations at Fort Union and then that of the company's successor.

When Denig arrived on the upper Missouri, the Plain's culture was in its full flower. His ethnological report on the Assiniboine, published posthumously in the Smithsonian Institution's *Forty-Sixth Annual Report of the Bureau of American Ethnology* provides a detailed picture of Plains Indian life in the nineteenth century. This map gives a glimpse of the way in which the Plains were conceived, populated, and enjoyed by the Assiniboines and their neighbors even as the army forts and trading centers of the whites became permanent features of the landscape.

The ancestors of the Assiniboine Indians migrated from the Ohio Valley in the fifteenth and sixteenth centuries. They were part of the Dakota peoples and lived for a while in the lake region of Minnesota. Drawn to the buffalos that inhabited the prairies to the west, the Assiniboines' ancestors organized communal hunts that required both the cooperation and the contribution of all the hunters in the tribe. In the 1600s other Indians migrating into this region put pressure on the Assiniboines. They broke from the larger Dakota tribe and migrated north and west, gradually arriving in the area north of the Missouri River in what is now the Canadian province of Alberta.

There they allied with their eastern neighbors, the Plains Cree, to protect themselves against the powerful Blackfoot Indians who lived west towards the Rocky Mountains. In the beginning of the eighteenth century the Assiniboines obtained horses. They quickly adopted the nomadic lifestyle of Plains hunters and warriors. By the 1800s the Assiniboines had spread south from Alberta to the north side of the Missouri River into what is now North Dakota and Montana. They hunted the buffalo across this plain and sent raiding parties into the territories of the Crow, Blackfoot, and Arikara Indians. This map shows much of the Assiniboines' territory.

The area pictured on the map includes the north side of the Missouri River from Fort Union, represented at the bottom of the map, past Fort Benton to the Rocky Mountains and the outlying ranges in central Montana. Denig presumably added the title and the names on the map,

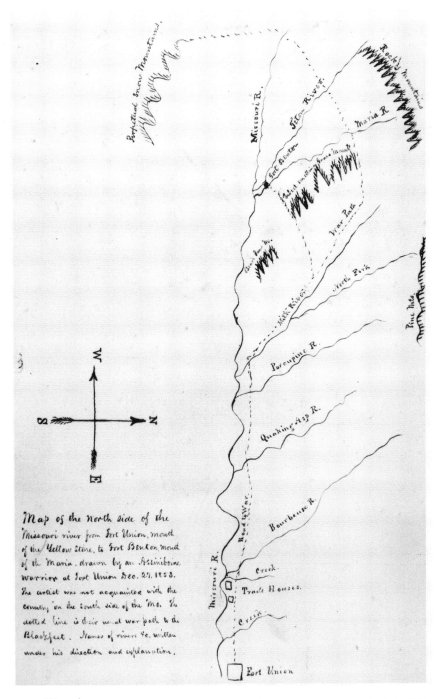

FIGURE 64. "Map of the North side of the Missouri river from Fort Union, mouth of the Yellow Stone to Fort Benton, Mouth of the Maria. drawn by an Assiniboine warrior at Fort Union Dec. 27, 1853." Courtesy of the National Anthropological Archives, Smithsonian Institution.

Another America

which he notes were written under the direction of his Indian informant, and he no doubt added the compass arrows to give the cardinal directions. The map is easily read by turning it on its side with north to the top, but the Indian's lines still do not correspond to western cartographic conventions. They reflect the way the landmarks and geography were conceived in the Plains oral traditions. The Missouri is represented as a wavy line going nearly straight across Montana, although in western maps a great bend occurs before Fort Benton and the Marias River ("Maria R" on the map). Similarly, the Milk River in the middle of the map is pictured continuing northwest when in western geography it turns and nearly parallels the Missouri River before reaching the Rocky Mountains. But the Assiniboine's map was not made to give a western oriented picture of the landscape; like much Plains picture writing it was made to record the warpath of the anonymous brave making a raid on the Blackfeet in Montana. The heart of the map is this picture of the warrior's exploits; out to bring glory to himself and the riches of stolen horses to his people.

Denig's annotations note that, "The artist was not acquainted with the country on the south side of the MO. [Missouri River]," but this may not be the case. The depiction of the northern Missouri tributaries is sufficient to tell the warrior's story, while the southern geography is irrelevant except where he crosses the river into Blackfoot territory. The "Road to War" begins at Fort Union, crosses two creeks, and skirts the Trade Houses (probably the establishment Denig was in charge of), and continues to the Milk River. It then follows the Milk west-northwest using well-known landmarks to show the route. The Bears Paw Mountains in north central Montana are still known by that name, and the "Pine Mts." are the Cyprus Hills of southeastern Alberta. Just as shown on the Indian's map, the Milk River passes between these two landmarks and then continues north of the Sweet Grass Hills ("Sweet Smelling Grass Mounts") in southern Alberta before turning west towards its origin in the Rocky Mountains. The warpath that the Indian records upon this landscape goes up and around Fort Benton, pictured between the Marias and Teton Rivers, possibly to avoid any concentrations of Indians camping or trading there. The warrior's path then heads south along the face of the Rockies, crossing the Missouri River into the "Perpetual Snow Mountains." These are believed to represent the Big Belt and Little Belt Mountains that lie east of the Missouri River in central Montana. The mapmaker has portrayed a route of over four hundred miles in a manner that could be easily read by any Indian familiar with the region and its landmarks.

Denig described the Assiniboine territory as "one great plain with hills and timber only on the rivers where the valleys offer good arable land." Despite having lived with the tribe and spending nearly two decades in their company, Denig still viewed the Assiniboine and the other tribes of the upper Missouri through the eyes of western civilization. He dutifully recorded aspects of their culture and seemed to understand that their way of life was sacred to them, but Denig nevertheless hoped to civilize these Indians. He contended that the trading interests that he scrupulously represented, had laid the foundation for the road to civilization. Unfortunately, Denig found his in-laws, the Assiniboines, to be one of the most recalcitrant tribes when it came to adopting the white man's ways. "They adhere with tenacity to the old customs and superstitions," he wrote, "which is most vexatious and discouraging."

To Denig, the grasslands of the Plains represented a resource to be used for raising horses and domestic cattle. The Assiniboines, on the other hand, saw the land as having been made for them by the creator. Unlike the whites who conceived of owning the land and transforming it to a higher purpose, the Indians looked upon the Plains as a gift created for their well being. Why else would the great spirit have made the prairie and filled it with buffalos and the other game? And why would he have made the Indians such strong riders, fierce warriors, and deadly hunters if they were not meant to hunt, fight over, and inhabit this paradise? Denig's understanding of the Indians made him sympathetic to the pleasure they took in their existence, and he viewed the fur trade as a means of sustaining the Indians' way of life while profiting the capitalists in the East. Denig also understood that the balance needed to maintain this trade-off was being threatened by the continual in-migration of whites.

Like the other hunters of the Plains, the Assiniboines camped in nomadic bands that migrated across their territory. They came together for communal hunts and to make war upon their enemies. Each band had one or more leaders or chiefs, men who had gained their position through brave deeds and the courageous and reckless behavior that won glory for the warrior. Without hereditary positions of leadership, one gained influence among the Assiniboine through success in battle and by having the insights needed to make a successful hunt or know where the game would be plentiful. Tribal decisions were arrived at in a council of the leaders, with the warrior societies and other divisions of the tribe coming to agreement on issues of mutual interest.

An Assiniboine male who wished to show his abilities as a leader would call his friends together and suggest a horse raid. Dreams and ritual chants would bring the warrior power, and he would read the signs and portends for the most auspicious time. Traveling to the enemy's territory, the small raiding party would trail the opponent's camp at night, timing its raid to be most effective. Those who wished to gain particular honors would steal the better horses, and with luck the raiders might encounter members of the enemy's tribe whom they could scalp and bring home as prizes for additional honors. Once the horses and any other spoils had been taken, the braves would ride back to their camp as quickly as possible, stopping before they arrived to arrange themselves in mourning if one of their comrades had fallen, or put on their finery and fire their weapons to announce their success.

When the Assiniboine went to war it was less of an individual undertaking. A council would be called to determine if it was time for the people to strike their enemies. Within the traditions of the Plains there was always a rationale for a fight——an offense to be revenged or territory to be retaken. When a tribe was weakened or preoccupied, it was understood that the Indians on any side of them would take advantage of this opportunity to strike and expand their territory. In this way the Plains were divided up in a shifting pattern of power and possession. The ability to repel one's enemies and defend one's territory determined which part of the Plains a tribe could claim. While the tribal territories changed hands depending upon who was strong and well supplied with horses, the buffalo ranges that made up the bulk of the land were there for the Indians' subsistence. Regardless of how they fought over its apportionment, the land was for all the Indians. To sell it would be the same as selling their only source of food, the source for their materialculture, and the landscape around which the principles and activities of their lives were organized.

In one section of his report on the "Indian Tribes of the Upper Missouri," Denig speculated on the Indians' future. He summed up the Indians' relationship with the buffalo, "If the buffaloes diminish, so do the Indians." But he saw no diminution in the great buffalo herds. Even allowing for the reduction in open range due to white emigration, Denig saw the buffalos increasing. He attributed this to the Indians' method of hunting——now dependent upon the horse and the gun——and to their way of life, which disturbed the buffalos' habitat much less than white ranchers or farmers would. Without estimating the size of the northern herd he noted that after more than twenty years of taking hides the buffalo were more numerous than ever. He speculated that because of imported diseases and white immigration the Indians would diminish and perhaps be destroyed long before their game. And, although he noted that the trade in hides may have increased the number of buffalos taken, the increase was too small "to hasten the destruction or even diminution of any game as plentiful as the buffalo." Denig concluded that the Indians in their current state, and the buffalos, would both ultimately disappear as a consequence of white immigration, "though the Indian, being the smaller number, would be the first to vanish."

In addition to foreseeing the effect of white settlement on the Indian and the buffalo, Denig was a first-hand witness to the destructive force of white diseases. He was stationed on the upper Missouri in 1837 when the small pox made its way up the river a second time. That summer, as the steamboat carrying the infected crew members docked to unload trade goods at the forts on the Missouri, the Indians would come to inspect the wares and make trades. Despite attempts to keep them away, the Indians entered the infected areas and brought the disease back to their families and villages. That fall the smallpox nearly destroyed the Mandans and spread to the Hidatsas, Arikaras, and Dakotas. By the spring of 1838 the disease had made its way to Fort Union. The Assiniboines trading at the fort caught the smallpox. Denig reports that members of an Assiniboine band consisting of two hundred fifty lodges all contracted the disease at the same time; only sixty-five men or about thirty lodges surviving by the time the scourge was done. Other bands of Assiniboine came to the fort and caught it as well. The strain of small pox was particularly virulent. It struck with a fury, throwing the Indians into deliriums and killing them from internal hemorrhages even before the characteristic spots appeared. Every day Denig had to supervise the dumping of cartloads of victims into the river.

The plague of 1837 and 1838 altered the life on the prairie. The Blackfeet were so reduced that they turned inward for a generation and no longer posed a threat to the Assiniboines. The Assiniboines themselves were reduced from over one thousand lodges to less then four hundred. Such destruction caused havoc within the tribe. Kinship relations were destroyed, property was lost, and only a few were left to mourn and record the death and destruction. An entire generation had to grow up before new leadership could appear and the bands could once more gather together. Denig reports that fifteen years after the plague the Assiniboines had only increased their number by one hundred lodges or approximately five hundred people.

The aftermath of the smallpox led to political changes as well. The Dakotas, although having suffered from the pox, remained the largest tribe on the Plains. They took advantage of the other tribes' weakness to steal their horses and drive them from their hunting grounds. This left smaller tribes like the Assiniboine permanently weakened. Those who did not have horses could not hunt with the same efficiency, and they lacked the basic commodity of Plains trade. To counteract the Dakota threat, the Assiniboines made an advantageous alliance with the Crow Indians. In exchange for Crow horses and the promise of mutual assistance, the Assiniboines allowed the Crows to hunt on their territory and to freely cross their lands to trade with the Hidatsas. In the new dynamics of the Plains, the two together provided a strength in numbers that neither could achieve alone.

Even more powerful than the trading posts, the small pox, and the other diseases was the influx of American emigrants. Within fifteen years of the 1837–38 epidemic the geography of North America had changed. In the aftermath of the Mexican War, the land area of the United States increased to include the Southwest from Texas to California and the area west of the Rocky Mountains north to Oregon Territory. These new areas lured settlers and prospectors. Pioneers crowded the Plains, their wagons and cattle destroying great areas of the grassland. When the Indians struck back, the government intervened. A number of military battles took place, but an even more insidious policy was being formulated in the plan to divide the Plains up into tribal territories, drawing boundaries and assigning Indians to tracts of lands where their way of life was to be contained. The treaties, land cessions, and agreements that began with the forced relocation of tribes from the East and continued with the council of Plains tribes at Fort Laramie remade the map of the Plains. It was no longer a shifting pattern of claims that followed the fortunes of the Plains tribes; a new division was being imposed upon the land by the government's authority. National policy evolved into one of containing the Indians in smaller and smaller territories where they would not harm the white settlements and could eventually be persuaded to adopt a western way of life.

The Assiniboine were represented at the 1851 council and treaty of Fort Laramie along with Oglala Dakotas, Northern Cheyennes, Crows, Arikaras, and Blackfeet. The council attempted to impose western-style boundaries and limits on the Indians' territories, and the government imposed its own political organization on the tribe by recognizing an official tribal representative. In the case of the Assiniboines, the government appointed Crazy Bears as chief, although even Denig admits that Crazy Bears's authority was not recognized within this egalitarian tribe. In the treaty that followed, the Assiniboines were assigned a territory to the south of their normal range. According to the treaty they were to occupy the area between the Missouri and Yellowstone rivers, bounded to the east and west by the territories of the Blackfeet and the Crows.

The artificial boundaries established by the treaty were not respected and the Assiniboines continued to occupy their territory north of the Missouri River. They eventually settled in the Fort Peck and Fort Belknap reservations of Montana. These two reservations lie within the territory described on this Assiniboine warrior's map.

(Figure 65) was made at about the same time as the Assiniboine's map and shows the warriors' path to the Blackfeet. Denig reproduced it in his ethnological report on the Assiniboine. The picture displays the characteristic use of profile drawings enhanced with details of costume or clothing, for instance the Assiniboine warrior's hairstyle, to identify the tribal affiliation. On a flat blank background the warrior has recorded his accomplishment of killing his enemy. Like the oral account that was affirmed and recorded by the tribe, this drawing was a record of the warrior's deed. The elaborate paint and costume of the warrior, and the feathered tail, painted rump, and fancy bridle of his horse, give an indication of the ritual preparation and pageant-like display that went into the warfare of the Plains.

(Figure 66) Lean Wolf, second chief of the Hidatsa Indians, made this map during his visit to Washington, D.C., in 1881. Using basic elements of Plains' pictography, Lean Wolf's map tells the story of his exploits as a young warrior even while the map documents the transformations that were

Another America

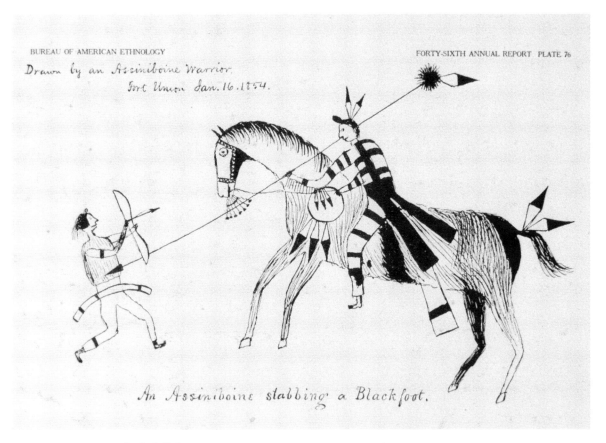

Drawn by an Assiniboine Warrior.
Fort Union Jan. 16. 1854.

An Assiniboine stabbing a Blackfoot.

FIGURE 65. **An Assiniboine** *stabbing a Blackfoot. Drawn by an Assiniboine Warrior. Fort Union Jan. 16, 1854.*

taking place on the Plains. Within the lifetime of Lean Wolf, the Hidatsa Indians had seen their villages nearly wiped out by imported white diseases; they had seen their neighbors the Mandans and Arikaras loose their prominent position in the trade network of the Plains; they had suffered the aggression of the Dakota Indians and seen the United States unable to deliver on its guarantees of safety; they had seen themselves and the other Indians of the Plains confined to reservations; and now the buffalo were disappearing and with them would go the Hidatsa's way of life. In the face of all he had seen, Lean Wolf remained a Hidatsa. On his trip to Washington he was asked to draw pictures recording his life. In keeping with the warrior traditions of the Plains, all of Lean Wolf's drawings record his exploits counting coup, stealing horses, and receiving his warrior honors.

Lean Wolf's map represents the area from the Hidatsas' village, called "Like a Fishhook," and up the upper Missouri River to Fort Buford at the confluence of the Yellowstone and Missouri rivers. This area, now part of west central North Dakota, encompasses the northern end of the Hidatsa, Mandan, and Arikara homelands. Because of their important position in the indigenous trade network of the Plains, the Hidatsa were one of the first tribes of Plains Indians to obtain and trade horses. While keeping their village culture they quickly adapted the horse to hunting on the

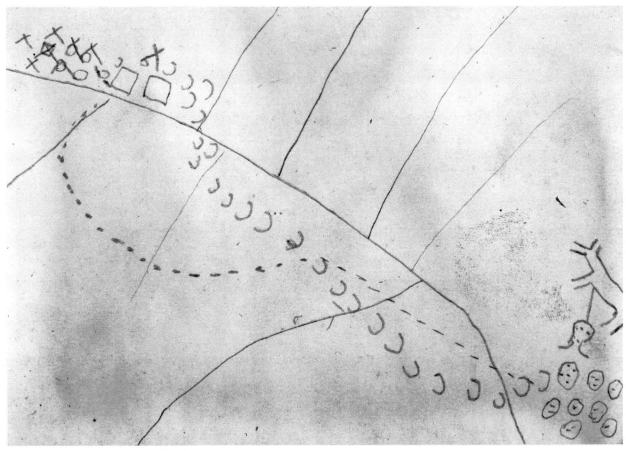

FIGURE 66. **Lean Wolf's** *map of his horse raid, 1881. Size of the original 3 x 5 inches (7.6 x 12.7 cm.), Courtesy of the National Anthropological Archives, Smithsonian Institution.*

buffalo plains and acquired the war and raiding traditions of other Plains tribes. The Hidatsas' important location on the Missouri River also brought them into early contact with European traders. French, Spanish, and later American traders visited them regularly from the 1730s on. Some, following the pattern of Edwin Denig with his Assiniboine wife, married into and lived with the tribe to serve as middlemen and interpreters. By the time of the events recorded on Lean Wolf's map, the processes of white economic and political encroachment had resulted in trading forts and Indian agencies at Fort Berthold, next to Like a Fish Hook village, and at Fort Buford to the west by the Yellowstone. Although Lean Wolf's map of the Missouri River is bounded by these two white settlements, the landscape he presents remains Native American. The Missouri is drawn from the lower right to the upper left with various northern and southern tributaries to provide a geographical setting. Like most Plains picture writing, the events portrayed are far more important than the geography. The landscape provides a background for Lean Wolf's depiction of

Another America

his raid upon the Dakotas living near Fort Buford. In the 1860s and '70s the Dakotas had continually raided the Hidatsas' village. Lean Wolf's raid upon these terrible enemies would have satisfied the Hidatsas' need for revenge and brought him high honors.

The map uses several conventions of Plains picture writing. Lean Wolf represents himself in the lower right using a generalized figure that is identified by the pictograph name connected to it. His pictograph signature is the wolf with a white body and the mouth unfinished to show that it is empty or lean. This symbol could be read by most Plains Indians, who would have known whose story was being told. The Hidatsas' Like a Fish Hook village, where Lean Wolf starts his raid, is pictured in the lower right, the circles representing the earth lodges of the Hidatsa. Lean Wolf has added dots and lines to representing the wooden beams of these semi-permanent homes. Lean Wolf began his raid on foot and represents his tract by the dotted line that crosses to the south side of the Missouri and then dips down farther south to cross the Yellowstone River and come up upon Fort Buford from the west.

The dwellings of the white residents of Fort Buford are represented by the two square buildings on the north side of the Missouri. Lean Wolf pictures the complexity of the mixed Indian and white community that had settled near the trading post. The Dakotas are represented by the "X"s that stand for the poles of their tipis, while Dakotas married to Hidatsas are represented by the "X" over the circle, and a white man married to a Dakota is represented by the "X" over the square. Most important of all to Lean Wolf's story is the track of hoofprints leading back to the Hidatsa village that indicates the success of his horse raid.

By 1881, when he made this map, Lean Wolf was no longer a young man. His warrior accomplishments had earned him a place of honor and responsibility among his people. He may have gone to Washington to represent his people and ask for the government's help as the Hidatsa faced an uncertain future. At the end of the nineteenth century the Hidatsas' traditional way of life was breaking up and the tribe's population reached its lowest ebb. In the two centuries since white contact, the Hidatsa had decreased from a group of perhaps five thousand Indians farming and hunting along the Missouri River to a small tribe who sought protection by affiliating itself with the Mandans and the Arikaras. As the nineteenth century drew to a close, these three tribes struggled to survive together on the reservation, and their combined populations amounted to just over one thousand.

The Hidatsas, sometimes called the Gros Ventre or the Minitarees, were a combination of peoples, some of whom claimed traditions along the Missouri River going back for many centuries. Other branches of the Hidatsa migrated from Manitoba and eastern North Dakota as part of the Crow people. They spoke a Siouan dialect, and by approximately 1775 had settled in three villages around the mouth of the Knife River where it meets the Missouri in central North Dakota. Here they practiced what has been called the "Plains village tradition." Unlike the image of Plains Indians as nomadic hunters in the style of the Dakotas, the Cheyennes, the Assiniboines, and the Blackfeet, the Hidatsa and the other farmers and hunters lived in semi-permanent villages. Like the Pawnees and Arikaras, the Hidatsas and Mandans built their villages of earth lodges on the terraces above the Missouri. Periodic floods deposited rich soil along the bottom lands and the Indians planted corn, beans, and squash. These crops provided the Hidatsa and their neighbors with staples that they could trade with the other Indians. In addition to their crops, the Hidatsa depended upon the buffalo, and they used the horses they acquired through trade and raids, like the one recorded on Lean Wolf's map, to go out on the plains in communal hunts that replenished the tribe.

In the second half of the 1700s the Plains horse culture began to flourish and the traditions of wars and raids began to take on their nineteenth-century characteristics. Soon the nomadic tribes began to make regular forays against the upper Missouri villages. Rather than trade for the Hidastas' corn, it was more honorable to steal it in the process of a horse raid or after counting coup and perhaps taking the scalp of an enemy. The Hidatsa and their neighbors gathered together in larger villages that afforded more protection from these raids. In the late 1700s the villages on the upper Missouri were home to the largest concentrations of American Indians on the Plains. These villages became important exchange points in the economic network of the Plains, and they continued to serve as a magnet for young braves wishing to make a name for themselves stealing horses and taking scalps.

In 1781, when the smallpox struck the Plains, the Hidatsas were living in their three villages along the Knife River. The Hidatsas are estimated to have lost a third of their population in this epidemic while the Mandans, living to the south, were reduced to almost half. The weakened Mandans moved up the Missouri River and established two new villages near the three Hidatsa settlements. Together, these became known as the "five villages." It is here that the tribes were visited by Lewis and Clark, George Catlin, and the European, Prince Maximillian, accompanied by the painter Karl Bodmer. In the first half of the nineteenth century these and other visitors left an impressive record in words, paintings, and drawings that helped document these unique cultures before they were once again changed by imported diseases and the pressures of white society.

Lean Wolf grew up in one of the Hidatsa villages along the Knife, and his uncle was serving as one of the Hidatsas' chiefs when the smallpox struck again in 1837. This time the Dakotas took advantage of the plague to raid the Mandan villages and attack anyone who tried to escape. Stuck in their villages, the disease nearly wiped out the Mandans, reducing their numbers to less then one hundred. The Hidatsas were able to leave their villages and flee up the river, where they were spared the worst of the epidemic. Greatly weakened and easily preyed upon by the larger Plains tribes, the Hidatsa suffered in the aftermath of the plague. It was during this period that Lean Wolf came of age; and like all warriors, he participated in the raids and fights that were central to the life of Plain Indians. Lean Wolf's pictographic records, made along with this map during his visit to Washington, D.C., give no hint of the Hidatsas' troubles. Rather, they revel in the deeds and accomplishments that brought him honor and position among the Hidatsa. Like a Davy Crockett of the Plains, Lean Wolf pictures how he drowned a buffalo "When aged 21." Other pictures record his surviving an attack by the Sioux, counting coup on his enemy, and riding as "Partisan" or the leader of a raiding party much like that recorded on his map.

In 1845 the Hidatsa abandoned their villages on the Knife River and moved upstream to establish "Like a Fishhook." Here they were joined by the remaining Mandan Indians, and their two cultures mixed even more than before. A trading post was established and the combined tribes afforded some protection. But the Hidatsas and the Mandans continued to suffer. In the competitive environment of the Plains, nomadic tribes would sweep in to steal the Hidatsa horses, raid their crops, and take scalps. Following the Fort Laramie Treaty of 1851, the Hidatsa agreed to grant safe passage to white immigrants. In return, the government recognized the Mandan,

Another America

Hidatsa, and Arikara claims to the right bank of the Missouri from the mouth of the Heart River to the Yellowstone.

But the territories assigned to the various tribes in the Fort Laramie Treaty meant nothing to braves born to hunt and raid across the Plains. The Oglala, Hunkpapa, Yankton and other Dakota groups were expanding their territories west of the Missouri. They fell upon the Hidatsas and their neighbors like a plague. Smaller, weaker, and without the wealth of guns and horses possessed by the nomadic tribes, the Hidatsas and Mandans had trouble holding their own. In 1862 the Arikara Indians, who had remained in villages further down the Missouri, yielded to the Dakota pressure and abandoned their village to join the Hidatsas and Mandans already living at Like a Fishhook. To protect themselves, these three tribes sought an agreement with the federal government. They entered into an alliance with the United States that led to the establishment of the Fort Berthold agency in 1867. One year earlier, Fort Buford had been built at the confluence of the Missouri and the Yellowstone rivers. This is the landscape reflected in Lean Wolf's map. Despite the white presence and the difficulties that accompanied the crowding of three different cultural traditions into one large village, the deeds that stand out in Lean Wolf's memory are those of a young brave. The coup of successfully raiding the Dakotas' encampment was more in keeping with Lean Wolf's concept of what was important than any of the treaties or agreements signed with the whites.

By 1881 raids like the one Lean Wolf's map recalls were largely confined to memory. Following the Battle of the Little Bighorn the army campaigned aggressively to shut down the Plains. The Dakotas and Cheyenne were confined to reservations; in 1877 Chief Joseph and the Nez Perces were forced to surrender; and in 1881 Sitting Bull, one of the heroes of the Little Bighorn, returned from his Canadian exile to surrender at Fort Buford. Open land and the buffalos were quickly disappearing. Following the completion of the transcontinental railroad, white hunters moved in to take over the buffalo trade. Killing at three or four times the rate of the Indians, they helped to wipe out the herds that only thirty years earlier the trader Edwin Denig had predicted would outlast the Indians. By 1890 only about one thousand buffalos remained on the Plains.

Without the buffalo, the Hidatsa and the other tribes faced a future that was the antithesis of their life on the Plains. To survive, the men were forced to take up farming, or to rely upon the rations distributed by the Indian agents and the trade goods received as part of the annual annuities. On the Fort Berthold reservation the Hidatsas slowly abandoned their traditional earthen lodge village and moved onto the parcels of land they had been issued through the policy of allotment. There is evidence that Lean Wolf lived through this period of transition, surviving into the first part of the twentieth century. One of the final records Lean Wolf made during his trip to Washington in the 1880s was a sign language demonstration given to the anthropologist W. J. Hoffman. "Lean Wolf's complaint," as the sign language is titled, translates: "Four years ago the American people agreed to be friends with Us, but they lied. That is all."

(Figure 67) The drawing, Lean Wolf as partisan, incorporates several aspects of Plains Indian picture writing. The horns on his headdress indicate Lean Wolf's rank of chief and the arrangement of the eagle feathers shows his high distinction as a warrior. The empty or lean wolf of his pictographic signature is attached to the picture. The pipe held in the upright position indicates Lean Wolf's authority as "partisan" or the leader of a war party, perhaps returning from a successful raid such as the one illustrated on his map.

FIGURE 67. **Lean Wolf** *as partisan. Reproduced from one of the biographical drawings Lean Wolf made during his visit to Washington in 1880–1881 in "Picture-Writing of the American Indians" by Garrick Mallery.* Tenth Annual Report of the Bureau of Ethnology to the Secretary of the Smithsonian Institution 1888-89.

*　　*　　*

White Bird, a northern Cheyenne Indian, painted this scene of the Battle of the Little Bighorn (Figure 69) approximately twenty years after the fact. Like many Plains Indian pictures it records historic events in which warriors earned honors by defeating their enemies. In western history this battle became known as "Custer's Last Stand." At the time, it was seen as a humiliating defeat. News of the battle was picked up by the popular press and fed the public outrage over uncivilized savages standing in the way of Manifest Destiny. Following the battle the army campaigned with renewed vigor to close the Plains and confine all the tribes on reservations.

Since then, the Battle of the Little Bighorn has become mythologized. As a symbolic event in American history it has been interpreted and reinterpreted to suit the times. The battle has been explained as everything from the savage massacre of brave soldiers to the just desserts for a nation whose pride, ignorance, and imperialistic policies were personified in the arrogant figure of George Armstrong Custer. White Bird's painting is only one of many American Indian depictions

Another America

FIGURE 68.
Portrait of *Lean Wolf.*
*During his trip to
Washington, D.C., Lean
Wolf was photographed wearing traditional clothing. His
Hidatsa name, Tce-caq-a-
daq-a-qic, is given in the
lower left. Lean Wolf was
about 60 years old when this
photograph was taken.*

of the battle, and like white historians, Indians have tended to emphasize their experience of it. The Battle of the Little Bighorn was a seminal event in the history of conflict between American Indians and the people and government of the United States. It is best seen in the context of the events leading up to it.

White Bird's painting is an accurate depiction. It is a map in that it uses geography to pro-

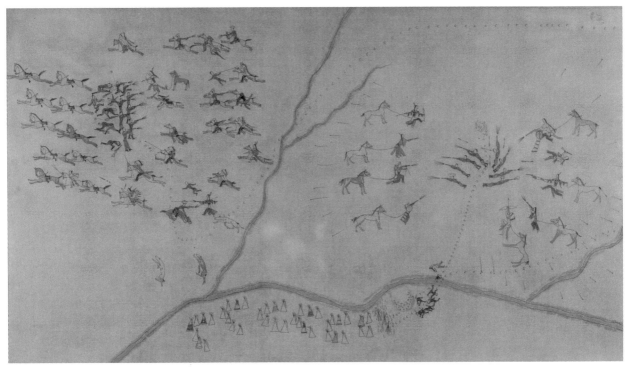

FIGURE 69. **White Bird,** *"Battle of the Little Bighorn, June 25, 1876," c. 1895. Size of the original 67.5 x 98 inches (171 x 249 cm), Courtesy of the West Point Museum, United States Military Academy, West Point, New York.*

vide a setting for the events being recorded. The Little Bighorn River, a tributary of the Bighorn and the Yellowstone rivers in south-central Montana, is represented across the bottom of the page. Two smaller tributaries flow into the Little Bighorn. Along the west side of the river White Bird has depicted the tipis of the Indian encampment that Custer attacked on the afternoon of June 25, 1876. In the visual shorthand of Plains picture writing, White Bird depicted the camp as a number of tipis spread along the winding banks of the river. In actuality this camp was made up of five bands of Plains Indians camped together and forming the largest village of American Indians ever recorded on the Plains. The bands of Dakotas, Cheyennes, and Arapahos were made up of Indians who had refused to obey the government's order to report to the reservation. They chose instead to stay out in the unregulated territory of the Plains and pursue the life they had known. The Hunkpapa, under the leadership of Sitting Bull, and the Oglala, led by the charismatic Crazy Horse, were joined by bands of Teton, Yanktonai, and Minniconjous Sioux, each with their leaders and chiefs. They in turn had been joined by Cheyennes and Arapahos rebelling against the army's attempt to sweep them off the Plains. As word of the Indians' defiance spread, Indians from the reservations, young men who saw a chance to win the honor and position that only warrior exploits could provide and others who craved one more season living the traditional life on the Plains, came out to join them.

Another America

The village White Bird pictures camped along the Little Bighorn may have totaled more than nine thousand people and included more then two thousand warriors. They had come together to make a stand against the force of arms, railroads, reservations, broken treaties, and white settlers that threatened to overwhelm them. Determined to fight for their way of life, the Indians' defiance is far more tragic in its nobility than are the consequences of Custer's hubris or his megalomaniac actions.

Ever since the 1851 Treaty of Fort Laramie, the United States had been attempting to restrict the Indians' territories, confining them to reservations while white emigrants and settlers slowly took over the ceded lands. The annexation of Texas, New Mexico, California, and the Oregon territory in the middle of the nineteenth century left the Indians of the Great Plains surrounded. An open frontier was no longer possible as settlers moved into the newly organized Kansas and Nebraska territory and California prospectors searched east into the Rocky Mountains for their mineral finds. Pressure was being exerted on the Indians from both sides. Wagon roads, railroads, forts, and telegraph lines were laid down, the new American network replacing the native landscape just as white settlers were replacing the Indians as the dominant population. At the same time what remained of the Indians' territory was becoming more crowded. By 1850 the United States had relocated nearly ninety thousand Indians west of the Mississippi.

For two decades the Plains Indians had fought against these incursions. When their lands were invaded or when army representatives and Indian agents pushed them too far, an uprising would occur. The Indians attacked settlements, killing civilians, scalping their victims, and taking hostages. The army and the settlers would respond with campaigns to wipe out the Indians, indiscriminately attacking whomever they could find. In 1864 such an incident occurred near the Arkansas River in the southern Plains. The Southern Cheyennes and Arapahos had resisted the railroad and the white hunters coming into their territories. The Colorado militia responded with an attack on Black Kettle's band of Cheyenne as they were camped along Sand Creek. Known as the Sand Creek Massacre, the militia killed more then two hundred Cheyenne men, women, and children, cutting off their scalps and limbs and displaying them as victory trophies back in Denver. The Indians hostilities that followed cut Denver off from the east until the army retaliated with a counteroffensive the following year.

Once the Civil War ended, the army focused its efforts on controlling the American Plains. One of those who came out to be an Indian fighter was Lieutenant Colonel George Armstrong Custer. Given a field commission in the Civil War, Custer had become a hero with his death-defying charges under fire. Now appointed second in command of the Seventh Cavalry, he crisscrossed the southern Plains helping the army perfect its Indian-fighting strategy. The army campaigns of the 1860s had proved largely ineffective. Slow moving, heavily armored columns of cavalry and infantry would march to meet an enemy that specialized in hit-and-run tactics. For several years the swift-riding warrior bands outwitted the army and scored surprising victories when they controlled the encounter. In the second half of the 1860s the army adjusted its tactics. It began employing converging columns to squeeze the Indians into smaller and smaller territories, and attacked the Indians' villages where the warriors were limited in their ability to retaliate by having to protect their women and children. The army also began raiding the Indians' winter villages. Here the usually mobile Indians were entrenched with their families and were even more vulnerable.

In November of 1868 Custer staged such a raid at the Battle of the Washita. He led the Seventh Cavalry in a dawn attack against a sleeping Cheyenne village. One hundred three Cheyennes were killed in the battle, including women, children, and old men, one of whom was Black Kettle, the southern Cheyenne chief who had escaped the massacre at Sand Creek. The raid was considered a great victory in the Indian wars and helped to increase Custer's fame.

On the northern Plains the Sioux or Dakota Indians dominated. From the Missouri River to the Platte and west to the Powder River territory they resisted all white attempts to enter their lands. In the decades before the 1860s they had fought with and subdued many of the other tribes of this region. They formed an alliance with the Northern Cheyenne and maintained the balance of power with raids and wars on their enemies. Partially as a result of the Sioux aggression, many of the smaller groups such as the Hidatsas and the Mandans accepted white forts and reservations. A stalemate occurred when the Sioux prevented the army and settlers from using the Bozeman trail that went from the Platte River north to the gold fields of Montana. Finally, in 1868, the Sioux accepted the treaty that established the "Great Sioux Reservation." The reservation lands extended west from the Missouri River through most of South Dakota. To the west of the new reservation, in what is now Montana, the land was declared unceded Indian territory. This area included the rich buffalo grounds of the Powder, Tongue, Bighorn, Little Bighorn, and Yellowstone rivers. Following the treaty, the army abandoned its forts along the Bozeman trail, and bands of Sioux, Cheyenne, and other Indians who rejected the reservation life moved on to the unceded territory. Among those who chose to live in this territory were Sitting Bull and Crazy Horse. They led their bands to the north and the west, away from the white man, to continue their traditional life.

The Sioux War of 1876–77 was preceded by the discovery of gold in the Black Hills. In 1874 George Custer led an expedition to the Black Hills, a sacred place for both the Cheyenne and the Sioux. The government justified this violation of its treaty with the Dakotas by saying that a fort was needed in the area to prevent Indians raiding into Nebraska. Custer's expedition found gold, and the United States spent the next year trying to convince the Dakotas to sell their sacred lands. In the meantime miners and prospectors, who had no patience for treaties or Indian land claims, swarmed over the Black Hills. When the Dakotas refused to sell, the government declared that it had a duty to protect these miners from the Indians marauding on the Plains. They ordered Sitting Bull, Crazy Horse, and the other Indians hunting in the unceded Indian territory to report to the reservation by January 31, 1876. After that date they would be considered at war with the United States. It was in order to enforce this bogus demand and push the Dakotas and their allies onto the reservation that Custer led his Seventh Cavalry towards the Little Bighorn in the summer of 1876.

The Sioux, Cheyenne, and Arapaho Indians camped along the Little Bighorn in White Bird's map were regrouping and planning for their next move. Eight days earlier, warriors from these bands had turned back the forces of General Crook at the Battle of the Rosebud. Now they camped together for protection. Each band had its own leaders and they camped in separate circles, but they counseled together and looked forward to a summer of raids, hunts, and fights with the white soldiers. In the meantime, Custer had followed the Indians' trail from Rosebud Creek. Using Crow and Arikara scouts, he hoped to catch the Indians napping and repeat the victory he had won on the Washita. When these scouts saw the smoke rising from the multitude of fires in

Another America

the Indians' village, they counseled caution rather than attack. But Custer would hear nothing of this. In a moment of hubris he neglected to scout the entire village. Custer had no idea of the meaning of his words when he told his officers, "The largest Indian camp on the North American continent is ahead and I am going to attack it."

Custer instructed Captain Reno to take his battalion across the river and attack the village from the south. Custer himself went north under cover of the ridges and bluffs on the east side of the river to make a two-pronged attack at the north end of the village. White Bird's map pictures both battles that took place as the Indians defended their camp. The track of Reno's battalion is depicted on the right side of the map. Their hoofprints cross the river to where Reno's men fanned out to charge. The shots of Reno's soldiers immediately roused the Indian camp. Women and children sought shelter, the braves prepared themselves for battle, and the older men shouted instructions. A number of warriors set up a skirmish line at the south end of the village. While they battled with Reno's battalion, the other warriors prepared for the fight. In the Plains traditions it was not wise to go into battle without one's medicine and the ritualized preparations for war. Among those who told stories of the battle were Indians recalling how the older men hurried them along in their preparations, urging them to join the battle.

When Reno and his men realized the size of the village they were about to attack, they pulled their horses up short. Their charge and fall-back is shown in the hoofprints of the horses. In the meantime, the warriors gathered their horses and rode to the battle. As the full extent of the Indians' avenging host rose up to repel the attack, Reno faltered. While he gave conflicting commands to mount and dismount, his troops were overrun by the Indians. The results of this first encounter are represented by the bodies of the dead soldiers littering the ground on the camp side of the river. Reno's battalion broke and ran, trying to ford the river and head for the high ground. White Bird shows their track recrossing the river. The Indians picked the soldiers off their horses as they crossed the river, while the young men of the village came out to count coup on the dead and wounded by the campground.

Reno's forces fled towards the rise with the warriors in hot pursuit counting coup, disarming, and killing the soldiers at random. At one point, it is said that Sitting Bull instructed his warriors to "Let them go, Let them live to tell the truth about this battle," perhaps hoping that the Indians' defense of their encampment would not be held against them. Reno's men eventually attained the rise, called "Reno's Hill," where they and the battalion of Captain Benteen, which had come forward on Custer's orders, held off the attacking Indians through the afternoon and into the next day. White Bird pictures the surrounded soldiers under cover and firing back at the Indians on the right side of his map.

While the Indians routed Reno's attack and left him entrenched upon the hill, Custer's forces began their attack on the north side of the village. White Bird depicts the track of Custer's battalion along the top and center. By the time Custer ordered his men to attack, the warriors were mounted and hungry for battle. The sound of shooting from Custer's forces at the other end of the village reached the braves who had come to fight the fleeing Reno. They took off in two groups. One, led by the warrior chief Gall, charged up along the riverbank to meet Custer head on; the other, led by Crazy Horse, rode through the village to go north and attack the soldiers from behind.

Before the battle, Custer divided his forces, about two hundred fifty men, with one unit attacking the village toward the center. White Bird depicts this attack with the hoof prints that approach the village near the center of the map. This battalion was quickly forced back in a defensive action as the warriors began their counterattack. When Chief Gall's warriors brought the battle to them, Custer's men retreated up a rise where they laid down defensive fire. Suddenly, Crazy Horse and his warriors appeared from the north. Facing overwhelming odds without horses and exposed on a ridge, Custer and his men were done for; they made what history has dubbed their "last stand."

Unfortunately, the popular image of Custer and his soldiers valiantly fighting to the last man, dying with their boots on, is not borne out in the archeology of the battlefield or in eyewitness accounts. Facing odds of twenty-to-one and in the confusion of a pitched battle, the soldiers evidently panicked. One Cheyenne witness told how the Indians would send their arrows arching up to rain down upon the soldiers, another describes how the soldiers were "besides themselves" shooting wildly and running in every direction. The Indians, strong with their war medicine and tasting a great victory, ran the soldiers down as they tried to escape. At one point it was reported that the soldiers turned their guns upon themselves, killing themselves and killing each other. Several witnesses testified to this behavior. One Indian account says that the Everywhere Spirit, to punish the white men for attacking a peaceful Indian camp, caused the soldiers to go mad and kill themselves. By the end of the battle, Custer and his five battalions had been wiped out on the ridge.

White Bird represents this part of the battle on the left side of his painting. Soldiers flee on horseback and on foot, Custer (pictured in the white uniform) and his men are surrounded, their horses are run off and the soldiers are left without enough cover to lie down and fire. The entire battle pictured on this side of the canvas took less then an hour—one of the Cheyenne chiefs described it as "as long as it takes a hungry man to eat his dinner."

There is no accurate record of who killed Custer and, contrary to the myth of the Indians' respect for the colonel, his body was stripped and looted in the Plains Indian custom. The mutilation of the soldiers' bodies following the battle has been used as evidence of the Indians' savagery. But such practices have been used to advantage by all cultures, including the U.S. Army in its war against the Indians. On the Plains, counting coup on the body of a fallen enemy was a way to gain honor. Following the Battle of the Little Bighorn, the Indian boys went out on the battlefield to shoot their arrows into the dead soldiers. Scalps were taken to add to the warriors' collections and the bodies looted of any goods. To show their contempt for their oppressors, the Indians mutilated their bodies.

Although Reno, Benteen, and the remains of their battalions were rescued the following afternoon—the Indians had foreseen the arrival of more soldiers and moved their camp towards the south—Custer's defeat was not widely publicized until July of that year. News of the battle, told with all the drama and exaggeration of the contemporary journalism, arrived in the middle of the country's centennial celebrations. The Indians' victory would be their ultimate defeat. The efforts of the western army were redoubled to hunt the savages down.

The Indians who had fought at the Little Bighorn continued towards the south and struggled for several days to keep their huge camp together. As no buffalo were found and the threat of the soldiers' retaliation kept the Indians on the move, remaining in one large camp became more difficult. Some of those who had come from the reservations began to leave; others broke up into smaller bands and went to hunt on their own. Despite their victory, it was clear to many of the Indians that the old way of life could no longer be recaptured. The bands broke up to hunt and flee the soldiers. The army slowly hunted down as many of the groups as possible. In 1877 Crazy Horse was captured and murdered while under guard. Sitting Bull led his band to Canada where they lived an increasingly difficult life until they returned to the United States and surrendered in 1881.

The Sioux were relentlessly pursued until they resigned themselves to the reservation. On the Great Sioux Reservation the United States no longer felt any compunction about honoring the Indians' claims. A treaty commission extorted the Black Hills from the Dakota chiefs by threatening to cut off the rations needed to feed the Indians unless they signed. In February of 1877, the Dakotas ceded their sacred Black Hills to the United States.

By the 1890s all the tribes of the Plains had been confined to reservations. The landscape that had once been the Great Plains was now defined by railroads, telegraphs, settlements, ranches, mines and white land claims. As the white settlements continued to grow, those lands remaining in Indian hands became the target of the endless white appetite for land. In the guise of civilizing the Indians, Congress passed the Dawes Act in 1887. The act institutionalized the policy of allotment, dividing tribally held lands into individual plots and alloting them to the members of the tribe. Those parts of the reservation that had not been alloted to individual Indian owers were confiscated and put up for sale to white settlers. Having held the military force of the United States at bay for over fifty years, the Indians of the Plains now faced the greatest threat to their cultures.

(Figure 70) Red Horse, a Sioux chief and a participant in the Battle of the Little Bighorn, made a series of drawings, including a map, to accompany his narrative of the battle. This drawing shows Custer's men killed, stripped, and mutilated in the aftermath of the battle. Two Indian dead are included in the picture, and horses' hoofprints partially surround the image. The translation of Red Horse's description of the battle includes his remembrance that "the Sioux had many killed. The soldiers killed 136 and wounded 160 Sioux. The Sioux killed all these different soldiers in the ravine." The drawing is reproduced from "Picture-writing of the American Indians" by Garrick Mallery in the *Tenth Annual Report of the Bureau of Ethnology, Smithsonian Institution.*

Howling Wolf, a Cheyenne Indian from the southern Plains, made this picture-writing letter (a map of the southeast coast) (Figure 71) during his imprisonment at Fort Marion near St. Augustine on Florida's Atlantic coast. The map demonstrates the flexibility of Plains picture-writing. Howling Wolf used picture-writing's graphic shorthand to represent a landscape far removed from that in which the system evolved. Even more interesting than the map is the story of Howling Wolf's life. Born around 1850, Howling Wolf began his life as a warrior on the Plains, only to be imprisoned and forced to learn the ways of white society. In prison Howling Wolf practiced his artistic skills and acquired an amount of fame that brought him into contact with the larger American society. By the time he was released from prison the world had changed. Howling Wolf returned not to the life of a warrior but to the dismal life of the reservation. His attempts to make sense of his experience and to find a path for himself in a world that no longer bore any relation to the one he had been born into parallels the experience of many Native Americans. Like a

BATTLE OF LITTLE BIG HORN. Custer's Dead Cavalry.

FIGURE 70. **Custer's dead** *Cavalry. Copy of an original drawing by Red Horse, c. 1887.*

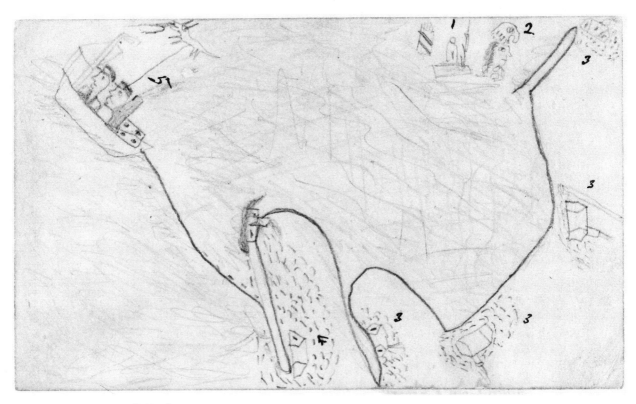

FIGURE 71. **Letter from** *Howling Wolf to his father Minimic, describing his voyage from Fort Marion. It was written at sea after leaving Savannah. 1877. Size of the original 3 x 5 inches (7.6 x 12.7 cm) Courtesy Massachusetts Historical Society.*

man without a map, Howling Wolf entered the difficult and confusing landscape of the twentieth century.

Howling Wolf was born into an important family. His father, Minimic or Eagle Head, was a distinguished warrior and a chief in Black Kettles' Cheyenne band. In the 1830s this group had migrated to the southern Plains, hunting the buffalo and bringing their hides to trade at Bent's Fort on the Arkansas River. They became part of the Southern Cheyenne, while their northern relatives continued to range in the area around the Black Hills. The Cheyennes acquired many horses and guns as well as the materials needed to maintain their nomadic life. They became a rich and successful tribe known for their skilled hunters and brave warriors. The Cheyennes had only abandoned their farming villages at the beginning of the century, but their superior horsemanship, warrior traditions, and success in the hunt made them synonymous with the life of the Plains.

Cheyenne society was strictly organized, with pressures exerted on the men to both succeed at gaining military honors and to sublimate themselves for the tribe. Tribal identity was reinforced by Cheyenne religious belief and through ceremonies like the Sun Dance, in which the whole tribe was needed to spiritually renew the world. Warrior or soldier societies structured the life of the young men and provided them with the ritualized means of preparing for battle, organizing raids, and gaining position within the Cheyenne. Howling Wolf came of age in this society. He was taught the Cheyenne ways and was prepared to gain honors in battle.

Around the time that Howling Wolf reached his adolescence Black Kettle's band was ruthlessly attacked in the Sand Creek massacre of 1864. Four years later, while Black Kettle's band was camped under a flag of truce, George Custer led the Seventh Cavalry in an attack on the Cheyennes' village at the Battle of the Washita, killing Black Kettle and indiscriminately shooting the men, women, and children of the tribe. It is not known if Howling Wolf or his father were with Black Kettle at either of these battles, but the story of the army's attacks must have been well known to the members of the Cheyenne, providing the young men with acts of violence to be revenged through attacks on the whites.

Throughout this period Minimic, like Black Kettle, counseled peace. After the treaty of 1867, in which the Cheyenne agreed to stay on their reservation, Minimic camped near the Cheyenne Agency and sought to dissuade the more militant factions of the tribe from attacking non-Indians. At the same time, Howling Wolf was out earning his honors as a Cheyenne warrior. Like his father, he had joined the Bowstring Society; with them he went on raids against other Indians, fighting with the Osage and counting his first coup in an attack on a wagon train in 1867. Such exploits were the only route to honor and position for a young Cheyenne. For several years Howling Wolf joined raiding and war parties, accumulating the honors of one who would be a leader like his father.

In the meantime, frustration grew among the Southern Cheyennes. Reservation life offered little except inadequate rations and restricted hunting grounds. Several factions within the tribe preached war as the only response to the increasing encroachment of the white man. By 1874 Minimic had been persuaded to this point of view and with his son, Howling Wolf, and many other of the Cheyenne, he left the reservation to raid on the Plains. Together with Comanche and Kiowa warriors they attacked forts and settlements throughout Kansas, northwest Texas, and Oklahoma, bringing in the army to suppress them. In the Red River War, as the southern campaign was called, the army employed the latest Indian fighting techniques. Two armed columns spread out across the Plains to converge upon the Indians. Throughout the winter of 1874–75 the army kept them constantly on the run. Starving, exhausted, and disillusioned, bands of Indians came in off the Plains to surrender to the military authorities. In April of 1875 Howling Wolf, his father and other Cheyenne, Comanche, and Kiowa Indians came in to give themselves up at the Cheyenne Agency.

In order to keep the Indians on the reservation and insure their cooperation, the army decided to imprison the ring leaders and war chiefs. Minimic, as a known leader of the Cheyenne, was immediately imprisoned. As an example to the rest, the army arbitrarily singled out young men from the line of surrendering Indians, labeled them ring leaders, and arrested them as well. Howling Wolf was placed in chains, and hauled away to prison with his father. To further debilitate the tribes it was determined that the Indians would be imprisoned at Fort Marion near St. Augustine, Florida. In May 1875, seventy-three of these so-called outlaws were placed in shackles and transported across the country by train. One of the older chiefs decided that it would be better to die than accept this unknown fate. He threw himself from the train and was shot while trying to escape. The rest found themselves imprisoned behind the walls of Fort Marion. There they were under the care of Lieutenant Richard Pratt. Pratt had been among the army officers cam-

Another America

paigning against the southern Cheyenne, and he had been their military escort on the journey east. Here at Fort Marion he was in charge of their welfare and improvement. Pratt would use the prisoners as subjects for his first attempt to systematically "civilize" the Indians.

Pratt's objective was to transform the Indian to the white man's ways. In an age when most of white society was happy to see the American Indians wiped out altogether, Pratt's efforts may be seen as humanitarian. He saw no value in the Indians' culture, saying, "the sooner all tribal relations are broken up; the sooner the Indian loses all his Indian ways, even his language, the better it will be." To this end Pratt instituted compulsory schooling for his inmates, providing them with lessons in English along with a generous dose of Christianity. Despite his desire to sever the Indians' ties to their traditions, Pratt was more than willing to use the Indians' culture to further his own ambitions. He encouraged the Indians to make bows, arrows, and other craft items to sell to the tourists who came to see the "savages" at Fort Marion. And he provided the Indians with paper, pencils, and colors so that they could make pictures to sell. Pratt's scheme provided the Indians with the opportunity to experience work for pay. To further the civilizing influence of capitalism, Pratt arranged outings for his charges. Under supervision, the Indians were allowed to go to town and make purchases at selected stores. Lieutenant Pratt's paternalistic policies gave the young men direction; in the confusing world of an eastern prison more than one brave turned his drive to win a warrior's honors toward the rigors of the white man's path.

Howling Wolf's artistic talents were immediately evident. His mastery of the Plains Indians' picture-writing language is evident in this postcard map. It contains several elements of Plains pictography, including multiple times and events recorded together and the characteristic economy of detail that focuses the viewer on the events and their meaning. The journey Howling Wolf depicts was undertaken in the third year of his imprisonment, after he had developed his artistic reputation and sympathetic whites were willing to pay for his transportation to Boston. Howling Wolf needed to go to Boston to see an eye surgeon and receive an operation to correct his failing eyesight. With a military escort, he traveled up the Atlantic coast by steamer, a journey that must have seemed fantastic to a young man who had grown up in the horse culture of the Plains.

Howling Wolf drew this postcard map during his journey and mailed it back to his father at Fort Marion. The map is accompanied by a key that is probably written in the hand of his military escort. The prison at Fort Marion is represented at "1." The flagpole and guardhouse are pictured behind the walls of the fort and the lighthouse is drawn to the left. This is where Howling Wolf began his journey. Howling Wolf's father, Minimic or Eagle Head, is pictured next to the fort at "2." He is portrayed in the Plains style with a profiled head connected to the pictographic signature of his name. Four settlements are labeled "3" and represented by dots and images of buildings. These are described as "Fernandina, Port Royal, and other places at which the steamer touches." Number "4" is Savannah, which Howling Wolf represented as a larger place by the increased number of dots. He also indicates that a change of steamers took place here, with the one docked outside the harbor and the dashed line of Howling Wolf and his escort's footprints going to the next steamer that is pictured at "5." Here Howling Wolf portrays himself on the boat next to his military escort. Howling Wolf's identifying sign, the wolf with the symbol of noise extending from his mouth, is drawn, attached to the figure's head in classic Plains picture writing style.

Since arriving at Fort Marion, Howling Wolf had been willing to learn the ways of the white man. Minimic had embraced Pratt's philosophy and urged the Indians at the fort and those back home to follow the road of the white man. Howling Wolf attempted to fit into the white man's world out of respect for his father.

While at Fort Marion, Howling Wolf evidently found an outlet for his nostalgia and frustration in the pictures he drew and painted. Several of the "Fort Marion Boys," as the imprisoned Indians became known, made drawings while at the fort. Their work represents an evolution in Plains Indian ledger art. Ledger art, so called because it was often drawn in accounting ledgers and other copy books, became popular among Plains Indians in the last half of the nineteenth century. Much easier to produce and transport than pictographs on hides or stationary objects and more versatile for recording historic events, picture writing on paper spread quickly among many of the Plains tribes. The pictographic language of the Plains was easily adapted to expressions on paper, and warriors used it to record their exploits in the same way that the oral tradition of the tribe recorded their achievements.

Most ledger art employed conventions that, like the Indians' sign language, were universally understood across the Plains. Rather than concentrate on the physical details of individuals, artists employed a graphic shorthand that used standard figures modified by dress or other distinguishing characteristics to identify tribal affiliation. Graphic name totems were used to identify individuals, and a host of conventions were developed to show the actions taking place on the flat picture plan. The subject matter of these drawings usually concerned counting coup, stealing horses, or battles with one's enemies. Other picture writing documents, like Howling Wolf's map, conveyed a message.

Separated from their cultural traditions, the Indians imprisoned at Fort Marion began to experiment with the form and subject matter they painted. Howling Wolf, among others, dropped the use of pictographic signatures and sometimes pictured individuals and action without specific identifiers. And, although he was entitled to record his warrior exploits, many of Howling Wolf's pictures concentrate on the pageantry and events of Plains Indian life, on historic occasions for the Cheyenne, and even on contemporary happenings such as the Indians attending classes at Fort Marion. While some of these subjects may have been drawn at the request of his customers, other changes Howling Wolf introduced into his drawings, such as background details, settings, and a near abstraction in the use of form, color, and pattern, show that he was experimenting with the medium.

In the 1870s Florida had already become a vacation destination for people throughout the United States. Howling Wolf's drawings and those of the other Indian artists were popular with the tourists visiting the fort. Well-to-do travelers from New York, Washington, and Boston would come down to St. Augustine and, because the Fort Marion Boys had been reported upon in newspapers and popular magazines, they would visit the fort to take in the sight of these wild men of the Plains. Howling Wolf's drawings were purchased by many of these visitors; as a consequence his works are spread throughout a number of museums, libraries, and historical collections. The money generated by the sale of this Indian art helped to pay for improvements in the prisoners' lives and the costs of their schooling.

The artists and society people who visited Fort Marion included politicians and eastern intelligentsia, advocates of liberal and humanitarian policies towards the Indians. Pratt cultivated this audience for his charges. He marketed the Indians' artistic creations to them and had the

FIGURE 72. **Howling Wolf** *attending classes at the Fort Marion prison. A picture of the Fort Marion Boys attending classes. Drawn sometime after Howling Wolf returned from his trip to Boston, he is pictured on the left seated alone and wearing his glasses. From* Harpers Weekly *XXII, No. 1115 (May 11, 1878) page 373.*

Indians stage dances for their entertainment. He would wine and dine influential visitors, trying to enlist them in his effort to bring the fruits of civilization to his prisoners. Among those who visited the fort were Alice Key Pendelton, the daughter of the composer Francis Scott Key, and her husband the politician George Pendelton.

While the Fort Marion Boys enjoyed their notoriety and the taste of the white man's life that Pratt programmed for them, all was not well in Indian territory. The Cheyenne and Arapaho reservation suffered from a chronic shortage of government guaranteed rations, and the Indians found it hard to adapt to the farming and other forms of labor the agents urged upon them. During their imprisonment, the Indians learned of the Sioux and Cheyenne victory at the battle of the Little Bighorn, of the flight of some Cheyenne to Canada with Sitting Bull, and of the Southern Cheyennes' last buffalo hunt in the winter of 1877–78.

Like the other prisoners, Howling Wolf attended school and learned some English. When his eyesight began to fail, saving Howling Wolf's eyes so he could lead his people to civilization fit in well with the sympathies and goals of Pratt and the well-to-do liberals that visited the fort. Alice Key Pendelton and several other philanthropists sponsored Howling Wolf's journey to Boston. There he saw a specialist who saved his right eye, and——as Lieutenant Pratt had hoped——he experienced an entirely different side of white civilization.

Howling Wolf spent five months in Boston, much of it outside the hospital. He is known to have visited many of the city's sights and the homes of several important persons. While still a curiosity to most of these easterners, Howling Wolf was nonetheless the object of their humanitarian sympathies. He probably received numerous encouraging remarks——the equivalent of a warrior's accolades——that may have encouraged him in his pursuit of the white man's way. When Howling Wolf returned from this bastion of civilization wearing corrective spectacles, an eastern tailored suit, and sporting the airs and accent of an eastern gentleman, Pratt recorded that he "had taken on altogether too much Boston for his resources and future good. . . . and I was forced to discipline him." Having gone to the big city and been shown off throughout the town, it is not surprising that Howling Wolf now embraced the ways of the white man and had trouble returning to the role of a prisoner awaiting his release from Fort Marion.

At the end of their three-year sentence, twenty-two of the prisoners were chosen to remain in the East for further education. As part of Pratt's plan they were to be educated and returned as missionaries to their people. In some cases this literally happened as several of the prisoners converted to Christianity and took religious training. But Howling Wolf was not among those who remained in the East. He had a wife and child back on the reservation, and in 1878 Howling Wolf returned to find a Plains that had been unalterably transformed.

The buffalo were gone and the Cheyenne were restricted to the reservation lands, unable to practice the raids and wars that had defined them. Without the ability to prove themselves in battle, the young Cheyenne men had no outlet for their warrior ambitions or the means to earn the privileges of adulthood. The path to courtship, marriage, and positions of authority, once clear and easily followed, was now a confusion that reflected the demoralized state of the tribe. A contemporary census shows that the Cheyenne population had sunk to less than three thousand and that adults now outnumbered children by nearly two to one. In these dire circumstances the reservation agent struggled to find food for the starving Cheyenne and looked for ways that the tribe could generate income.

Minimic, now an important leader among the Cheyenne, continued to urge his people to adopt the ways of the white man. He attempted to farm, wore western dress, and practiced the Christian religion. Howling Wolf attempted to follow his father's example, sending his daughter to the reservation school and working for a while at various jobs on the reservation. But these things did not bring the rewards and position Cheyenne men required. Life on the reservation was hard and difficult, and preaching Christian humility and acceptance did not make it any more tolerable.

When he was first arrested, Howling Wolf's future had held the promise of a position of leadership among his people. Now the warrior was faced with the choice of the dismal, repressed life of the reservation or adopting a culture that disdained the traditions and beliefs he was raised on. It was during this period that Howling Wolf produced another book of sketches. One of only two former prisoners that are known to have created art after their captivity, Howling Wolf may have produced the pictures in the hope that he could sell them. The drawings reflect both the

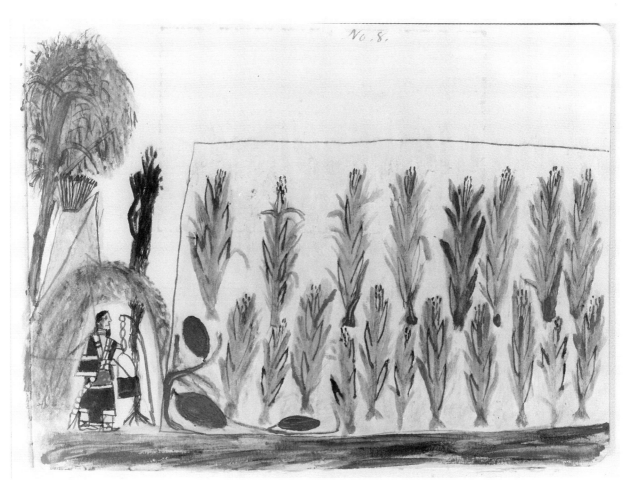

FIGURE 73. "Cheyenne corn *field of the olden time,*" Howling Wolf, c. 1880. *Courtesy of the Joslyn Art Museum, Omaha.*

artist's and the man's displacement. Even further evolved in style than Howling Wolf's Fort Marion drawings, they seem to be a visual attempt to make sense out of the Cheyennes' experience. The three pictures that open the book are of particular interest. The first portrays the Cheyennes greeting a white man along the banks of the river. The caption by Ben Clark, a scout who knew the Cheyenne well, describes the picture as "The first White men seen by the Cheyennes, over 100 yrs ago on the Missouri River . . ." The second drawing shows a meeting between Cheyenne and Kiowa Indians; Clark's caption describes this as "The first horses owned by the Cheyennes which they are trading for from the Kiowas on the Arkansas. . . . Supposed to be 150 yrs ago." The third picture is even more telling. In it Howling Wolf depicts a Cheyenne woman tending a corn field in the days before the tribe had moved out on to the Plains and adopted the life of nomadic hunters (Figure 73). Through these drawings Howling Wolf chose to go back to a time that encompasses the entire life of the Cheyennes on the Plains. With the closing of the Plains and the dismal life of the reservation, things had come full circle for the Cheyenne. Like the woman in his drawing they were now attempting to grow corn and other food crops in the garden plots and farmers' fields of the reservation.

The other pictures in this sketchbook evoke the life of the Plains. War dances, the return of victorious raiding parties and the Cheyennes' celebrations are depicted along with scenes of hunting, courtship, and social dancing. Howling Wolf also drew a picture of the Cheyennes participating in the Sun Dance, a ritual of social and spiritual renewal for the tribe. In 1879 Howling Wolf wrote to his former jailer and benefactor, Captain Pratt, that "When I hunted the Buffalo I was not poor . . . but here I am Poor. I would like to go out on the planes a gain whare I could rome at will and not come back. . . ."

When Minimic died in 1881, Howling Wolf rejected the ways of the white man. He forgot his English, went back to traditional dress, and gave up his attempts at farming. The next year he joined the Dog Soldiers. Reminiscent of the most warlike of the pre-reservation soldier societies, the Dog Soldiers practiced their traditional responsibilities of policing the reservation, keeping the peace, and enforcing the Cheyennes' laws. Because of their ability to deliver when the agent's Indian police could not, the Dog Soldiers gained power on the reservation. In 1884 Howling Wolf became the chief of the Dog Soldiers and with them helped to rule the reservation. They levied charges on the white men who drove cattle on to the reservation lands, and they exacted tolls from the freight trains that crossed the Cheyennes' territory. These activities provided an outlet for warrior ambitions; the Dog Soldiers galvanized part of the tribe. Under Howling Wolf's leadership, the Dog Soldiers attempted to compel members of the tribe to participate in the Sun Dance. Such ceremonies were frowned upon by the reservation authorities. But the Sun Dance was one of the central ceremonies of Cheyenne life, requiring the participation of all the people in order to achieve the tribe's spiritual renewal. Policing this ceremony, guaranteeing renewal and reaffirming the Cheyenne identity, had been a task of honor for the Dog Soldiers. The task appealed to the young braves yearning to establish their credentials as Cheyenne men.

The crisis brought on by Howling Wolf's behavior required army intervention. A new agent was appointed, the cattlemen who had taken over most of the reservation's grazing land were driven off, and the young men were given a chance to prove their manhood as scouts in the army. But the threat to the Cheyennes' way of life was soon to increase with the policy of allotment.

In the late 1800s U.S. Indian policy sought to civilize the Indians by repressing their traditional cultures. Native religious and cultural practices were outlawed, and the Dawes Act, passed in 1887, attempted to change the Native Americans' relationship to the land. First, the act broke up the Indians' tribal lands and assigned them to individual owners. Second, the act authorized the sale of unassigned Indian lands to the whites. Qualifying members of the Indian tribes each received a 160-acre plot as their allotment, the left over lands—some sixty million acres—being opened to white homesteaders. This policy destroyed the land base of the Southern Cheyenne. The reservation they shared with the Arapaho had once been nearly four million acres; after allotment only five hundred thousand acres remained in Indian hands.

Howling Wolf was among those who opposed allotment, but the government and the tribe overruled them. In the end Howling Wolf was assigned his 160 acres. Here he was supposed to adopt white culture and lose his Cheyenne traditions, but Howling Wolf clung to his heritage. For the next thirty-five years Howling Wolf went back and forth between the worlds of the Indian and

Another America

the white man. He rejected Christianity and joined the Native American Church. He spent time in jail and hid out among the Kiowas and Comanches for several years while charges were pending against him. He remained a representative of the conservative faction of the Cheyenne.

In 1927 Howling Wolf prepared to return to the Cheyenne area of Oklahoma after spending the summer in Houston. He had been hired to reenact the life of the Plains in a tipi village the city had erected as a tourist attraction. Twice a day Howling Wolf entertained his audience with authentic Indian dances. His son drove the seventy-seven-year-old Howling Wolf home. As they headed towards the Cheyenne Cantonment they were hit by another car and Howling Wolf's car was turned over in a ditch. The next day the warrior who had started his life counting coup and hunting buffalo on the Plains died from his injuries.

6.

Water-Chief

Mida aduikwa atis ...
Village of woulives on influence
Mandan Town

Mida aduineh ait
Wood bending creek

High-Eagle

Contemporary Native American Maps

THROUGHOUT THIS BOOK MAPS HAVE been viewed as cultural and historical records, documents of inhabitation that reflect the centuries of Native American heritage in the North American landscape. They have been examined for what they reveal about the Native American experience of the European encounter: the five centuries of invasion, war, and repression that completely transformed North America. By the end of the nineteenth century the world that Native Americans once knew no longer existed. Their lands and their way of life were gone. Their populations had been reduced to their lowest ebb and the remaining American Indians were confined to reservations.

That Native American cultures survived in the face of this oppression is testimony to the strength of their traditions and beliefs. That native peoples are emerging as important social, political, and economic forces in contemporary society is testimony to the Native Americans' continued evolution. Today Native American societies are a part of the people, events, and concepts that shape our experience of the world. The map of North America is once again undergoing a transformation. The image of exclusion that took shape in the last five hundred years is slowly being replaced by one of inclusion. The maps described here are contemporary images of a North America that include the heritage and experience of Native Americans. They represent an emerging social and cultural landscape in which Native Americans are included in the larger society.

This process of inclusion is by no means complete, and an understanding and acceptance of Native American nations as autonomous peoples within the larger society is far from assured. But maps do reflect the way a society sees the world. These maps, which include native territories and native place names, are akin to the earliest western maps of North America. They are a glimpse of uncharted territory; they portray the edges and faint outlines of a new way of seeing the world and one's place within it.

Two countervailing forces, one historical the other evolutionary, have helped to shape this new North American map. For most of recorded history the processes of mapping have worked to exclude and erase the Native American presence from the continent. Disease, wars, forced relocations, and exploitative treaties accomplished the physical removal of the American Indian presence, while mapmakers were busy making it look as if they had never been here. Native American geography was replaced with western cartographic conventions and western symbols of inhabitation and possession. On the early editions of his map of "New England" John Smith went so far as to instruct his reader to replace the list of "Barbarous" (Native American) place names with ones supposedly supplied by King Charles, transforming the indigenous geography into an Anglicized landscape.

The systematic exclusion of Native Americans continued through the colonial era and into the nineteenth century. In the view of western history, North America had been discovered by and belonged to the peoples of western Europe. Mapping the continent in the language of western cartography went hand in hand with taming the American wilderness and removing the savages who stood in the way of civilization. Maps became tools of repression and appropriation in the same way that colonial militias and frontier armies forcibly removed Native Americans.

History was the story of the European powers and the North American nation states. Native Americans were only recognized as footnotes in the more important western saga. Western society's exploration, settlement, and control of the continent has been the dominant history of North America, and western maps have reaffirmed this history with their image of a blank landscape slowly being brought to life with the settlements, roads, and plat-lines of western ownership. Despite the millennia of human inhabitation, North America's significance in western social history does not begin until its "discovery" in the late-fifteenth century.

The exclusion of Native American history from our map of the past is a loss for all of North American society. Native American oral traditions contain perceptions and experiences that go far deeper in time than the few centuries of western contact with North America. Their place names are a record of the ways in which people traveled, used, and understood their land; they reflect the adaptations and technologies that enabled Native American societies to grow and flourish.

Contemporary Native American Maps

Excluding the Native American presence from the map limits the larger culture's understanding of North America to only one or two hundred years. Rather than integrate the Native Americans' history into a continuum of human traditions, their history has been condemned to a shadowy and mythologized past disconnected from the stream of western history.

The irony of this picture of exclusion is that the Native Americans have not confined themselves to the past. Despite the confinement of their cultures, and policies that have made Native Americans the most impoverished people in North America, Native Americans have not lost their traditions. Native American societies have continued to evolve and adapt. Today they have begun to emerge from the past with their identities intact and with the formidable tools of western culture and technology at their disposal. Native Americans have adapted these tools to their own ends and are using them to once again assert their place, to demand that their heritage be recognized, and that their historical experience become a part of this land.

Understanding the evolution of Native American societies is essential to understanding contemporary Native American maps. Throughout their history Native American societies, like all societies, have absorbed and adapted the ideas and technologies of others. In the past the adaptation of guns and other western technologies changed the native practices of hunting and warfare; today the adaptation of western political, legal, and economic practices has changed the Native Americans' position in the larger society. To argue that the Native American identity is frozen in time and that rights and recognition guaranteed in treaties no longer apply once Native American societies have adapted new materials and technologies, is to ignore the natural evolution of all societies.

Contemporary Native American societies are the result of their experiences and adaptations, and central to this evolution is the persistence of their identity. Instead of diminishing their identity through the use of new technologies and social or political structures, Native Americans have adapted these tools to preserve their identities. American Indian rights organizations have adapted western practices of lobbying and protest to successfully defeat anti-Indian legislation. The adaptation of western-style media has enabled Native Americans to maintain their identities in the same way that the rendezvous on the Plains once reaffirmed Indian traditions. And that most quintessential of western professions, the lawyer, has been adapted by Native Americans through the creation of law centers, legal services, and Native American rights foundations to aid in their fight for the land, water, and cultural rights guaranteed in their treaties.

These adaptations are a response to the attacks upon Native American culture and lands that have continued throughout the twentieth century. Government policies provided incentive for Indians to relocate to urban areas, education programs provided training for jobs in non-Indian society, and the policy of termination ended the trust relationship between Indian tribes and the United States. All these policies were aimed at getting Native Americans to assimilate. Today the problems and inequities that characterize the relationship between western society and Native Americans have not been eliminated, but Native Americans have evolved the legal and political structures to help protect their cultures and rights. And the perceptions of the larger society have also begun to change. While not denying that conflicts over rights and resources lie at the heart of problems between Native American and white societies, and that prejudices and misconception mar many of the Indian–non-Indian interactions, contemporary Native Americans are slowly coming to be seen as an asset by the larger society. The addition of their traditions, their heritage, and their contemporary experience enriches all of North American culture.

Contemporary Native American maps are a symbolic expression of the move to reassert the Native Americans' place on the map of North America. The process presents a risk to Native American societies. Some fear that the information will be used to appropriate their lands, or that the revelation of sacred sites and holy places will result in an influx of white "wannabes" to disturb their traditions. But in balance the benefits of recognition outweigh the risks for many Native American groups. They have begun a cartographic dialog with the larger society. In South Dakota the Lakota people have suggested that adding their place names to the state map would be an appropriate gesture of reconciliation. The Hopi have begun interviewing their elders and collecting their oral geography with plans to preserve it in a new map of their nation. And Native Americans throughout the continent have begun to make their own maps, once again applying their traditional names to the land. As these individuals and societies assert their place in the larger culture it is appropriate that the medium of the western map, with its power to shape our conception of the land, be used to preserve and pass on their cultural heritage.

The maps presented here provide examples of three different approaches to making the contemporary Native American presence known. The "Historical Map of Temagami" is a re-creation of the nineteenth-century Native American landscape upon a western cartographic base. The map integrates the Ojibwas' perception and experience of the region into the western history of the place. It makes visible the routes of the Ojibwa geography that once defined the land. The objective of the map, prepared by an Ojibwa and officially published by the Ontario Geographic Names Board, is to make the Native American regional history a part of contemporary experience.

The second map, the "Map of Zuni Land Claims," demonstrates the adaptation of western technology and legal structures to Native American ends. The map was compiled as evidence in a land dispute between the Pueblo of Zuni in New Mexico and the Government of the United States. The map displays the Zunis' history of inhabitation. Unlike the western record, which begins with the Zunis' land grant from the Spanish in the seventeenth century, the Zunis' perception of history begins with their thousands of years of southwestern inhabitation. By using the technology of Geographic Information Systems (GIS), the Zunis were able to make visible their experience with the United States. The map starts with the full extent of the Zunis' ancestral territory and traces the history of "takings" that led to the present reservation. It is a map where the contrasting experiences of history in Native American and western society are vividly displayed.

The third map, the map of Inujjuaq from the *Inuit Place Name Map Series of Nunavik,* is an example of the merging of the Native American and western landscapes. Nunavik, now officially recognized as the Inuit region of northern Quebec, is one of the aboriginal territories that are being incorporated into the official map of Canada. The Inuit Place Name maps are a product of the Inuits' cultural revival and their move towards self determination. Having won recognition for their distinct heritage and the ability to control their economic and cultural future, the Inuit of Nunavik began an aggressive campaign to establish their place in contemporary Canadian society. The maps were compiled from the oral traditions and they represent the most effective means of preserving and passing down the Inuits' geographic heritage. They are a western innovation that the Inuit have adapted to their cultural ends. Perhaps more important, the maps proclaim the

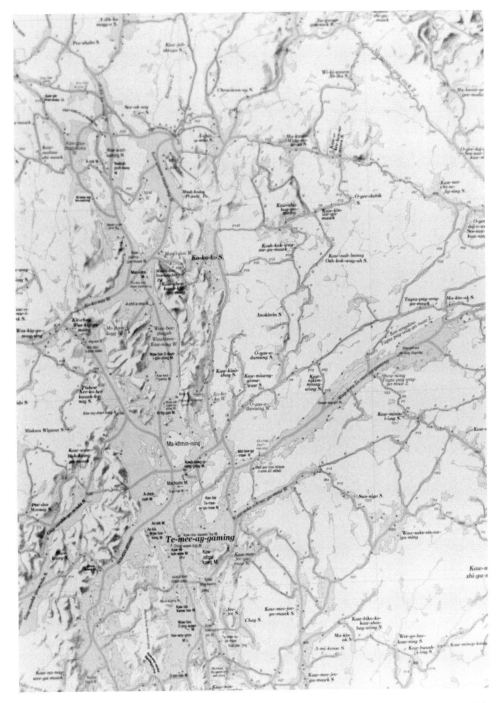

FIGURE 74. Craig K. *Macdonald, detail from the Historical Map of Temagami, 1978. Published by the Ontario Geographic Names Board, August, 1985. Size of the original 58 ½ x 38 ½ inches (148 x 98 cm). Courtesy of Craig K. Macdonald.*

Another America

Inuits' contemporary political and cultural presence. Published in English, French, and Inuktitut these trilingual maps present a new image of the American landscape. It is a picture of a land in which the various human traditions and perceptions of the land can coexist, a landscape enriched by the native heritage as well as western history and experience.

The Historical map of Temagami (Figure 74) is a visualization of the native landscape in a section of Ontario, Canada. Compiled from information supplied by Anishinawbeg (Ojibwa) elders and from nineteenth-century surveys and notebooks, the map makes the Native American oral geography visible within the conventions of a western map. The Native names for places and features have been placed on the map and the Native network of routes and trails re-created to show the history of this place. They document a landscape that was intimately known and fully named within the traditions of the Ojibwa people. The map was created to provide a unique perspective on the historic geography of the Temagami region and the Anishinawbegs' link to the land. It is a graphic statement of how their history is a part of our mutual history. The mapmaker invites others to use the map as a guide to exploring and understanding this landscape.

The Temagami area is located north of Georgian Bay on Lake Huron. It extends from Canada's Ottawa River at the boundary between Quebec and Ontario, where Lake Temisk-kaw-ming (Temiskaming) forms part of the provincial boundary, and continues south and west to the area around Lake Wawn-a-biay-bing (Wanapitei). This is the historic home of the Temagami band of Ojibwa or Anishinawbeg Indians. Today they reside at the Bear Island reserve within Lake Temagami (Te-mee-ay-gaming). The map pictures their home as it was known before 1900; even the river courses and shorelines have been drawn to show how they existed before the introduction of water control projects and modern dams.

Other geographic features that provide a western orientation to the map include the Montreal River that borders the text in the upper right. Called the Moi-ang Z(ee-beng), roughly translated as "at the place of the Moi-ang river," this flows from the northwest above Lake Temagami. Similarly, the river route represented along the bottom of the map includes part of the Sturgeon River, called the Nah mang Z(ee-beng) on this Anishinawbeg map. On the map these rivers are pictured as part of routes that include portages, lakes, and trails all connected together to show the way they were used by the Native Americans at different times of the year and in different conditions.

The names and places highlighted on the map include many that have no corresponding designation in English or French maps of the region. When the search for western counterparts is suspended, the map can be more easily seen as an integrated picture of how the indigenous Anishinawbeg experienced the region. But the map is to be understood as more then just the record of a landscape that has been lost; the annotations note that much of the indigenous trail system still exists; underneath the western geography the cultural geography of Native Americans continues.

The original map of Temagami was held in the oral traditions of the Anishinawbeg, but to document its existence, to make it a part of the historical geography of this region, it was necessary to visualize this landscape in a form that could be read by others. Representing the information within the conventions of a western map gives it the same power of naming and describing that modern atlases, road maps, and topographic surveys carry. Portrayed in this western idiom the "Historical Map of Temagami" fulfills the need for a picture of the landscape in which orientation and navigation are possible. The Anishinawbegs' oral geography becomes the landscape. It is a functional map that integrates the historic experience of the Anishinawbeg into the spatial concepts of the larger society. The Native American past and present become part of modern culture, in much the same way that the traditions of the continent's European immigrants have been assimilated and adapted into North American society.

Compiling the "Historical Map of Temagami" required more than twenty-seven years of research. In an ironic reversal of the western process of surveying and mapping——collecting Native place names and then replacing them with Anglicized versions——the mapmaker had to go back to the notebooks, diaries, field journals, and maps of the early western surveyors and explorers to pry out the Native American place names. The compiler, Craig Macdonald, personally explored and traveled over one thousand miles of the trails and routes that are pictured on the map. Finally, the oral geography of the region was reconstructed, checked, and confirmed in consultation with more than two hundred Anishinawbeg elders. The information was then transferred to a western base map. The result is a unique picture of the region's geography. A key of 661 Anishinawbeg geographical names has been added to the map and a phonetic key for the transcribed Anishinawbeg words has been provided. The exclusive use of the Anishinawbeg place names within the map indicates how completely the region was known, organized, and utilized by the Native Americans. With this map it is no longer necessary to use western place names in order to understand, travel within, or describe the region.

The Temagami Indians who named this landscape were part of the Anishinawbeg tribe. Known as the Ojibwa in western culture, bands of Anishinawbeg occupied the region north of the Great Lakes beginning in the seventeenth century. The Anishinawbeg integrated themselves into their environment. They subsisted on fish from the abundant lakes and rivers, on game hunted in the forest, and on wild rice, maple sugar, and other foods gathered in their seasons. Birch bark was used for making shelters and canoes, and the plant and animal resources of the environment were adapted to meet their material needs. Bands like the Temagami consisted of a few hundred people headed by a chief. The entire Anishinawbeg population numbered between three and four thousand. These peoples migrated between their fishing, hunting, and gathering spots, and some planted gardens to supplement their diet. The Anishinawbeg would gather where food was abundant, coming together to fish the rapids at Sault Sainte Marie or to gather maple sap to boil in the sugar camps. These gatherings of great numbers of Anishinawbeg helped to maintain their tribal identity.

In the late sixteen and early seventeen hundreds the Anishinawbeg began trading with the Europeans, bringing in furs to exchange for manufactured goods. The routes and trails on the map show that from Lake Te-mee-ay-gaming (Temagami) the Anishinawbeg had access to the Great Lakes and east to the St. Lawrence River. With their strategic position they became important participants in the Native American trade and communications network of the region, and regularly brought their furs, pelts, and native-made goods to the trading posts.

In the 1700s the region began to be visited by missionaries and fur traders. They were followed closely by European settlers. By the early 1800s the Anishinawbeg began to cede their lands to the British Crown. In 1850 the Robinson-Huron Treaty transferred the remaining Indian lands in southern Ontario, including the region of Temagami, to the government. The reserve for the

Temagami Indian band was established on Bear Island, and they were urged to confine themselves to the smaller area despite their guaranteed right of access to the region's resources. The move to reserves changed some of the Anishinawbegs' ways. The concentration of populations meant that hunters had to go further to the west to gather their furs, and family trapping areas were established to manage the supply of game and furs. Some of the Anishinawbeg even became farmers, although hunting, gathering wild rice, and making maple sugar continued to be important sources of food throughout the nineteenth century.

In the twentieth century this region has continued to evolve. The Temagamis' area became part of the western map. Canadian cities and towns and the network of roads and highways replaced the indigenous landscape. Except for a few place names, the geography depicted here was ignored or forgotten. But the Anishinawbeg of Ontario continued. Their population grew to an estimated twelve thousand and many of the members migrated to U.S. and Canadian cities and worked in western jobs. The Anishinawbegs' migrations and their position in the modern cash economy do not necessarily mean that the Ojibwa have become completely assimilated. Today the Anishinawbeg are said to have integrated themselves into the larger society while retaining much of their traditional culture and beliefs.

The map, published in the 1980s, is symbolic of the continuing Anishinawbeg presence. Their historical experience persists. The map is both a western and an Anishinawbeg statement of that history. Through maps such as this the mutual heritage of the land is slowly expanding to encompass more than one culture's experience. By representing this Indian geography on a map that anyone can use to explore and travel, the Anishinawbegs' traditional way of looking at this land becomes part of the larger society's way of seeing.

(Figure 76) The Pueblo Indians of the North American Southwest represent one of the oldest continuing cultural traditions in the world. In the 1960s a Pueblo elder noted how his people "have lived upon this land from days beyond history's records, far past any living memory, deep into the time of legend. The story of my people and the story of this place are one single story."

Evidence of native inhabitation in what is now the American Southwest goes back at least ten thousand years. The ancestors of today's Indians hunted and gathered across the region's varied landscape leaving a record of their tools, campsites, and dwellings. About four thousand years ago the Indians of the Southwest began to adapt the maize and squash agriculture that had originated among the Indians of Mexico. The culture that evolved is known as the Anasazi. Anasazi traditions can be linked to those of today's Pueblo Indians. The Anasazi lived in permanent dwellings, and developed and used pottery. By the beginning of the Christian era, agriculture had replaced hunting and gathering as the source of Anasazi subsistence. With this stable source of food the Anasazi population grew, and they began to build large urban centers like Mesa Verde, Chaco Canyon, and Casa Grande. Many hundreds of people would live in these villages, and at the height of the Anasazi period more than three hundred thousand people occupied the region. This was the largest concentration of people north of the Mexican civilizations, and they were linked by a network of communication and trade routes that was still in existence when the Spanish and American settlers entered the Southwest.

Around 1300 the Pueblo culture began to evolve out of the Anasazi. Drought and the invasion of peoples from the north made it difficult to maintain villages where there were no longer

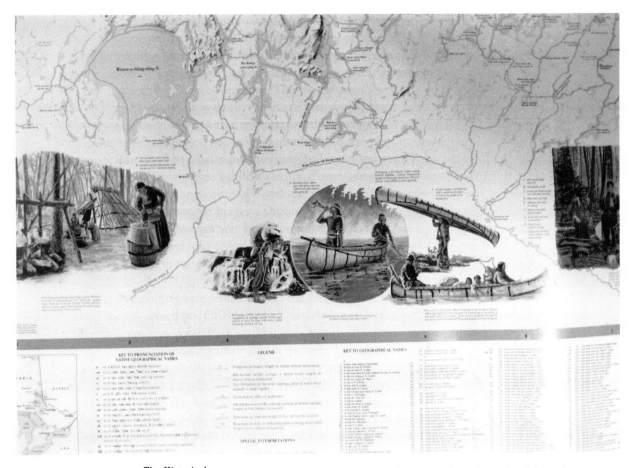

FIGURE 75. **The Historical** *Map of Temagami includes vignettes of traditional Anishinawbeg life in the region. The representations of transportation by canoe and snowshoe depict some of the ways the Anishinawbeg lived within this landscape.*

dependable sources of water. As the population declined, the Pueblos began to concentrate themselves in settlements along the Rio Grande and other rivers to the west. There they continued to develop their complex religious beliefs and ceremonial systems. In the Pueblos' view, their world consisted of both physical and mythological landscapes. They shared the world with spiritual beings and together they were entrusted with keeping nature in balance and seeing to the continuance of their people. The Pueblos shared a legacy of their millennia of inhabitation. Within this time frame the intrusions of the Spanish and American empires were only phases in the continuing history of the Pueblos.

Today Pueblo Indians live in seventeen settlements located within the valley of the Rio Grande River and its tributaries. To the west, the Laguna and Acoma Pueblos are located on the Rio San Jose, and the Pueblo of Zuni is along the Zuni River at the border of New Mexico and Arizona. The Pueblos' encounter with western society began more the four hundred years ago with

Another America

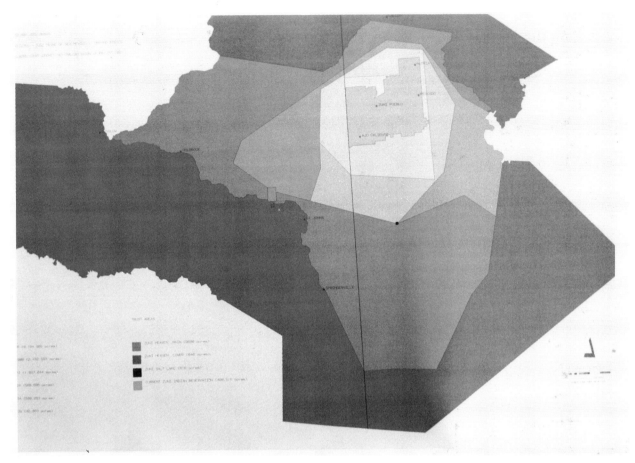

FIGURE 76. **Areas of** *"Zuni Land Taken Since 1846," 1987. Size of the Original 25 x 43 inches (6.5 x 109 cm). Courtesy of the Pueblo of Zuni and the Environmental Research Institute, Institute of the North American West.*

the intrusion of the Spanish Empire and has continued with their current relationships to the United States. This encounter has always centered around different views and perceptions of the land. In response to western culture's appetite for land, Native Americans have had to adopt the tools, methods, and technologies of the West to maintain their own way of life. This map of "Zuni Lands Taken Since 1846" (Figure 76) is a contemporary adaptation. Represented in the cartographic language of the west and using recent mapping technology, the map was created to aid the Zuni in a land claim against the United States.

The map of "Areas of Zuni Lands Taken Since 1846" was made by the Environmental Systems Research Institute using a digital database called a Geographic Information System (GIS). Maps of the areas of lands taken over time were generated using this database, and the concentric areas were laid one on top of the other in the final map. This technology enabled the Zunis to graphically display and quantify the changes in their lands over time. Attorneys representing the

Zunis used the map to provide a clear and accurate description of the total acreage of the Zunis' aboriginal area and the six zones in which land had been taken between 1846 and 1939.

The map is centered on what is now the border of New Mexico and Arizona. The contemporary Zuni reservation is represented east from the border of Arizona to their settlements at Nutria and Pescado. This area includes the Pueblo of Zuni, which lies at the heart of the Zuni territory. The Zunis' original lands extended far beyond these borders. Within the area represented on the map Zuni settlements and those of their Anasazi ancestors go back nearly two thousand years. Their villages and farms extended west into what is now Arizona and south along the tributaries of the Little Colorado River to the boundary formed by the hills and mountains that separate the Zunis' lands from that of other Indians. To the east, their lands extended to the Zuni Mountains and the territory of the Acoma Pueblo.

Throughout this area the ancestors of the Pueblo Indians farmed the canyons and bottom lands. Their economy and subsistence patterns favored concentrated settlements or pueblos, and villages of several thousand people developed. The Zuni pueblos were important points of trade and exchange in the region's economic network. Corn, tobacco, domestic goods, pottery technology, and cultural or social tradition spread from Mexico to the Southwest. The Zuni pueblos were one of several trading centers where these ideas and innovations were taken and adapted to the cultures of the Southwest and then disseminated throughout the continent.

In the twelfth century the Zunis began to gather in larger and larger towns. Like the other Pueblo peoples, the Zunis contracted their settlements during the drought that struck in the fourteenth century. They abandoned their outlying settlements to concentrate their villages along the Zuni River with its reliable source of water. Around 1500 an estimated ten thousand Zunis lived in six villages spread out along the banks of the Zuni River in what is now New Mexico and Arizona.

In 1540 the Zunis encountered western society in the form of Francisco Coronado. The conquistador had entered the region to search for the "Seven Cities of Cibola," rich opulent cities that the Spanish believed existed in this region. Coronado captured the Zuni village of Hawikuh and set up his headquarters. He spent two years exploring the region, quartering his soldiers in various of the pueblos and supplying his troops with the Indians' crops. Those Indians who offered resistance to the Spanish demands were shown the force with which the Spanish exacted their tribute. Several of the pueblos were attacked and the inhabitants burned at the stake. When Coronado could find neither gold nor fabulous riches, his expedition returned to New Spain. For the next fifty years the Zunis were left relatively untroubled by the imperial presence to the south. In the late-sixteenth century Spanish explorers and missionaries again entered the region. They were followed by Juan de Oñate in 1598. He came to establish the colony of New Mexico and put the Pueblos under Spanish rule.

In the colony of New Mexico the civil authorities imposed systems of tribute and forced labor while the missionaries began to repress the Native religious practices. To maintain their ties to the spirit world the Pueblos began to practice their religion in secret. During this first century of Spanish colonialism many of the Pueblos became depopulated. The Indians suffered famine and disease, and nomadic tribes from the north and east took advantage of the Pueblos' weakness to raid their villages and crops. In order to administer the Pueblos the Spanish called for the creation of a Pueblo civil authority. These civil officials were to be elected without interference by the Pueblos' religious authorities. The resulting "governors," although often guided in secret by the

Another America

religious hierarchy of the Pueblo, contributed to factionalism within what had been an integrated and unified social system.

In 1680 the Pueblos organized and executed one of the most successful Indian revolts in North America. They simultaneously attacked missionaries and colonists within each village and drove the survivors to Santa Fe. There the Indian warriors laid siege to the Spanish stronghold and drove the governor and his followers from the district. The successful revolt revitalized the Native cultures and their political and religious structures reemerged. The spoils of victory included the large herds of Spanish horses, and in the aftermath of the Pueblo revolt the horse culture spread rapidly throughout the West.

The Zunis had joined in the revolt and driven the Spanish from their territory. But the deprivations they had suffered, their fear of Spanish reprisals, and the threat posed by Indian raids caused the Zuni to leave their separate villages and take refuge together on a defensible mesa. This move assimilated six autonomous Zuni villages into one, and spurred the evolution of the Zunis' complex systems of ritual and belief.

When the Spanish returned to reconquer New Mexico, the Pueblo unity that had driven them out was no longer in place. Factionalism among the Pueblos enabled the Spanish to enlist the Indians as fighters in the reconquest. From 1692 to around the end of the century the Spanish campaigned to reestablish colonial rule. The Zunis, outside much of the fighting that took place among the Pueblos, made a token submission to the Spanish in 1692 and returned to their village. Rather then reoccupy all six of their villages, the Zuni moved together into one village, the Pueblo of Zuni.

The Spanish had learned from the revolt of 1680. They stopped forced labor and tribute among the Pueblos, and the Franciscans no longer had the numbers or the resources to actively persecute the Native religions. In 1689 the Spanish crown granted the Pueblos title to small tracts of land. These areas enabled the Pueblos to administer their own affairs within the Spanish realm. Under Spanish rule the Zuni and other Pueblos recovered from the loss of population in the previous century. Pueblo agriculture was expanded and their farms began to supply the growing Spanish settlements of the region. Throughout the eighteenth century the Pueblos gradually assimilated various Spanish material and cultural traits. The two societies were drawn together by the need to protect themselves from the Apaches, Navajos, and other Indians who attacked Spanish settlements and Indian villages alike. It was during this period that the Pueblos perfected their defensible architecture of terraced dwellings with easily defended rooftop entrances.

In addition to the Catholic Church, the Spanish introduced many items that became important parts of the Pueblo cultures. Wheat, oats, peaches, and domesticated sheep and burros were added to the agricultural resources of the region. The new crops increased the agricultural output of the Zunis and helped to revive their population. Sheep became an important resource for their wool, which was used to produce the characteristic southwestern blankets. And burros enabled the Zuni to reintegrate themselves into their territory. With the added mobility and carrying capacity of the burros it was possible to farm further and further from their central Pueblo. Farming lands that were a day's journey from the pueblo were used again as they had been for centuries. Around the beginning of the American era the Zuni developed two summer villages for tending their outlying farms. These eventually became the permanent Zuni villages of Ajo Caliente and Nutria, shown on the modern Zunis' map.

In 1846 the United States occupied and annexed New Mexico. The map of the "Areas of Zuni Land Taken Since 1846" begins with this occupation of the Pueblo lands. Following the official transfer of New Mexico to the United States in 1848, the Zunis and the other Pueblo Indians faced a century of assault. The map, with its successive rings of lands taken in the Zunis' dealings with the United States, is a graphic record of the history of events and policies that reduced the Zuni estate. It is symbolic of the difference between the world views of Native Americans and the western culture of the United States. To the Zunis, the map begins with the full extent of their ancestral territories, the heritage that they brought with them when they were once again annexed by a foreign power. To the United States, the legally recognized Zuni lands were the minuscule territory, 17,636 acres, that the Zuni had been granted by the Spanish Crown back in 1689. In the western world of documents and possession, the Spanish land grant constituted the official definition of Zuni lands, not the Native Americans' oral history or centuries of inhabitation. The Zunis' experience is one of successive land "takings" that reduced them to their current reservation. The western experience of this process is the legal record of recognition and land grants that increased the Zunis' estate from the original Spanish grant to the more than four hundred thousand acres that make up the Zuni reservation. The landscape on which these two opposing views met was one on which the unfortunate Zuni and their Pueblo neighbors had neither the tools nor the strength to make their views succeed. It was necessary to adapt western tools and methods for the Zuni to reassert their place.

The map of Zuni lands taken is divided into six chronological sections that correspond to changes in the legal status and land rights of the Zuni and other Pueblo Indians. The widest boundaries represent lands taken between 1846 and 1876, the initial period of Zuni–United States relations. In the treaty that ended the war with Mexico, the United States had recognized the Zunis' territory, but it was not considered a reservation with the same rights and protections as Indian reservations established by the United States. Rather, the Zunis' lands were considered disposable property and open to purchase by non-Indians. Between 1846 and 1876 local courts, interested in promoting New Mexico for statehood and development, ruled that the Zuni were not "tribal" and therefore not eligible for the protection of the federal Indian department. Their lands could be disposed of at will. During this period the Zuni record that over 60 percent of their lands were taken.

The second chronological section of the map, "Lands Taken 1876–1900" begins with the Supreme Court's 1876 decision upholding the state law exempting the Zunis and other Pueblos from federal protection. Following this decision, the Zunis had little defense against the continued attempts by Americans, both local residents of Mexican descent and whites streaming in from the East, to take over, purchase, and in other ways usurp the Zunis' lands. By the time the first century of U.S. occupation came to a close, the Zunis had lost more than twelve million acres of their ancestral lands.

The lack of recognition of Zuni sovereignty continued into the twentieth century. The "Lands Taken," during the periods 1900–1912 and 1912–1924 comprise more than a million and a half acres of Zuni ancestral land. Ironically, this latter period coincides with western legal developments that, from the United States' point of view, actually increased Zuni land holdings. In 1913 the Supreme Court reversed its decision of 1876 and ruled that the Pueblo Indians were entitled to the same protections as other Indian tribes in the United States. The Pueblos' lands were put in trust and the Pueblos were granted the right to regain lands that had been taken. The decision meant that the Americans' title, rather than the Indians', was to be extinguished. While the numbers of non-Indian landowners and the amounts of lands they possessed were relatively small, they represented the prime irrigable lands on the reservations. For eleven years Indians and non-Indians were in conflict over the effort to reacquire these Indians lands. For the Zunis, this time period is marked by the continued taking of their lands.

The period of 1924–1934 is recorded as a time when nearly six hundred thousand acres of Zuni lands were taken. In 1922 a senator from the State of New Mexico sponsored a bill that called for the recognition of all non-Indian land claims filed before 1902, ten years before New Mexican statehood. This policy would have decimated the Zuni lands and deprived them of the few gains made since the Supreme Court decision of 1913. In response to this threat the Indians and their non-Indian allies made successful use of western political and legal structures to protect their lands and resources.

With the help and urging of non-Indian advocates, the Pueblos organized themselves in an all-Pueblo council to lobby against the proposed bill. They were joined by a proactive group of artists and intellectuals sympathetic to the Pueblos' way of life, by Indian rights organizations, and by the General Federation of Women's Clubs. Together these organizations lobbied to defeat the proposed legislation. Instead of a bill that would have taken more of the Indians' land, the Pueblo Lands Act of 1924 established a commission to investigate and settle the Pueblos' land disputes. By adapting western means to Indian ends the Pueblos had successfully used the cultural, legal, and technological structures of the larger society to defend and protect their rights.

The final section of lands taken on the map, 1934–1939, coincides with the passage of the Indian Reorganization Act in 1934 and the end of title litigation. The Indian Reorganization Act gave Indians throughout the United States more autonomy over their external affairs and protected their cultural traditions. By establishing constitutional governments through popular elections, the Indians could move toward self-determination. At the same time that the Zunis' map records the last of the land takings, western documents record that non-Indians without legitimate title had been evicted from the Pueblos' territory, and that land acquisitions increased the Zuni and other Pueblo holdings.

With these changes in the Pueblos' legal status came changes in their culture as well. As viable and evolving societies, the Pueblos have continued to adapt technologies, concepts, and social forms from those they come in contact with. Like all modern societies their cultures reflect a combination of traditional values and contemporary experience. Despite these western adaptations, Native American groups remain separate and distinct peoples with traditions, histories, and world views that make them fully functional modern cultures.

In 1970 the Zunis took a decisive move towards self-determination when they assumed self-governance over the tribe's internal and external affairs. This development was paralleled by the Zunis' adaptation of a secular government structure to replace their traditional religious-based government. The change was not without reaction—like other Native American groups the Zuni have had to pick their way through the difficult landscape of modern society while retaining those essential things that make them a people.

The Zunis' ability to continue as a viable economic and cultural entity requires that they control their land and their resources. To do so the Zunis have had to adapt the tools of western

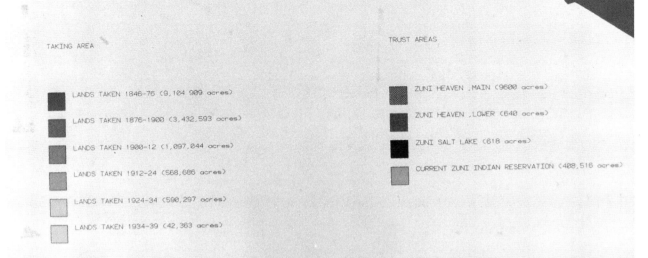

TAKING AREA

◼ LANDS TAKEN 1846-76 (9,104,909 acres)

◼ LANDS TAKEN 1876-1900 (3,432,593 acres)

◼ LANDS TAKEN 1900-12 (1,097,044 acres)

◼ LANDS TAKEN 1912-24 (568,686 acres)

◻ LANDS TAKEN 1924-34 (590,297 acres)

◻ LANDS TAKEN 1934-39 (42,363 acres)

TRUST AREAS

◼ ZUNI HEAVEN, MAIN (9600 acres)

◼ ZUNI HEAVEN, LOWER (640 acres)

◼ ZUNI SALT LAKE (618 acres)

◻ CURRENT ZUNI INDIAN RESERVATION (408,516 acres)

FIGURE 77. Detail from *the map of "Areas of Zuni Land Taken Since 1846" showing the key and acreage taken in each successive time period.*

culture. The use of Geographic Information System data and western cartographic techniques is just another example of these adaptations. The map illustrates the persistence of the Zunis' vision. Their desire to assert their place and be recognized as a part of the larger society is reflected in the words of the governor of the Pueblo when he announced the Zunis' comprehensive development plan:

> "We live in accord with Zuni Pueblo concepts and, in the past, have asked or expected little of those not of our pueblo. Now we want to achieve a level of living such as other Americans enjoy. We have a long way to go in a short period of time.
>
> "Zunis want to retain their identity——not the moccasin and feather image——but the cultural and historical identification any man uses to reflect pride of his forefathers and their accomplishments and contributions to society."

This map of Inujjuaq (Figure 78), on the east coast of Canada's Hudson Bay, is one of a series of trilingual maps prepared by the Avataq Cultural Institute of Nunavik, the Inuit homeland in Northern Quebec. Printed in three languages——English, French, and Inuktitut——and two orthographies——Roman letters and the Inuit syllabic writing——these maps are symbolic of a developing relationship between Native Americans and western society. As the first of its kind in North America, the Inuit Place Name Map Series of Nunavik is an expression of a new phase in the encounter between the Native American societies and the cultures that arrived on this continent five hundred years ago.

For several decades the Inuit people of Northern Quebec, like Native peoples throughout North America, have been undergoing a cultural renewal. They have struggled to determine their

Another America

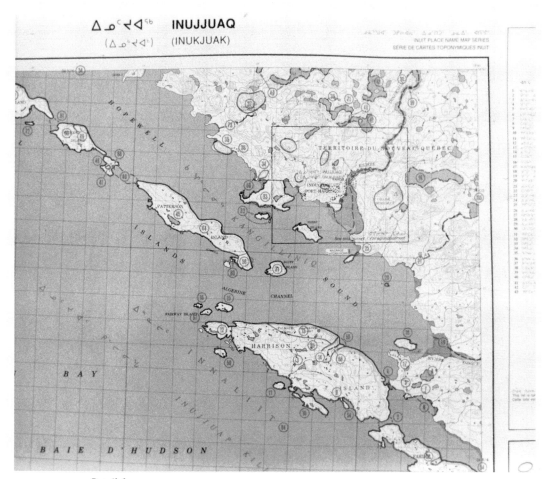

FIGURE 78. **Detail from** *the map of Inujjuaq, from the Inuit Place Name Map Series of Nunavik, 1991. Size of the original 27 x 25 inches (68.5 x 63.5 cm). Courtesy of Ludger Müller-Wille and the Inuit Elders of Nunavik.*

own fate and break the bonds of government control over their lives. Part of this struggle has been the reemergence of their cultural identity as unique peoples with a unique heritage. These maps of their homeland are a reassertion of this identity. The Inuit place names have again been applied to the landscape, only this time they are a contribution to the larger society's conceptualization of this land.

In the 1980s the Inuit elders mandated that the names of the land be recorded so that the Inuit's geography would not be forgotten. The Inuit Place Name maps compiled from this survey are not meant to be curiosities or pictures of a past geography; they are meant to be functional documents in the contemporary world. They have been researched, compiled, and printed so that the Inuit can continue to use and exploit their traditional environment using the new technologies and ways of life they have adapted from western society. The maps also include English and French translations of the Inuit place names so that "even Qallunaat (non-Inuit) can use them."

The map of Inujjuaq is one of seventeen sheets printed in 1991. Inujjuaq, called Inukjuak on western maps and known as Port Harrison during the French and English colonial regimes, is one of the largest settlements in the region. Here the Inuit have concentrated themselves in a contemporary community that includes modern housing, services, and communications networks, along with cultural and social organizations that help to maintain the Inuit identity. The map, at a scale of 1:50,000, represents the immediate area and islands around Inujjuaq. A smaller inset map shows a more detailed picture of the settlement of Inujjuaq with its modern roads and airport. On the original, the Inuit information is given in red using a combination of Inuktitut syllabic writing, transliterated place names, and a numerical key. English and French place names have been left on many features and the accompanying key provides western descriptions for the Inuit features. The map is a mixed or hybrid landscape. The shape, execution, and technology of production are all borrowed or appropriated from the West. The information, the place names, are the persistence of a traditional geography that goes back for several centuries. Included in the place names are numerous sites for hunting and trapping camps, geographic features, and the names for the village, plus such modern additions as docks, landings, and lighthouses. It is at once both foreign and familiar, a map neither totally western nor totally Inuit.

Inujjuaq represents only a small part of the Nunavik region. Nunavik itself covers the entire Peninsule D'Ungava and the area surrounding Ungava Bay. The region extends from the east shore of Hudson Bay to the entrance of Hudson Strait and includes many of the offshore islands.

In a larger cultural and political sense, the Inuit Place Name Map Series is a part of the continuing evolution of the North American landscape. It is a process one scholar describes as a cartographic dialog——a dialog in which the image and conception of the North American landscape continues to change. In the past, western mapmakers portrayed the continent in western terms of reference using place names, orientations, and symbols of inhabitation and possession that excluded Native Americans. The Inuit Place Name maps are maps of inclusion. Nunavik and other Native American homelands are to become part of the official map of Canada and form the larger society's visualization of this land.

But the Inuit of Nunavik did not wish to wait for the Canadian government to put them on the map. At the request of the Inuit elders they began a survey of Inuit place names. With the help of Ludger Müller-Willie and the Indigenous Names Surveys at McGill University, nearly eight thousand Inuit place names were collected. These place names not only correspond to features and places that have been given western names; they include places that only the Inuit have named. The Inuit then adapted the tools of western mapmaking to portray their oral landscape. This melding of the two geographic traditions can be seen on the map where the Inuit place names have been applied to a standard western topographic base.

The first Inuit place name maps of the Nunavik region were printed in 1990. They were so popular with the inhabitants of Nunavik that the first print run sold out in one day. In symbolic recognition of this addition to the landscape of North American, the first maps of the series were selected as part of the Canadian exhibit at the meeting of the International Cartographic Association in 1991. The Inuit's geography had not only become a part of the contemporary map of Canada, its reemergence on the North American landscape was an international event.

This reemergence of the Inuit's cultural presence has not been without its price. Adapting to western society meant changes in the Inuit traditions. In the agreement that the Inuit struck with the national and provincial governments to gain their political and economic independence, they had to agree to give up some of their aboriginal rights to the land.

Nunavik has been home to Native Americans for nearly five thousand years. The process of naming the places and features of the region began with these first people, and the oral map of the region continued to evolve as new technologies and cultural traditions succeeded one another. From the very beginning, the Inuit of northern Quebec were great travelers. The Inuit technologies included specialized weapons, hunting and trapping equipment, temporary houses, dog sleds, boats, and an elaborate transportation network that enabled them to move through the region. Using umiaks——large boats that could accommodate several people along with their dogs, sleds, and camp provisions——the Inuit rowed and sailed up the inland rivers, along the coast, and out to the islands. Individuals would accompany the travelers in kayaks and dogs would be employed to pull sleds and boats or to carry provisions over the ice and along the waterways. The Inuit even built specialized sleds that could be transformed into kayaks and back to sleds again to enable them to cross the area's varied terrain.

The oral traditions provided the map for these travels. Inuit place names provided orientation, they outlined the routes of travel and trade, they identified the sites of the culture's heritage, and they marked the meeting places where the Inuit gathered to dance, sing, and pass on their traditions.

Until the middle of the nineteenth century, the Inuit's patterns of land use and their social structures made it possible for them to maintain this knowledge in their oral traditions. The oral account was the primary means of communicating spatial information. Maps were only drawn when they were needed to clarify or illustrate the information.

Even with the Inuit's centuries of adaptation and their knowledge of the regional geography, Nunavik was a hard land. There were times of famine and starvation, and the mortality rate was so high that simply replacing one generation with the next sometimes proved difficult. At the beginning of prolonged European contact only about two thousand people inhabited the region.

In the nineteenth century fur traders and whalers visited the area, introducing western goods and western vices. Guns increased the efficiency of the Inuit's hunts, but alcohol and syphilis affected their well-being. In the twentieth century trading posts opened in the region, including two at Port Harrison (Inujjuaq), and the Inuit were drawn into the fur trade. The wealth of goods available from the trading posts brought a change in the Inuit's traditional hunting patterns. Fur-bearing animals were emphasized over the traditional range of resources and the Inuit subsistence patterns changed. As they became dependent on imported trade goods, the Inuit began to migrate to the permanent villages that grew up around the trading centers. They adopted a more sedentary life without the traditions or resources to maintain it. In the 1920s, when fur prices reached their peak, these trading villages became centers of Inuit activity. With the influx of money and goods, traditional Inuit technologies and materials were replaced with western goods. Kayaks and harpoons were being replaced by guns and wooden boats, and manufactured clothes replaced skin clothing .

The precipitous fall of fur prices during the Depression of the 1930s put the Inuit economy into turmoil. Many of the trading posts closed, and the food and goods necessary to sustain the Inuit were no longer available. The Inuit's dependence on western goods was complicated by the influence of Christian missionaries. The missionaries condemned the Inuit's beliefs and practices, further alienating them from the knowledge and traditions that had sustained them. By the middle of the twentieth century the Inuit of Nunavik were lost in the transformation of North America. The Depression, the closing of trading posts, and the government's preoccupation with the Second World War put many of the Inuit families into crises. Despite the abundance of the culture that was overtaking them, numerous cases of death from starvation were reported.

Following the Second World War, the government presence in Nunavik became more pronounced. The Canadian government began to provide family allowances and established medical facilities in some of the villages. The Inuit population began to grow. These improvements in the economic and physical health of the Inuit were part of an exchange between the two cultures. The benefits of welfare and medical care were purchased at the price of a move to permanent villages and the continued loss of traditional culture. The self-sufficient migratory hunters of the nineteenth century were becoming a sedentary and dependent minority.

In the 1950s and '60s the provincial government of Quebec and the Canadian national government became interested in the mineral resources of northern Quebec and instituted policies to contain the Native populations. Permanent villages were constructed with improved housing and medical and educational facilities, and with government agents offering welfare payments and western trade goods. For the majority of the Inuit this new environment still required that they hunt and fish for a major part of their subsistence. Because they were now concentrated in permanent villages, hunters had to go farther and farther to find the animals on which they depended. A network of family-owned traplines soon crisscrossed the region and the individual hunter on his snowmobile became the more common means of interacting with the Arctic environment.

As the Inuit adapted these western technologies, their relationship to their environment changed. Previously, groups of hunters or family bands moved through the environment following the routes described in the oral tradition. With these new technologies, hunters utilized different routes and their perception of the environment (viewed from the seats of their snowmobiles) had literally changed. Throughout these changes the Inuit identity and their knowledge of their environment remained. The adaptation of modern technologies did not negate Inuit history and traditions. Rather, like their social and material culture, the Inuit's "map" needed to evolve. It was this situation that the Inuit elders wished to address when they mandated the collection and recording of Inuit place names.

The Inuit's knowledge of their environment is a legacy of their centuries of living on this land. The oral traditions were no longer effective for passing these riches on to a new generation living in new villages and using the land in new ways. The adaptation of western map technology enabled the Inuit to preserve their detailed geographic knowledge. In preparing the Inuit Place Name maps an edition was printed on waterproof fibers specifically for use by those wishing to travel and hunt in the region.

The research and production of the Inuit Place Name maps are the result of political and economic developments that accompanied the revival of Inuit interest in their traditional culture. In the 1970s, the national government moved to turn over administration of Native populations to the province of Quebec. The Inuit protested. They did not want to be wards of "the little government." Two Inuit organizations formed to lobby for self-determination. The cooperative movement favored the preservation of Inuit traditions and land rights. The Northern Quebec Inuit

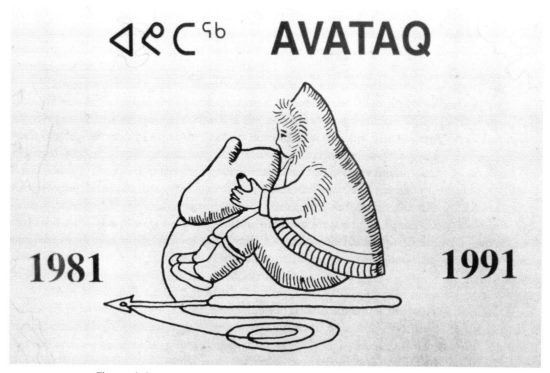

FIGURE 79. The symbol *of the Avataq Cultural Institute represents an Inuit in traditional dress with a harpoon and seal float. The symbol refers to the traditional technologies and subsistence economy of the Inuit, the roots from which their culture has grown.*

Association formed as a political movement with the aim of political and economic autonomy for the Inuit.

When the Quebec government announced plans to develop a large hydroelectric project for James Bay and Northern Quebec, the need to extinguish aboriginal title and expropriate the Natives' land arose. In the negotiations that led to the James Bay and Northern Quebec Agreement of 1975, leaders of the Northern Quebec Inuit Association were the only Inuit representatives at the bargaining table.

The terms of the James Bay and Northern Quebec Agreement reflect the bureaucratic and political accommodations the Inuit had to make as they negotiated a place for themselves in the larger society. In the agreement, the Inuit gained political control over their lives and the resources of the local communities. Their unique culture was recognized and given special rights for fishing, trapping, and hunting. The Inuit were granted control over the educational system within their communities and given the ability to shape educational curriculum to reflect Inuit traditions and preserve the Inuit language. In local affairs they were able to administer justice and social services in keeping with their traditions. The largest part of the agreement involved monetary compensation, and the Inuit received dozens of millions of dollars with which they could direct their economic future and development.

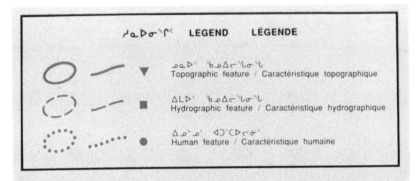

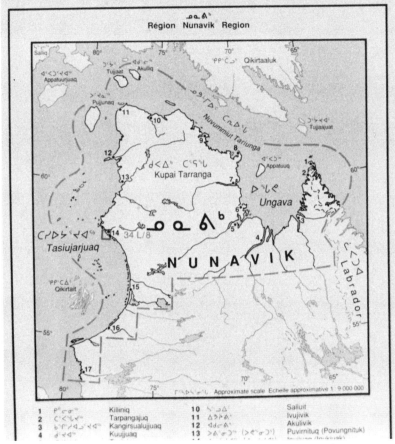

The trade-off for political and economic autonomy involved extinguishing the Inuit's rights to much of their aboriginal territory. The recognition of Nunavik acknowledges the historical experience of the Inuit and their contemporary presence in northern Quebec, but the Inuit's ability to determine the future of much of their aboriginal lands has been limited. In the James Bay and Northern Quebec Agreement the Inuit were granted exclusive rights over 1 percent of the territory. Within these lands, labeled category one, the Inuit have rights to the animal and other resources and the ability to approve or disapprove, and reap the benefits of, any mining or development projects. Within the lands designated category two the Inuit retain exclusive rights to hunt, fish, and trap, while outside interests wishing to develop the land must respect and accommodate these rights. In the third and largest category of lands the Inuit have the same rights as non-Inuit citizens, and government projects such as James Bay's hydroelectric development can proceed.

This agreement was arrived at within the context of national, provincial, and Native American politics, and not all Inuit have accepted its terms or outcome. Some continue to live on the land and maintain traditional ways in opposition to the agreement, but the majority of the Inuit accepted the agreement and the new political structure of Inuit life. Following the agreement, the Inuit established corporations to manage their funds and resources. They used part of their compensation to begin a program of economic development. Fourteen villages were developed in the region, some at the site of traditional campsites. These villages contain modern houses, electricity, oil heat, water supplies, and sanitary services along with communications and travel links, satellite connections, schools, and hospitals.

In the 1980s the Inuit of Nunavik turned towards cultural development. A conference of Inuit elders from all the villages of Arctic Quebec called for a program of cultural revival. The Avataq Cultural Institute was established and resources were dedicated to the development of an Inuit museum and to the survey of Inuit place names that resulted in the map series. Bilingual publications in English and Inuit syllabic writing were produced and radio broadcasts were conducted in Inuit. This reevaluation of the Inuit traditions extended to a revival of the hunting economy, a return to traditional technologies and clothing, and a renewed interest in traditional beliefs.

This cultural revival is part of the Inuit's effort to find a balance between their traditions and the opportunities and difficulties of the modern world. Adapting the tools and methods of the West to assert their presence and making the compromises that led to their recognition as part of modern Canada are now part of the Inuit's culture. They are part of a dialog between two societies that are evolving together——an evolution in which the Inuit can assert their identity and claim their place in the larger society. While challenges and difficulties remain, the publication of the Inuit Place Name Map Series of Nunavik represents an unprecedented recognition of the Native American presence as part of contemporary society.

Bibliography

Ambrose, Stephen E. *Crazy Horse and Custer; the Parallel Lives of Two American Warriors.* New York: Meridian, 1986.

Anson, Bert. *The Miami Indians.* Norman: University of Oklahoma Press, 1970.

Barbour, Philip L., ed. *The Complete works of Captain John Smith.* Chapel Hill: University of North Carolina Press, 1986.

Barrow F.R.S, John. *A Chronological History of Voyages Into the Arctic Regions.* London: John Murray, 1818.

Blaine, Martha Royce. *The Ioway Indians.* Norman: University of Oklahoma Press, 1979,

Boas, Franz. "The Central Eskimo." *Sixth Annual Report of the Bureau of Ethnology to the Secretary of the Smithsonian Institution 1884–85.* Washington: Government Printing Office, 1888.

Bourne, Russell. *The Red King's Rebellion Racial Politics in New England 1675–1678.* Atheneum, New York, 1990.

Burt, Jesse and Robert B. Ferguson. *Indians of the Southeast: Then and Now.* New York: Abingdon Press, 1973.

Bushnell, David. "The Account of Lamhatty." *American Anthropologist N.S.* 10 (Oct–Dec 1908), pp. 568–574.

Butler, B. Robertin. "Prehistory of the Snake and Salmon River Area." *Handbook of North American Indians,* vol. 11, *Great Basin.* Washington: Smithsonian Institution, 1986.

Cash, Joseph H. and Gerald W. Wolff. *The Three Affiliated Tribes (Mandan, Arikara, and Hidatsa).* Phoenix: Indian Tribal Series, 1974.

Cohoe, *A Cheyenne Sketchbook.* Commentary by E. Adamson Hoebel and Karen Daniels Petersen. Norman: University of Oklahoma Press, 1964.

Conrad, David E. "The Whipple Expedition On The Great Plains," *Great Plains Journal,* Spring 2/2 1963, pp. 42–66.

Cumming, William Patterson. *The Southeast in early maps, with an annotated check list of printed and manuscript regional and local maps of southeastern North America during the colonial period.* Chapel Hill: University of North Carolina Press, 1962.

————————R. A. Skelton, and D. B. Quinn. *The Discovery of North America.* New York: American Heritage Press, 1972.

D'Anglure, Bernard Saladin. "Inuit of Quebec." *Handbook of North American Indians,* vol .5 *Arctic,* pp. 476–507.

————————"Contemporary Inuit of Quebec." *Handbook of North American Indians,* vol. 5 *Arctic,* pp 683-688.

Day, Arthur Grove. *Coronado's Quest: The Discovery of the Southwestern States.* University of California Press, 1940.

De Forest, John W. *History of the Indians of Connecticut.* (first edition published in 1851), Archon Books, 1964.

Denig, Edwin Thompson. "Indian Tribes of the Upper Missouri." *Forty-Sixth Annual Report of the Bureau of American Ethnology to the Secretary of the Smithsonian Institution 1928–1929.* Washington: Government Printing Office, 1930.

De Vorsey, Louis. "Amerindian contributions to the mapping of North America: A preliminary view," *Imago Mundi,* vol. 30 (1978), pp. 71–78.

————————. "Silent Witness: Native American Maps." *The Georgia Review,* Winter 1992, pp. 709-726.

Drake, Samuel G. *Biography and history of the Indians of North America, Book III.* Boston: Antiquarian Institute, 1837.

Easton, Mr., of Rhode Isld. *A Relation of the Indyan Warre.* 1675.

Ewers, John C. *The Blackfeet: Raiders of the Northern Plains.* Norman: University of Oklahoma Press, 1958.

Fairbanks, Charles H. *Florida Indians III Ethnohistorical Report on the Florida Indians.* New York: Garland Publishing Inc. 1974.

Flexner, James Thomas. *Lord of the Mohawks: A Biography of Sir William Johnson.* Boston: Little, Brown and Company, 1979.

Foreman, Grant. *Indian Removal: The Emigration of the Five Civilized Tribes of Indians.* Norman: University of Oklahoma Press, 1972.

——————. *A Pathfinder In The Southwest: The Intinerary of Lieutenant A. W. Whipple During his Explorations*. Norman:University of Oklahoma Press, 1941.

Gibson, Arrell M. *The Chickasaws*. Norman: University of Oklahoma Press, 1971.

Gilman, Carolyn and Mary Jane Schneider. *The way to independence: memories of a Hidatsa Indian family, 1840–1920*. St. Paul: Minnesota Historical Society Press, 1987.

Goetzmann, William H. *Army Exploration In The American West 1803–1863*. New Haven: Yale University Press, 1959.

Gussow, Zachary. "An Ethnological Report on the Historic Habitat of the Sauk, Fox, and Iowa Indians," *Sac, Fox, and Iowa Indians, I*. The Garland American Indian Ethnohistory Series, New York: Garland Publishing, 1974.

Hamilton, Charles. *Braddock's Defeat: The Journal of Captain Robert Cholmley's Batman, The Journal of a British Officer, Halkett's Orderly Book*. Norman: University of Oklahoma Press, 1959.

Haines, Francis. *The Plains Indians*. New York: Thomas Y. Crowell, 1976.

Hammond, George P. *Don Juan de Oñate and the Founding of New Mexico*. Historical Society of New Mexico Publications in History, Vol. II. Santa Fe: El Palacio Press, 1927.

——————., and Agapito Rey. *Don Juan de Oñate Colonizer of New Mexico 1595–1628*. Coronado Cuarto Centennial Publications. The University of New Mexico Press, 1953.

Harley, J. B. and David Woodward, eds. *The History of Cartography, volume one, Cartography in Prehistoric, Ancient, and Medieval Europe and the Mediterranean*. Chicago: University of Chicago Press, 1987.

Hauptman, Laurence M. and James D. Wherry, eds. *The Pequots in Southern New England: The Fall and Rise of an American Indian Nation*. Norman: University of Oklahoma Press, 1990.

Helm, June. "Matonabbee's Map." *Arctic Anthropology*, vol. 26, No. 2, 1989, pp. 28–47.

Henry, Jeannette, Vine Deloria Jr., N. Scott Momaday, Bea Medicine, and Alfonso Ortiz, eds. *Indian Voices: The First Convocation of American Indian Scholars*. San Francisco: The Indian Historian Press, 1970.

Hertzberg, Hazel Whitman. "Indian Rights Movement 1887–1973," *Handbook of North American Indians*, vol. 4, *History of Indian-White Relation*. Washington: Smithsonian Institution, 1988, pp 305–23.

Hoebel, E. Adamson. *The Cheyennes: Indians of the Great Plains*. New York : Holt, Rinehart and Winston, 1978.

Howley, James P. *The Beothucks or Red Indians: The Aboriginal Inhabitant of Newfoundland*. Cambridge: Cambridge University Press, 1915.

Hyde, George E. *Life of George Bent: Written from his Letters*. Savoie Lottinville, ed. Norman and London: Univeristy of Oklahoma Press, 1968.

——————. *The Pawnee Indians*. Norman: University of Oklahoma Press, 1974

Hudson, Charles. *The Juan Prado Expeditions: Explorations of the Carolinas and Tennessee, 1566–68*. Washington: Smithsonian Institution Press, 1990.

Iverson, Peter. "Taking Care of the Earth and Sky." *America In 1492: The World of the Indian Peoples Before the Arrival of Columbus*. Alvin M. Josephy Jr., ed. New York: Alfred A. Knopf, 1992.

Jennings, Francis. *The Invasion of America: Indians, Colonialism, and the Cant of Conquest*. Chapel Hill: University of North Carolina Press, 1975.

—————. "Susquehannock." *Handbook of North American Indians,* vol.15, *Northeast.* Washington: Smithsonian Institution, 1978.

—————. *The Ambiguous Iroquois Empire: The Covenant Chain Confederation of Indian Tribes with English Colonies from its beginning to the Lancaster Treaty of 1744.* New York: W. W. Norton & Company, 1984.

—————. *Empire of Fortune: Crowns, Colonies, and Tribes in the Seven Years War in America.* New York: W. W. Norton & Company, 1988.

Joutel, Henri. *A Journal of the Last Voyage Perform'd by de la Sale.* Originally printed in translation by A. Bell and others, London, 1714.

Kehoe, Alice B. "How the Ancient Peigans Lived." *Research in Economic Anthropology* 14 (1993).

Kenner, Charles L. *A History of New Mexican-Plains Indian Relations.* Norman, University of Oklahoma Press, 1969.

Keyser, James D. *Indian Rock Art of the Columbian Plateau.* University of Washington Press, 1992.

LaFantasie, Glenn W., ed. *The Correspondence of Roger Williams,* 2 vol. University Press of New England, for the Rhode Island Historical Society, 1988.

Lewis, G. Malcolm. "The Indigenous maps and mapping of North American Indians." *The Map Collector,* 9 (1979), pp. 25-32.

—————. "Indian Maps," *Old Trails and New Directions: Papers of the Third North American Fur Trade Conference.* C. O. Judd and A. J. Ray, eds. Toronto: University of Toronto Press, 1980, pp. 9–23.

—————. "Indian maps: their place in the history of Plains cartography." *Great Plains Quarterly,* 4 (1984), pp. 91–108.

Lyon, George F. *The Private Journal of Captain G. F. Lyon of HMS Hecla During the Recent Voyage of Discovery Under Captain Parry.* London: John Murray, 1824.

Moodie, D. W. and Barry Kaye. "The Ac Ko Mok Ki Map." *The Beaver, Magazine of the North,* spring 1977, pp. 5–15.

Mallery, Garrick. "Sign Language Among North American Indians . . . ." *First Annual Report of the Bureau of Ethnology to the Secretary of the Smithsonian Institution 1879–80 by J. W. Powell, Director.* Washington: Government Printing Office, 1881.

—————. "Picture-Writing of the American Indians." *Tenth Annual Report of the Bureau of Ethnology to the Secretary of the Smithsonian Institution 1888–89 by J. W. Powell, Director.* Washington: Government Printing Office, 1893, pp. 25-822.

Marozas, Bryan. "The Role of Geographic Information Systems in American Indian Land and Water Rights Litigation." *American Indian Culture and Research Journal,* vol. 15, no. 3, fall 1991, UCLA., pp. 77–93.

McKenny, Thomas L. and James Hall. *Biographical sketches and anecdotes of Ninety-five of 120 Principal Chiefs from the Indian Tribes of North America.* Washington: United States Department of the Interior, Bureau of Indian Affairs, 1967.

Merrell, James H. *The Indians' New World: Catawbas and Their Neighbors from European Contact through the Era of Removal.* Chapel Hill: University of North Carolina Press, 1989.

Murphy, Robert F. and Yolanda Murphy. "Northern Shoshone and Bannock." *Handbook of*

North American Indians, vol. 11, *Great Basin.* Washington, Smithsonian Institution, 1986.

National Archives of the United States. "Journal of proceedings at a council held in the City of Washington D.C. with a delegation of Chiefs and braves of the confederated tribes of Sacs and Indians of the Mississippi and a delegation of Sac and Fox and Ioway Chiefs and braves of the Missouri." Document re negotiations of Indian Treaties, 1801–89, Ratified Treaties 1833–37,

Nash, Philleo. "Twentieth-Century United States Government Agencies." Handbook of North American Indians, vol. 4, *History of Indian-White Relation.* Washington: Smithsonian Institution, 1988.

Parry, William E. *Journal of a Second Voyage for the Discovery of a North-west Passage from the Atlantic to the Pacific; Performed in the Years 1821–22–23, In His Majesty's Ships Fury and Hecla, Under the Orders of Captain William Edward Parry, R.N., F.R.S., and Commander of the Expedition,* London: John Murray, 1824.

Pargellis, Stanley, ed. *Military Affairs in North America 1748–1765, Selected Documents From the Cumberland Papers in Windsor Castle.* Archon Books, 1969.

Pennsylvania State Historical Society. *Minutes of the Provincial Council of Pennsylvania,* vol 7. Harrisburg, 1851.

Peterson, Karen Daniels. *Howling Wolf: A Cheyenne Warrior's Graphic Interpretation of His People.* Palo Alto: American West Publishing Company, 1968.

—————. *Plains Indian Art From Fort Marion.* Norman: University of Oklahoma Press, 1971.

Peirce, Ebenezer W. *Indian History, Biography, and Genealogy: Pertaining to the Good Sachem Massasoit of the Wampanoag Tribe.* Freeport, New York: Book for Libraries Press, 1972.

Pratt, Richard H. *Battlefield and Classroom: Four Decades with the American Indian, 1876–1904.* Robert M. Utley, ed. New Haven: Yale University Press, 1964

Randolph, J. Ralph. *British Travelers Among the Southern Indians, 1660–1763.* Norman: University of Oklahoma Press, 1973.

Rogers, E. S. "Southeastern Ojibwa." *Handbook of North American Indians,* vol. 15, *Northeast.* Washington: Smithsonian Institution, 1978, pp. 760–71.

Rountree, Helen C. *The Powhatan Indians of Virginia: Their Traditional Culture.* Norman: University of Oklahoma Press, 1989.

Rowe, Frederick W. *Extinction: The Beothuks of a Newfoundland.* Toronto: Mcgraw-Hill Ryerson Limited, 1977.

Rundstorm, Robert. "Review of Inuit Place Name Map Series of Nunavik." *Cartographica,* vol. 29, no. 1, spring, 1992, pp. 60–61.

—————. "A Cultural Interpretation of Inuit Map Accuracy." *Geographical Review,* vol. 80, no. 2, April 1990.

—————. "Mapping, Postmodernism, Indigenous People and the Changing Direction of North American Cartography." *Cartographica,* vol. 28 no. 2, Summer, 1991, pp. 1–12.

Schaafsma, Polly. "Rock Art." *Handbook of North American Indians,* vol. 11, *Great Basin.* Washington, Smithsonian Institution, 1986.

Sipe, C. Hale. *The Indian Chiefs of Pennsylvania.* New York: Arno Press & *The New York Times,* 1971.

Slotkin, Richard and James K. Folsom, eds. *So Dreadfull a Judgment: Puritan Responses to*

Another America

King Philip's War, 1676–1677. Middletown, Connecticut: Wesleyan University Press, 1978.

Speck, Frank G. *Beothuk and Micmac.* New York: Musuem of the American Indian Heye Foundation, 1922.

Stands In Timber, John and Margot Liberty, with the assistance of Robert M. Utley. *Cheyenne Memories,* New Haven: Yale University Press, 1967.

Sundstrom, Linea. *Fragile Heritage: Prehistoric Rock Art of South Dakota.* National Park Service through the South Dakota Historical Preservation Center, 1993.

Swagerty, William R. "Indian Trade in the Trans-Mississippi West to 1870." *Handbook of North American Indians,* vol. 4, *History of Indian-White Relations.* Washington, Smithsonian Institution, 1988, pp. 351–74.

Szabo, Joyce M. *Howling World and the History of Ledger Art.* Albuquerque: University of New Mexico Press, 1994.

Szasz, Margaret Connell and Carmelita Ryan. "American Indian Education." *Handbook of North American Indians,* vol. 4, *History of Indian-White Relations.* Washington: Smithsonian Institution, 1988.

Theissen, Thomas D., W. Raymond Wood, and A. Wesley Jones. "The Sitting Rabbit 1907 Map of the Missouri River in North Dakota." *Plains Anthropologist* 24–84 Pt. 1, 1979.

Tillett, Leslie, collector and ed. *Wind on the Buffalo Grass: The Indians' own Account of the Battle of the Little Big Horn River, & the Death of their life on the Plains.* New York: Thomas Y. Crowell Company, 1976.

Turnbull, David. *Maps Are Territories Science Is an Atlas.* Geelong, Victoria, Australia: Deakin University Press, 1989 (University of Chicago Press edition 1993).

Underhill, John. *News from America; or, A New and Experimental Discoverie of New England: Containing, A Trve Relation of Their Warlike Proceedings . . . with a Figure of the Indian Fort, or Palizado . . . by Captaine John Underhill. . . .* London: Printed by J. D. for Peter Cole, 1638. (Reprinted: Da Capo Press, New York, 1971).

Villagra, Alcala-Gaspar Perez de. *A History of New Mexico.* 1610. Translated by Gilberto Espinosa. Chicago: Rio Grande Press, 1962.

Viola, Herman J. *The Indian Legacy of Charles Bird King.* New York: Smithsonian Institution Press and Doubleday & Company, Inc. 1976, pp. 101–5.

Wallace, Anthony. *King of the Delawares: Teedyuscung 1700–1763.* Philadelphia: University of Pennsylvania Press, 1949.

Wallace, Paul A. W. *Indians in Pennsylvania.* Harrisburg: The Pennsylvania Historical and Museum Commission, 1964.

Waselkov, Gregory A. "Indian Maps of the Colonial Southeast." *Powhatan's Mantle, Indians in the Colonial Southeast.* Peter H. Wood, Gregory A. Waselkov and M. Thomas Hatley, eds. Lincoln: University of Nebraska Press, 1989, pp. 292–343.

Welch, James with Paul Stekler. *Killing Custer: The Battle of the Little Bighorn and the Fate of the Plains Indians.* New York: W. W. Norton & Company, 1994.

Weslager, C. A. *The Delaware Indians: A History.* New Brunswick: Rutgers University Press, 1972.

Wheat, Carl I. *Mapping the Transmississippi West, 1540–1861.* San Francisco: Institute of Historical Cartography, 1957–1963.

Bibliography

Whipple, Lieut. A. W., Thomas Ewbank, Esq. and Prof. Wm. W. Turner. *Pacific Railroad Survey,* vol. 3, pt. 3, *Report Upon the Indian Tribes.* Washington: Government Printing Office, 1855.

Wilke, William E. *Dubuque on the Mississippi, 1788–1988.* Loras College Press: Dubuque, 1988.

Williamson, Ray A. *Living the Sky: The Cosmos of the American Indian.* Norman: University of Oklahoma Press, 1984.

Winter, Kieth. *Shanaditti.* North Vancouver: J. J. Douglas Ltd., 1975.

Wright, Louis B., ed. *A voyage to Virginia in 1609; two narratives: Strachey's True reportory and Jourdain's Discovery of the Bermudas.* Charlottesville: Published for the Association for the Preservation of Virginia Antiquities by University Press of Virginia, 1964

Wood, W. Raymond, compiler. *An Atlas of Early Maps of the American Midwest.* Springfield: Illinois State Museum, 1983.

Another America

Index

Index